THE
JUNCTION
BOYS

ALSO BY JIM DENT

King of the Cowboys

You're Out and You're Ugly, Too!
(with Durwood Merrill)

THE JUNCTION BOYS

HOW TEN DAYS IN HELL WITH
Bear Bryant
FORGED A CHAMPIONSHIP TEAM

JIM DENT

St. Martin's Press ✹ NEW YORK

THOMAS DUNNE BOOKS.
An imprint of St. Martin's Press.

THE JUNCTION BOYS. Copyright © 1999 by Jim Dent. All rights reserved.
Printed in the United States of America. No part of this book may be
used or reproduced in any manner whatsoever without written permission
except in the case of brief quotations embodied in critical articles or
reviews. For information, address St. Martin's Press, 175 Fifth Avenue,
New York, NY 10010.

Library of Congress Cataloging-in-Publication Data

Dent, Jim.
    The Junction boys : how 10 days in hell with Bear Bryant forged a
championship team at Texas A&M / Jim Dent.—1st ed.
        p.   cm.
    ISBN 0-312-19293-2
    1. Bryant, Paul W.   2. Football coaches—United States Biography.
3. Football—Coaching—United States.   I. Title.
GV939.B79D46   1999
796.332'092—dc21
    [B]   99–22179
                                                              CIP

Design by Michael Mendelsohn/Design 2000, Inc.

First Edition: September 1999

10   9   8   7   6   5   4   3   2   1

To the memory
of the great Doug Todd

Contents

CONTENTS

Author's Note

All of the material from this book, including the scenes and dialogue, was derived from interviews, official records, books, newspaper and magazine articles, and my own observations. It was amazing how Bear Bryant's former pupils were able to quote his worn phrases and manner of speech as if he somehow still spoke to them.

Dialogue was based on my research, which on and off covered about fifteen years and involved more than a hundred interviews with persons intimate with the subject. Many of Bryant's quotations were taken from the three great books written on his life—*Bear* (by John Underwood and Bryant), *The Legend of Bear Bryant* (by Mickey Herskowitz), and *Coach* (by Keith Dunnavant). Other books that provided greatly to the research were *The Time It Never Rained* (by Elmer Kelton), *When Catfish Had Ticks* (by Rana Williamson), *Heart of a Champion* (by Steve Pate and Dan Jenkins), *The Fifties* (by David Halberstam), *A Centennial History of Texas A&M* (by Henry C. Dethloff), and *Aggies Handbook* (by Sam Blair).

The idea to write *The Junction Boys* was born out of numerous conversations during the eighties with Gene Stallings while he was the defensive secondary coach of the Dallas Cowboys. At the time, I was the Cowboy beat writer for the *Dallas Times Herald,* spending six weeks each summer in Thousand Oaks, California, where the team prepared for the season.

Stallings and I spoke at length on several of those summer nights, and also during Cowboy road trips, about the Junction experience. I can still hear his rich bass voice saying, "Jimmy, did I tell you about the time in Junction . . ." I would listen and scribble mental notes. My memory files were quite thick years later when I decided to tackle the project. By then, Stallings had transformed Alabama back into a national football power.

The force that drove me to research and write the book was Stallings's passion for Junction. You would expect a rational man to feel differently about a ten-day march through hell, drought, and cactus. Bear Bryant's preseason camp inspired seventy-six players to quit and almost killed two or three others. But Stallings truly felt that Junction had molded his character and forged his winning spirit. Funny thing. As I traveled around the country, interviewing other Junction survivors, I heard many of the same sentiments and opinions.

Dozens upon dozens of former Texas A&M players and coaches contributed their time and their insight. I would like to thank all of them. Those who put up with me quite frequently and walked the extra mile for this book were Dennis Goehring, Don "Weasel" Watson, Bill Granberry, Bobby Drake Keith, Bill Schroeder, Jack Pardee, Marvin Tate, Elwood Kettler, Lloyd Hale, Billy Pete Huddleston, Don Kachtik, Bum Phillips, Troy Summerlin, trainer Billy Pickard, and, of course, Stallings.

In Junction, research and texture were provided by Rob Roy Spiller, Charles Hagood, and town historian Frederica Wyatt. Friendships were made in Junction that I hope will last a lifetime. It is a wonderful place with wonderful people.

At Texas A&M, I would like to thank staff members of the sports information department, the Letterman's Associations, and the *Twelfth Man* magazine. A special thanks goes to Dr. Don Beck for helping to sort out the social significance.

Without my literary agent, Jim Donovan, and Pete Wolverton, the associate publisher of Thomas Dunne Books, this book would have never happened. Thanks, Pete, for grasping the value of the story line when others failed. Donovan provided the first edit on the book and was a driving force from start to finish.

As always, Rolly Dent sat at my feet during the long hours of writing and kept my seat very warm during the coffee breaks.

Foreword

In 1954 the Texas A&M football team went to a little town called Junction for preseason training camp. We went in two buses and we came back in one. Shoot, that one bus was half full with dog-tired players. By the time we left, Coach Paul Bryant had left an indelible mark on our lives.

I am proud that I was one of the thirty-five players to make the bus trip back to College Station. Surviving the sandspurs, the cactus, the heat, and the practices without water was tough on me and my teammates. But I also felt that Junction helped mold us into the football team we would become—undefeated Southwest Conference champions two years later. In 1954, we played most of the season with about twenty-five guys. We lost a lot of games, but Coach Bryant knew what he was doing. Out of the yellow dust and the broiling heat of Junction, he forged a team of champions.

Now that I look back on that experience, I realize that it helped build my character. I learned that you never quit. We were only out there ten days, but I must have wished a thousand times that we would pack up and leave. But quitting was never an option with me. A lot of players quit and left in the middle of the night, hitchhiking back to A&M. Others would wait by the water fountain after lunch and you knew they were trying to get up the courage to tell Coach Bryant they were leaving.

Junction was much more demanding than any camp. We practiced every day, even on Sundays, before church, and our only breaks were to eat, hold meetings, and rest. Sometimes it was too hot to sleep. Since I was a skinny sophomore, I got stuck with a top bunk in one of those oven-hot Quonset huts and my nose was parked about two inches from the corrugated steel roof. That roof was hotter than a breakfast griddle and I could barely breathe.

When our bus pulled out of Junction, we knew we would be winners.

Bobby Drake Keith and I agreed that we were going to win the conference championship that very season. Instead, we won one game. Coach Bryant caught a lot of criticism from the media and the Texas A&M administration. They didn't realize he was just trying to find out who really wanted to play. Toughness was what he was really looking for.

I played for Coach Bryant, coached under him, and eventually followed in his footsteps as the head coach at Texas A&M and also at the University of Alabama. He remains one of the most powerful influences on my life. He's my hero.

After winning his sixth national championship in 1979, one of the reporters asked him what he would like to do next. He said he would like to hold a reunion of the Junction survivors. It was important to Coach Bryant that those players still respected him. In truth, though, we loved him.

Years ago, when I was the defensive secondary coach of the Dallas Cowboys, I started telling Jimmy Dent many of the stories about Junction. Obviously, he listened. He then interviewed most of the Junction survivors and dozens of people close to the subject. He has written a powerful and honest account about the era that none of us will ever forget. This is a book for the ages.

—Gene Stallings

THE
JUNCTION
BOYS

1

Baptism

If you believe in yourself and have dedication and pride—
and never quit—you'll be a winner. The price of victory
is high, but so are the rewards.

—PAUL "BEAR" BRYANT

FEBRUARY 8, 1954

A bonfire licked the night sky as the mob surged in waves toward a
grove of trees. Pvt. Gene Stallings sprinted across the campus, his spit-
polished shoes stabbing the sidewalk. He heard the snare drums and the
"yee-haws" and watched the rows and rows of handheld torches bobbing
and flickering in the brisk wind as two hundred horns belted an old school
song across the prairie. Half a football field away, Stallings joined the
singing in a rich baritone voice:

"Good-bye to Texas University,
So long to the Orange and White.
Good luck to dear old Texas Aggies,
They are the boys who show the real old fight."

That morning, the skinny freshman from the Agricultural and Mechanical College of Texas had heard the name. It hadn't rendered up a face. It seemed that Stallings had been too occupied with practicing football, marching to meals, saluting upperclassmen, catching hell, polishing his shoes, and rising to reveille. Texas A&M's search for a successor to Ray George had turned up a man with a peculiar name—Bear Bryant. But it didn't ring a bell.

Stallings stuffed a black tie into the third button of his olive green military shirt and tucked his shirttail tightly into his light brown slacks. He'd be doing military push-ups until Sunday lunch if his uniform failed to meet code.

As a young boy, Stallings had sat mystified beside the family's RCA radio back in Paris, Texas, listening as the words and descriptions flowed from the melodic voice of Kern Tips on the Humble Oil Football Network. He grew to be tall and rail-thin, but with enough athletic skill and savvy to catch the eye of recruiters. He believed that both his destiny and his birthright were to play in the Cotton Bowl on New Year's Day and then to someday coach the Aggies to that ultimate game. He had committed to memory the names of players and coaches in the Southwest Conference. But Bear Bryant, he wasn't from Texas, was he?

Bryant had arrived that night from Kentucky on a rocking windblown twin-engine plane just after dark and had been escorted onto campus by a howling, torch-waving contingent of Aggie cadets who drove their cars on both sides of the highway. There was much to know about this man. In eight years, he'd transformed a basketball institution into a football powerhouse and then quit when he didn't get his way. He'd coached a habitual loser and conference stepchild to a 60-23-5 record, a Sugar Bowl upset over one of Bud Wilkinson's great Oklahoma teams, and a Cotton Bowl victory against TCU—a top-ten squad. In eight seasons, his Kentucky Wildcats finished in the Associated Press Top Twenty five times. Given the sorry facilities and the absence of football tradition, along with the specter of basketball baron Adolph Rupp, the state's most powerful man, no one in the history of the Southeastern Conference had done more with less.

Now he was running the hell away from Rupp.

The second-biggest divorce case of 1954 after Monroe versus DiMaggio might have been Bryant's split with Kentucky. A mandate from the governor was required to free Bryant from the final twelve years of his contract, and with that accomplished, he was apprised that all of the

2

big-time and high-paying college jobs were filled. About the only thing left was at Texas A&M, where the Aggies hadn't clinched a conference championship since the week before Pearl Harbor. Now Bryant had a mess on his hands—not to mention a team that had lost its last five games in '53 by a combined score of 133–41.

"God, I guess I've gone and flushed down eight years of hard work," he told his wife, Mary Harmon, on the day he quit Kentucky. "All because Adolph Rupp gets the gravy." Mary Harmon cried.

Situated on the flat belly of central Texas, Texas A&M was what most folks called a pissant little place. The campus possessed all of the glamour of a stock show—an all-military, all-male institution that looked like a penitentiary and boasted the color scheme of a grocery bag. Some folks called it a cow college. The only thing missing was a cattle guard at the front entrance. It was ninety miles from Houston, the closest big city, and had little to offer to a driven man like Bryant.

The University of Texas over in Austin was a country club compared to A&M. Texas students, known as teasips, liked to say that "A&M is where the men are men and the sheep are scared shitless." Football recruiters told top stud blue-chip prospects, "Hell's bells, son, you don't wanna go down there. They blow a horn to get you up, ring a bell to put you to sleep. No girls. No nothin'." No wonder they called the place Old Army. Texas A&M chancellor Marion Thomas Harrington feared that Bryant would take one look at this cold, colorless, and womanless world and run all the way back to Kentucky. So Harrington scheduled his interview for Dallas, more than two hundred miles to the northeast.

When Harrington strolled into the suite of the fashionable Fairmont Hotel on Ross Avenue that cold January morning, he quickly pulled the drapes. He took a seat near the center of the boardroom table and was flanked by Jack Finney and W. T. "Doc" Doherty—both members of the A&M board of directors. The carpet was thick and a broad crystal chandelier lit the room.

Bryant pulled an unfiltered Chesterfield from his shirt pocket, stamped it on the silver flip-top lighter, and quietly analyzed the men in dark suits.

"I don't know what y'all are tryin' to hide here," he drawled, flipping the lighter closed. "But you oughta know that when I was in Kentucky, me and Mary Harmon lived right next to the Idle Hour Country Club— I'm sure you've heard of the place. We were members. Hell, we had about the only air-conditioned house in Lexington. They paid me a good wage. You should also know, Dr. Harrington, I had lots of offers from schools all over the country. The Arkansas people flew me in and offered me an oil-and-gas deal about three years ago. I'd be a millionaire today if I'd took it. Anyway, boys, I want to be head football coach and athletic director. So, you see, I ain't comin' to Texas for no bullshit.''

Harrington cleared his throat. ''I can assure you, Paul, that our offer will be competitive with anything you'll find in any part of the country. In case you didn't know, Gen. Sam Houston's son himself was in our very first class. You'll just not find a finer place in America than College Station. You're going to fall in love with the place. It will grow on you, Paul.''

Finney was the athletic committee chairman and a well-heeled oilman. ''Tell me, Jack,'' Bryant said. ''If we could offer any boy in Texas the same scholarship deal as the University of Texas and there were twenty good studs out there, how many'd we get?''

Slapping a flat palm on the table, Finney looked like a bulldog about to break his chain. ''Ten, and I can guaran-god-damn-tee you that,'' he said.

''OK, boys, let's ante up,'' the coach said, leaning back and rocking his chair onto its rear legs. ''How much money we talkin' here?''

''We've got $15,000 to offer,'' Harrington said quickly.

''You know that won't do,'' Bryant shot back, the chair tumbling forward.

Doc Doherty, an independently wealthy man, spoke up: ''I'll write you a $10,000 check from my company every year.''

''What about oil wells—things of that nature?'' Bryant asked, his eyes narrowing.

''We've got a man living outside Austin who'll take care of you,'' Finney said. ''You'll have a beautiful house, two Cadillacs to drive, and all the damn money you and Mary Harmon can ever spend.''

Bryant stood slowly and cracked the drapes. Fourteen stories below, the Dallas morning traffic buzzed along Ross Avenue. He gazed at Pegasus, the flying red horse that adorned the rooftop of the Mobil Building. Through the haze, he could see all the way to the tall tower with WFAA-TV emblazoned on it.

''Boys,'' Bryant drawled, turning toward the men. ''I guess I'd better get on back to Kentucky and try to explain all of this to Mary Harmon. She's already cried her eyeballs out once. But you can look for me in early February.''

Swaggering toward the door, Bryant turned and looked at Doherty. ''By the way, Doc,'' he said. ''I hear your campus looks like a prison. I'm sure everything'll be locked up pretty tight when I get down there.''

. . .

Six thousand cadets packed the Grove theater as Stallings elbowed his way through the sea of military uniforms. One of the torches cast its light on Billy Schroeder, a tall, square-jawed boy of German descent who'd been a starting end as a sophomore in 1953. Billy's eyes seemed to be propped open with toothpicks, and he was smiling like he'd just chugalugged a keg of Lone Star beer.

''Bebes, we've been saved!'' he shouted to Stallings.

Stallings had been called Bebes since infancy, when his older brother couldn't pronounce Baby Gene. He could never remember being called Gene and was even registered as Bebes Stallings on his Social Security card.

''I know it looks pretty good!'' Stallings tried to shout over the crowd. ''But I've never heard of this man!''

''Never even heard of him—how's that possible?'' Schroeder said in disbelief. ''This man's the greatest coach in college football! Shoot, Bebes, he's bigger than Frank Leahy. He's gonna put A&M football back on the map!''

Stallings had lived with constant and painful infections in his left ear since infancy, confounding doctors and causing almost total deafness. He turned his right ear toward Schroeder as the large boy hollered above the crowd, ''Come on, Bebes! The rest of the team's up front.''

Five students bounced onto the stage wearing white shirts, white pants, white belts, white socks, and white shoes. A stranger who'd just wandered onto campus might have thought they were orderlies from the funny farm. The yell leaders each wore flattops and had eyes bigger than flying saucers. They cavorted across the stage, shouting, ''Whoa ha, gig 'em, Aggies!'' They rolled up their sleeves and placed hands on their knees as the Aggie Band roared into the second chorus of the ''Spirit of Aggieland.''

''T-E-X-A-S, A-G-G-I-E,
Fight! Fight! Fight-Fight-Fight!
Fight! Maroon! White-White-White!
A-G-G-I-E, Texas! Texas! A-M-C!
Gig 'em, Aggies! 1! 2! 3!''

From a rear corner of the stage, tucked into the shadows, Bear Bryant was bemused by the entire scene—the torches, the chanting, and five men dressed like Mr. Clean. The yell leaders twirled their hands and punched the air. The cadets, now swaying arm in arm, began to sing again. Next to Bryant stood Jones Ramsey, the affable sports information director who was fondly called the world's tallest fat man. Ramsey was there to coach Bryant on his speech.

"How many ya figure are here?" the coach asked.

"Best I can tell, about six thousand. Best damn turnout I've ever seen."

"How many we got in school right now?"

"Last count, sixty-two hundred."

"Then where in the hell are the other two hundred turds!"

"Don't know, Coach. Maybe we could send a posse out and hang 'em."

Crushing a Chesterfield beneath his large right shoe, Bryant said, "OK, what should I say to these toy soldiers?"

"My advice," Ramsey said, "is give 'em what they want. Hell, you could bring down the damn house with a loud burp."

This arena, this stage, was what Bryant had coveted since growing up dirt-poor in the Arkansas creek bottoms. Even on frozen mornings when he built the fire, slopped the hogs, and hooked up the team of mules to the family wagon, the boy kept dreaming. He recognized things about human nature long before anyone knew this about him. He often told himself, even on the darkest and saddest days, that someday he would be somebody.

At age forty, the face was dark and chiseled. He stood six-foot-two and weighed 220 pounds, and the frame bespoke a toughness. After fifteen years of chain-smoking unfiltered cigarettes, the voice had sunk to a gravelly bass, and he spoke with a heavy southern drawl that promoted an air of authority. For years Bryant had practiced and then perfected the art of walking slowly and talking slowly and of punctuating public speeches with stops and pregnant pauses so the crowd could hang on his every word. In spite of the drinking, the cussing, and the hard attitude, here was a man who could warm the pulpit.

Back in Kentucky, a good friend, Bull Hancock, had brought it all into focus one night as they were knocking back a bottle of Bryant's favorite bourbon. A hugely successful Thoroughbred breeder and owner, Hancock slapped Bryant's shoulder and said, "Paul, I don't think it's so much that you coach football as you coach people. You just have a way with folks."

That first night in Aggieland, Bryant wore a dark flannel suit with cuffed pants. A dab of Brylcreem mixed with his dark curls. Walking slowly to the front of the stage, he could see rows and rows of cadets far into the darkness. The army ROTC boys wore olive shirts with black ties, and the air force ROTC boys had donned dark shirts with green ties. Several flags signifying the colors of the squadrons and the companies were held aloft, and for a time Bryant could feel himself drifting back to his own naval days on the USS *Uruguay,* sailing to North Africa during World War II.

The torchlights created strange flickering flames that cast long and jerky shadows. Suddenly the adrenaline kicked in and his charisma bubbled to the surface. Bryant ripped off his suit coat and glared at the crowd like a man ready for a back-alley fight. He slammed the expensive fabric down on the stage and stomped it with both shoes. Whipping off his tie, he twirled it above his head and threw it down. He kicked and stomped the tie like a menacing rattlesnake and then danced around it. He mimicked the yell leaders by rolling up his sleeves almost to the elbows. Then he cradled the silver microphone in both hands and waited for the silence.

"Boys," he drawled deeply and resonantly and then paused. "It's time to win some damn football games."

Not since 1939 had there been such a thunderous roar on the spartan prairie. That year, A&M beat Texas 20–zip and the Aggies were voted number one in the final Associated Press poll. The sound washed over Bryant. Bebes Stallings, standing just below him, felt a piercing pain in his left eardrum, and he rubbed the lobe with his hand. The loudest cheers came from the Aggie players, standing just a few feet from the stage. Don Watson, a scatback from Franklin, pulled a tiny silver flask from his rear pocket and pumped a shot of bourbon down his throat. "I just saw God!" Watson squealed. Dennis Goehring, a stumpy guard, rammed a sawed-off little finger into the sternum of Bobby Drake Keith, who jumped more than a foot off the ground.

"Take that, you little sonofabitch!" Goehring hollered in a sandpaper voice before turning and grabbing at Watson's flask. Players backed away from Goehring, who possessed a devilish humor. Big Jack Pardee had a big smile plastered to his face and, as usual, said nothing. Marvin Tate was awestruck by the entire scene. Standing almost a head above the crowd, Schroeder tried to catch Bryant's eye, flashing him the thumbs-up "Gig 'em, Aggies" sign.

Bryant had grudgingly accepted a sad reality—that the stepchild he'd adopted was ugly. He still wasn't sure, though, how far the Aggies had fallen. Many of these boys still hadn't been to the first grade when the Aggies last ascended to the Cotton Bowl. But as he looked into their bright eyes and eager faces, he could see hope.

"I want to tell y'all one thing," he said. "We'll win again. We *must* win again."

A cannon rolled in the distance and horns blared and Bryant knew he could have spoken all night and the cadets would have stood and cheered and waved their torches and sung their songs and boosted their banners. But the coach had learned a vital secret about communicating; a leader should carefully limit his time with the troops so that every syllable counted and every word was remembered. He could have promised them a championship that night. But he was certain he didn't have the livestock to back it up.

Bryant scooped up the tie and wrapped it loosely around his neck. He smoothed the lapels and stuck a hand in his left pocket. Tucking the folded coat between his hip and left wrist, he slowly swaggered away. Descending the stairs behind the stage, he set his eyes on Ramsey, who seemed besotted by the show. "You know, it was like strange voodoo out there," Bryant said. "They'd a hollered and cheered if I'd peed on the stage."

Turning toward the crowd a final time, Bryant said, "I know one thing about those fellers. Ten of 'em can out-yell a hundred of anybody else's."

Bryant paused once more to watch the bonfire and to feel the power of his own presence.

"I sure as hell lit a fire tonight, didn't I?" he said, slapping Ramsey on the shoulder.

• • •

The knock came softly at first and Bryant decided to ignore it. Anybody that limp-wristed wasn't coming into his temporary living quarters on the second floor of the Memorial Student Center, a low-slung brick building that had been completed three years earlier.

Fifteen seconds later, he heard another knock. "Go away, wimp!" he barked. "Come back when you get a gut in your body."

Then came the pounding. "That's better!" he yelled. "Open the goddamn door and come in."

It was Willie Zapalac, a fresh-faced assistant coach who'd played for the Aggies in the forties and was full of spunk. He was the only coach still hanging around from the days of Ray George. Willie thought he still had a job and in fact, Dr. Harrington had told him that he'd be retained regardless of who was hired. That seemed like a solid promise since Dr. Harrington was the chancellor of Texas A&M College.

But assistant athletic director Bones Gates had told Willie to pack his bags a few days after Bryant was hired. Zapalac persisted and Gates suggested that he take it up with the headman himself.

"Let me ask you a couple of things?" Bryant said after Willie took a seat. "What would you think about winning the Southwest Conference with this sorry bunch?"

"I think it could—"

"You *think*," Bryant hollered loud enough to be heard across the street at G. Rollie White Coliseum. "I don't want a bunch of people around here who *think*. Now goddammit, answer the question."

"Based on what I know about the team, we could. I think—"

"Mister, you've got one more chance."

"Yes, sir, it *will* happen," Zapalac said, jumping to his feet and saluting.

"Now get your ass out of my office. You're the only coach I'm keepin'. So don't screw it up. And *never* salute me again."

"Yes, sir."

Bryant's eyes almost burned a hole in Zapalac's flannel shirt. "Son," he said. "On your way out, tell the next man in line to come on in." This puzzled Willie to no end. When he'd arrived at Bryant's door, no one else was waiting outside. Returning to the hallway, though, he bumped into head trainer Bill Dayton, who was leaning against the wall, checking his watch.

"Coach said g-go on in," a rattled Zapalac said. "Good luck, Bill."

For a hardworking man who dealt in bruised and battered bodies, Dayton was sharply dressed and starched. He wore khaki pants and a white button-down shirt with two silver ballpoint pens neatly aligned in the shirt pocket. His black shoes shone like mirrors, and his flattop was freshly buzzed.

"Bill, tell me about yourself," the coach said flatly, clearly in no mood for boasting or fanfare.

"Coach, as you know, I've been here six years and I have a degree in kinesiology. I have one year of medical school remaining and then I'll be a medical doctor. I am one of three licensed trainers in Texas. I go to work at six in the morning, and a lot of nights I don't go home until past ten. I love my work, I love Texas A&M, and there's nothing I'd rather do than work with Aggie athletes.''

Bryant leaned back in his chair and tapped his forehead with a pencil. He reached for the cigarette pack, lit one, and then left it burning in the ashtray. He gazed through the window where he could see one of the companies marching to lunch. Turning toward the trainer, Bryant locked his gaze on the man's dark eyes.

''I'm going to make it short and sweet, Bill. I don't want a medical man messin' with my football players. I don't want a man who knows somethin' called kinesiology pampering my boys. I don't need a man telling my boys what's wrong with them. I need a man who'll stick 'em in the whirlpool, give 'em an aspirin, or tell 'em to take a shower when they've got a pulled muscle. I've heard all about you, Bill. You sit players out two weeks with a pulled hamstring. You sit players out two weeks with a hip pointer.

''Did they ever tell you that when I was at the University of Alabama, playin' football, I played a whole game against Tennessee with a broken leg? And, by God, it probably was my best game. I was an ol' slow boy, but I caught a long touchdown pass. I lateraled off to our quarterback for another one. And I got their quarterback three times behind the line. We won 25 to nothin'. Hell, Bill, I didn't need two weeks off. I just needed somebody to cut the damn cast off my leg so I could get out there and bust some ass!''

Dayton's heart had sunk into his glossy shoes. When first summoned by Bryant, he had figured it to be a get-acquainted meeting. Now, he was getting canned for reasons that seemed confusing.

''Get your ass out of my office, Dr. Dayton. You've got ten minutes to clean your shit out of my locker room and ten more minutes to get off campus. I'll mail your last check.''

Minutes later, Dayton hustled through the trainers' room. He waved at student assistant Billy Pickard. ''I'm going home, son. Go ahead and lock up tonight, Billy.''

''But, Bill,'' Pickard said as Dayton shot through the door. *''You've got the only keys!''*

Pickard, a skinny sophomore with a peeled head, didn't know what to make of the panic in Bill's eyes. He couldn't imagine what had overcome his boss, a man rarely off the clock. Billy thought Dayton was the best trainer in Texas. Why, he had brought players back from injuries in two or three weeks and most had played the rest of the season without a limp.

Across campus, on the second floor of the MSC, Bryant paced restlessly. He felt alone and out of place at Texas A&M and, for the first time in many years, was experiencing some self-doubts. He'd made three bad career decisions in the last three years—turning down the Arkansas job because the timing wasn't right; telling Alabama to come back later because he didn't want to undercut his former coach and old friend Red Drew; and stomping out of Kentucky, where Adolph Rupp would forever be king.

Bryant had gone ballistic when he thought Kentucky president Herman L. Donovan lied to him—privately promising to fire Rupp after a shameful point-shaving scandal rocked the basketball team. Instead, Donovan had awarded Rupp a contract extension and given him a new Cadillac. In turn, Bryant got a new cigarette lighter.

The last few days, Bryant had worried if A&M was where he was meant to be. Frank Thomas, his mentor and former head coach at Alabama, had told him long ago that he should be making his way in coaching by age forty. So, here he was at the magic number, wanting more than he'd already gotten and wondering if he'd already blown it. The Kentucky scene was still replaying in his mind when the two shiny sedans and a new pickup pulled up to the curb outside the MSC and parked. He watched from above as the men made their way through the front door, and for the first time that day Bryant smiled.

Then a ringing phone interrupted his good mood. On the line was assistant coach Elmer Smith, who'd been dispatched to recruit players at an Alabama high school all-star game.

"Got any boys worth a damn there, Elmer?"

"Yeah, Coach, there's one."

"Then sign him up."

"Coach, there's only one problem."

"What's that?"

Smith paused. "He's only got one arm."

Bryant had barely hung up the phone when there was a loud knock. He was still chuckling when he opened the door and greeted five of the biggest powerbrokers that A&M had to offer. These men would be called "suits" in most places. But not in Texas, where bigwigs liked to wear boots, jeans, and hats and many of them chewed Red Man. Rich guys also liked to drive pickups—nice ones with air-conditioning.

Since the first year of recruiting was going nowhere, Bryant had called a meeting of the big wallets. He shook hands with Johnny Mitchell, a local

11

oilman who once had hit 151 consecutive wells, missed 1, and then hit 18 straight. Also invited was Jack Finney, who had attended Bryant's job interview in Dallas. From Houston came Bobby Don Crockett, and from his ranch near Austin came Herman Heep, a rich oilman who had jumped the Aggie ship during the losing years but was lured back by Bryant's charisma. Heep had enough money to completely rebuild Texas A&M if he felt like it. The last man through the door wore jeans and a work shirt and hadn't shaved in about a week. He extended his right hand to Bryant, who knew very little about him. "Name's Sid Banker," he said in a cigarette baritone. "Some folks just call me the banker. You just call me Sid."

Bryant had ordered a table for the meeting, hoping to create a kind of boardroom effect; that wasn't working. The head of the student center had sent up an old dining table that was covered with mustard and ketchup stains. It didn't seem to bother the Aggie sugar daddies, though. Some broke out cigars and flasks and didn't even ask for ice.

"Men. I don't need to tell you fellas that our recruiting's down. Just got a call from Elmer Smith. Sent him to Alabama on a recruiting mission and all he's coming back with is this one-armed boy. That's kind of been the sad story. Right now, we're in the fight of our lives to get John Crow out of Louisiana. Elmer's been baby-sitting him about every day. But the LSU people've offered John Crow everything but a saloon on Bourbon Street."

Two other targeted blue chippers were Ken Hall, a running back from Sugar Land, and Charlie Krueger—probably the best lineman to come out of Texas in ten years. Hall, who had gained 4,000 yards as a senior, was called the Sugar Land Express. Krueger had grown up dirt-poor on a sharecropper's farm where the windows were covered with croaker sacks. Bryant suspected that Texas and Rice had already offered Charlie some cash and, as he liked to say, "It's mighty hard to turn down something if you've never had nothin' at all."

Bryant drew on a cigarette and turned toward Jack Finney. "A few weeks ago, Jack, I asked you a key question. And you told me that of all the big studs in Texas, you thought we could get at least half."

"Yeah, and I still believe it."

"Well, we're runnin' out of time."

Placing both hands on the table, Bryant assessed each face.

"I think that each and every one of you is sick and tired of the losing. A&M hasn't won a damn thing since before the war, and there's a lot of negative recruiting goin' on. All they gotta do is tell the top recruits that A&M's got no girls and we've lost the boy.''

Bryant dropped a silver spittoon on the table. ''I made my commitment when I took this job. Now it's time for you to make yours.''

Nobody moved.

''Boys. Just think of this as going to church and dropping the dough in the plate. Let's see how much commitment you got in your hearts.''

The first two rolls of hundred-dollar bills were bundled by rubber bands. They amounted to $5,000. From the corner of the table came another $5,000. When the tithing stopped, the spittoon was almost full. It all amounted to $30,000. Not bad. He'd never collected that much money in one sitting in Kentucky, where the bluebloods kept that much cash around for cab fare or for betting the daily double. He knew it would buy two or three good players.

Bryant smiled.

''Boys, with this kind of money, we might just be able to fix the wagon and paint the barn. One more thing before you go. A couple of years ago, the NCAA got cute and started an enforcement division. Seems they've got their backs up. When I was at Kentucky, they put the basketball team on probation for shavin' points. Now, I sure as hell know the NC-double-A boys will come sniffin' when we start winning. They'll be checking our boys' rags and their rides. Every coach in the Southwest Conference will be pointing the finger at us. So I'm asking you boys to keep your mouths shut. There's nothin' wrong with a little discretion ever' now and then.''

Bryant stood at the door and shook every hand. Sid Banker, the last man out, winked at him.

An important lesson Bryant had learned through the years was that you don't buy every boy. Studs with big up-front bonuses tended to develop an attitude you could spot a mile away. Clothes, cars, and pretty girls normally spoiled a boy. Bryant thought about a line from a Hank Williams song that had climbed the charts to number one in 1954: ''Your cheatin' heart will tell on you.''

At four that afternoon, the single-engine crop duster took off from a cow pasture about five miles from campus. It banked near the student center so Bryant, gazing from his window, could see it. The pilot dipped the wings twice. Then the plane disappeared into the high white clouds. The bagman had carved out a square block in a bale of hay. Ten thousand dollars in hundred-dollar bills had been tightly wrapped inside a Texas A&M flag. The hope was that the bale would break apart when it hit the ground. They damn sure didn't want it cracking open in midflight. Hundreds and hundreds of dollars raining down from the heavens might be confused with divine generosity.

The engine whined loudly as the plane flew low over the house. Strapped tightly in his seat, the bagman grunted and then pushed open the passenger door. The bale tumbled from the plane and rolled end over end as it plummeted toward the field of brown weeds. To assure the mission was accomplished, the pilot banked the plane once more and soared over the house. Through the bare trees, the men could see two people running from the front porch. The maroon-and-white A&M flag was lying in clear view amid the broken pieces of straw. The pilot and the bagman smiled as the plane hummed toward home above the flat, barren countryside of central Texas.

Back at A&M, Bear Bryant gazed at the drab buildings and watched the cadets marching in the fading afternoon light. He wondered if the mission had been accomplished—and if they'd gotten their man.

· · ·

The old man sauntered into the training room, his crude hearing aid hanging from his neck by a worn and tattered shoelace. His back pocket bulged with a flat longneck pint of brown liquid.

"Hey, Smokey, what you got there in your pocket?" Billy Pickard said.

"That's my cousin I. W. Me and him are gonna have a long talk after a while."

In more than thirty years of athletic training, Smokey Harper was known as much for guzzling I. W. Harper as for rehabilitating players. There were three rules in Smokey's training room. "If the pain's above your neck," he'd say, "take an aspirin. If the pain's below your neck, take a hot whoolpool. If that don't work then, shit, son, take a hot shower."

No one was sure of the extent of Smokey's medical studies. He'd played some basketball at Mercer College and some backwoods semipro baseball in South Carolina with Shoeless Joe Jackson after the former Chicago Black Sox outfielder was banned from the major leagues for agreeing to fix the 1919 World Series.

"Shoeless Joe's the best damn hitter I ever saw," Smokey would say. "And the second-best drinker behind me."

From across the room, Billy Pickard observed old Smokey and wondered how he had been picked to replace a fine man like Bill Dayton. Now the locker room was alive with the clacking of cleats and the slamming of metal lockers. So many boys were trying to get dressed for the afternoon practice that they were knocking into one another. Players were sharing lockers, helmets, and jersey numbers. Dennis Goehring, his chubby face turning crimson, yelled across the room, "I'm gonna kick your ass today, Marvin Tate! Don't turn your back on me today."

Goehring then checked the team roster that was taped to the bulletin board. He was still a seventh-team guard, and Tate was a first-teamer.

"That shit's gonna change," Goehring muttered to himself.

Spring drills at Texas A&M were more like a calf scramble than football practice. Bryant had proudly scripted all of his drills to the minute, only to have the players trip over one another as they ran from station to station. A student manager would blow his whistle every nine minutes, igniting total chaos. Bryant was the first college coach in America to develop such a schedule, and the result at Kentucky had been a national ranking and bowl games. At A&M, it was causing heartburn.

Bryant had worked the boys until their tongues hung out—and this was only spring practice. The season was still six months away.

"Ain't ever seen football players this bad," he said, standing at midfield, hands on hips, talking to assistant coach Pat James, a thick man with a chest like a beer keg. "Where in the hell'd they get these puke stains?"

"Coach, you won't believe this. But they've been signing up over a hundred boys every year for the last four years. If you're a high school kid in this state and your daddy's an Aggie, or if your daddy knows an Aggie, you get a free ride to A&M. Just like that."

"That's another thing buggin' me. Those dad-gum alums are callin' and writin' me every day. They're comin' out to our practices in busloads. I'd like to march over there and say, 'I'm the chief and you're the Indians and get your asses off my goddamn field.' "

Bryant and James quietly assessed the Aggie men who stood on the sidelines with their buzz haircuts and their short-sleeve shirts. Many appeared fat and out of shape, and Bryant thought they looked like beer swilling red-baiters. These were not the country clubbers that were being produced at SMU and just down the road at the University of Texas. These were members of the Rotary Club and the Cibango Club—an all-male organization for Aggies. You were never sure if these guys actually graduated from A&M or not. They did brag a lot, though, even when the Aggies were losing.

15

James spit tobacco and smiled. "Coach, know how you can tell when an Aggie's been raking leaves?"

"No."

"He's got two broken legs from falling out of a tree."

Bear smiled for the first time that day.

In truth, Bryant had bigger problems than a bunch of meddling alums. Of the 200 players in uniform, no more than a handful could even spell football. It was almost whittling time, he thought. Otherwise, he wouldn't be able to distinguish the keepers from the turds. One boy who'd caught his eye was Fred Broussard, a muscular six-foot-two, 220-pound center from Cajun country in Louisiana. He was the biggest player on the field, and, at his size, Bryant thought he could be playing for the New York Giants.

The coach had logged mental notes on the big center—some good and some bad. When Fred felt like practicing, he could mow down anybody on the field. Other days, when his heart wasn't in it, he was mediocre, like most of the boys. Bryant didn't mind if a player was a little short in talent or stature if he compensated with a big heart. The players he hated were heavy on talent and light on guts. That was Fred all right.

Fred was jogging down the field on punt coverage when he stuck out a big paw and managed to trip Billy Pete Huddleston, a rabbit-quick half-back who was one of the best kick returners in the conference. Billy Pete hopped to his feet and, without warning, smacked Broussard in the nose with a left jab. Blood now smeared on his face, Fred was no longer just a lazy, overfed boy. He hit Billy Pete with a left-right combination that knocked his helmet flying. Billy Pete retreated and Fred landed several punches, knocking him down before the coaches could pull him away.

Later, as they stood on the sideline, Broussard approached his small tormentor. In a high, soft voice, Fred said, "Billy Pete, why'd you do that? Billy Pete, I like you."

Billy Pete cracked a smile that hurt immensely. "Believe me, Fred. It'll never happen again."

Day by day, Bryant was becoming more and more confused. He didn't expect the Aggies to match the talent he'd had in Kentucky. Still, some of the boys played as if they'd never had good coaching. Some couldn't block or tackle and he'd never seen more botched snaps. Some of the boys, like Billy Pete and Goehring, at least had the scrappiness to pick fights, but others were so polite that they didn't cuss, belch, or even smell bad after practice. A perfect example was Billy Schroeder, a tall, dark-haired end who wouldn't say shit if he had a mouthful.

At the end of practice, from the corner of his eye Bryant saw Billy approaching him. His helmet was tucked beneath his left arm, and his head was held high. Schroeder extended his right hand. "Coach, I just want to tell you how proud I am to be playing football for such a legend. I called my mom and dad last night and told 'em how excited I was." Schroeder wouldn't let go of the coach's right hand.

Finally yanking free, Bryant mumbled, "I wouldn't get too carried away, son. You might not feel the same after fall drills."

Schroeder's smile was frozen even as Bryant coolly turned his back and walked away.

About an hour later, the fresh drinks arrived, and it took Bryant about five seconds to knock back the first tumbler of bourbon. They had chosen the White Way Cafe across the main drag from campus. Jones Ramsey knew he was losing ground when he saw Bryant slam down his first drink.

The White Way Cafe was more a saloon than a restaurant, but a Greek cook there turned out the best chicken-fried steak and turnip greens in central Texas. Bear loved to soak his corn bread in the thick white gravy. On this warm, humid spring afternoon, though, they hadn't come to eat. They'd come to pound bourbon.

"You know that big-assed Fred Broussard?" Bryant said.

"Yes, sir, I do believe I helped make him first-team All–Southwest Conference last year," Ramsey replied, his chest swelling.

"Well, if it happens again, you're fired."

Ramsey almost dropped his drink. "Yes, sir."

Broussard had received film grades in the 80s and 90s from the previous coaching staff. But Bryant's top mark for him in any game was a 37. But that's not what really pissed him off. Fred had been allowed to come back to the team three times after quitting.

Bear turned up the second bourbon and slammed down the tumbler. "There's gotta be some changes around here. I'm gettin' ready to cut the squad, to yank some boys off the field. I can't see around the trash. I'm gonna tell about thirty of 'em that they can't play football anymore. Oh, they can keep their scholarships. But they'll have to work around the locker room, do odd jobs like cutting the grass. We need some boys to chalk the field and such."

Ramsey stared into his drink. This was preposterous, he thought. Given

Bryant's temper and the manner in which he was putting away bourbon, he decided to approach the matter slowly and with caution.

"They'll come out of the woodwork—the alums, I mean. You see, Coach, the old Aggies have been runnin' the program since the end of the war. You start cuttin' their boys and you're messin' with their nuts."

Bear groaned and lit a Chesterfield. He'd stomped off and quit jobs at Maryland and Kentucky for reasons that didn't begin to approach this.

"You know what I think," he said, knocking an ash to the floor. "I think we should blow it up and start over. The wrong people've been runnin' the joint for too long. Let's just torch the barn and kill the rats."

Ramsey was accustomed to putting out grass fires. But now the phone would be ringing off the wall. Bryant would be axing boys who had oil and political ties. Rich Aggies from Texarkana to El Paso would scream into the phone, "What in the hell is this man doing to our football team?" Ramsey would try to be patient: "I'm not sure, but, you know, the man won a lot of football games in Kentucky. So let's give him some time." Newspapers from Dallas, Fort Worth, Houston, and San Antonio would publish tall headlines about the radical changes. They'd be laughing in their martinis at the University of Texas.

The second drink hit Ramsey's stomach like a bombshell. Meanwhile, Bryant was ordering another round. The coach from Kentucky was just getting warmed up. Soon folks in Texas would know much about this man. Some would love him. Others would rue the night he dropped in from the dark, roily sky.

2

The Boys

In a crisis, don't hide behind anything or anybody
They're going to find you anyway.

—PAUL "BEAR" BRYANT

SUMMER OF 1954

The young cowboy had rattled along in the bobtail pickup all the way from the dusty little town of Sinton, where he'd stuck out his thumb. The driver, a roughneck with thick, long sideburns, turned up the radio every time a Hank Williams song came on. Now they were singing along to the number-one country-and-western hit of the year.

"Hey, good-lookin'
What ya got cookin'
How's about cookin' somethin' up with me."

For three months, Texas A&M halfback Don Watson had pretended to be working in the Heep oil fields in South Texas. Oh, he'd painted a couple of oil rigs and dug a few shovels of dirt one afternoon when it turned

19

cloudy. Mostly, he'd played and romped like a bull, beating the other boys at high jumping and broad jumping and climbing the water tower.

Every day, Aggie fullback Bob Easley tried to beat the sassy little Watson at some little game. Easley always lost, because Watson was too quick and agile and was considered the fastest player in the Southwest Conference, having been clocked at 9.5 seconds in the 100-yard dash on a cinder track. Today Watson had proposed another race. He and Easley would shinny up twin twenty-foot iron pipes, and the first one to touch the water tank was the winner.

Watson won easily, and as Easley slid back down the pipe he pointed a finger at his little buddy and hollered, "You ain't nothin' but a goddamn weasel!" The little running back cocked his head backward and laughed, exposing his tiny teeth. Hardly anyone called him Don for the next three years.

The Heep oil fields, just north of Corpus Christi and about thirty miles from the Gulf of Mexico, had for several years been the summer home for several Aggie footballers trying to earn a few bucks between the spring semester and fall two-a-day practices. Herman Heep paid the boys $1.50 an hour, a good wage for 1954, for not doing much. Every afternoon after "work," part-time Aggie coach Lou Carreker sent them through football drills on a grassy field adjacent to the compound. Jerry Claiborne and Phil Cutchin, two of Bryant's most trusted coaches, drove from College Station once a week to ride herd on the workouts. Among the players who'd made the Sinton trek were Jack Pardee, Davey Smith, Joe Schero, Herb Wolf, Bobby Jack Lockett, Dee Powell, Billy Schroeder, Easley, and Watson. They slept in a large wood-frame house on the Heep property where the refrigerator was filled with an odd mix of Kool-Aid and beer.

When the boys weren't trying to beat Watson in a footrace or tossing around the pigskin, they were talking about the Man back in College Station. They were feeling a little anxious about this coach called Bear Bryant, a man who had walked into their lives six months earlier.

"That sucker seems meaner than a javelina," said Bobby Jack Lockett, referring to the wild boars with razor-sharp teeth that roamed the Rio Grande Valley near the southern tip of Texas.

Pardee pulled a dry weed from between his teeth and said, "I thought the toughest men I ever met were roughnecks. Danged if I wasn't wrong about that."

As September approached, the boys spent more and more time pondering their fate with their new coach. They had heard about Bryant's reputation at Kentucky and witnessed his temper during spring practice. God, they dreaded the two-a-day workouts that would be held in this Texas oven.

Restless and ready for some fun, Watson was the first player to say good-bye to Sinton that August. He had no trouble hitching a ride up Highway 77. Folks were friendly and unwary of strangers in that part of the country. He wore cowboy boots, blue jeans, and a freshly washed T-shirt. In his duffle bag, he carried a toothbrush and a football. As they were rolling north up the two-laner, the discussion between Weasel and the roughneck turned to the upcoming season.

"I hear Bear Bryant's a mean sonofabitch," the driver said.

"Nix," Watson said. "He ain't no meaner than any man I ever met."

Tough times had been like a sidekick to Weasel, whose dad had vanished one day from their home in the tiny town of Franklin when the boy was only fifteen. His mother didn't have the prospects for a good-paying job. So Don and Dick, his younger brother, moved into a storage building behind a house belonging to his aunt and uncle. The place wasn't heated and had no bathroom. The boys were expected to pee in a large pot and carry it to the back of the property for dumping. Instead, they whizzed through the back windows until the screens started to rot.

Football recruiters came in droves to Franklin, drawn like moths to a light by Weasel's speed. He chose A&M because the Aggie coaches made a lot of promises.

Now, as the pickup rolled along the lean two-laner, they spotted the CITY LIMITS signs of La Grange. The Texas A&M campus was still another seventy miles up the highway, but Weasel was feeling an itch.

"Let me off up here by this train trestle," he told the roughneck.

"Son, you know I'm goin' all the way to College Station. But I see you're aimin' to sow some oats. Son, I really can't say that I blame ya."

Watson was so small and agile that he leaped through the window of the passenger door without opening it, landing gracefully as his boots smacked the asphalt in unison. He waved good-bye to the driver and took off running across the railroad tracks and down the long, dusty road toward the large white wood-frame house where he could hear fiddles and steel guitars wailing through open windows. He ran through a pecan grove and down the white fence line with his duffel bag tucked to his ribs like an oversize football. God, he was excited to see the Chicken Ranch again— its fresh paint and front porch swing and the large upstairs bedroom shaped like a spire. It was the best whorehouse in Texas, he thought, or at least that's what he'd heard. His sexual experiences had been limited to a few visits. He ran past a windmill and a barking dog and up the steps, where a large black woman met him at the door with a warm smile. She reminded him of the lady on the front of the flour box—Aunt Jemima.

"Well, hello, Don, haven't see you in some time," she said, her eyes gliding from the tip of his flattop to the soles of his dusty black boots.

"Shoot, Miss Mona, everybody's callin' me Weasel now. I don't know if I like it. But I guess everybody needs a nickname."

"Well, I'm quite sure that one fits you just fine."

"How're the girls? Can I come in?"

"Are you goin' to behave? You know I've had some complaints about you, Weasel."

Watson was a polished deal maker. He loved talking the girls into cut-rate deals. He rarely had enough money for the girls and beer, too, and he liked to have both. One just seemed to enhance the other.

"I promise."

"Then sweep yourself off, cowboy."

As she swung open the front door, Weasel saw the grand establishment unfolding before his eyes. He considered it the prettiest place in Texas. Marble tile beneath his feet led to a carpeted stairway that seemed to rise to the sky. To the right of the drawing room was a dark saloon where an old farmer in overalls snuggled up to a girl in her early twenties. She wore a see-through gown that revealed black panties and a black bra. They were trying to slow-dance, but the farmer's feet seemed glued to the hardwood floor. From the jukebox came the saddest song Weasel had ever heard, the voice belonging to the great Western Swinger himself, Bob Wills:

"I miss you, darlin', more and more every day
As heavens would miss the stars above
Through every heartbeat, I still think of you
And remember our faded love."

The Chicken Ranch was a fabled institution to desirous men from Austin to Houston and all of the bus stops and train depots in between. For almost a hundred years, the girls had been satisfying senators, soldiers, governors, cowboys, oilmen, farmers, bank robbers, train robbers, and, according to lore, even a couple of presidents. It was no secret that legislators from the state capital had been burning up the highway for years between Austin and La Grange.

After the market crashed in 1929, the depression came early and stayed late in Texas. A drought almost killed the ranching, and about the same time wildcatters started punching dry holes all over the state. Because times were bad and money was lean, men came to La Grange with little or no cash. So they started exchanging chickens for sex. Pretty soon, the back pasture was overrun with chickens and the place had a name that had stuck for almost twenty-five years—the Chicken Ranch.

A celebrated tradition in this haven for sin was the party that followed the Thanksgiving game between Texas and A&M. Rich alums from the winning school would spring for the booze and the bedroom frolicking. Texas A&M had won the big game only once since 1939. Weasel was pretty sure the bad run would continue in 1954, since the Aggies were slim on talent. That's why he was bankrolling his own visit and why he was following Miss Mona as she walked along the red carpet into the parlor, where he was greeted by several sexy young girls who stood, smiled, and formed a straight line. They wore revealing lingerie and enough perfume to make Weasel's eyes burn. One girl, Patsy, exposed a large portion of her immense and perfectly shaped right breast. He quickly chose Patsy.

After they ascended the stairs, Weasel squeezed her left elbow and steered Patsy into the first bedroom on the right.

"Where the hell you been?" she said, a frown forming at the corners of her mouth. She slammed the door. "And when are you gonna pay me the money you owe me?"

"Look, darlin,' " Weasel said, shucking his dusty boots. "I been out workin' all summer. I got some money coming. But all I've got to pay right now is two dollars and fifty cents. That's all the money I have in this dang world."

Patsy pouted. "You know it cost three dollars. Every time you come in here, you try to cut-rate me." She fell into the chair by the side of the bed and gazed at Weasel with sad brown eyes. "You know I'm trying to get back into the University of Texas, honey. I gotta pay tuition in two weeks. I don't have a big football scholarship like you do."

Weasel put two one-dollar bills and two quarters on the bedside table. He promised to do better next time. Patsy didn't know if she felt sorry for him or just thought he was cute. But the springs were soon creaking and the farmer downstairs heard a "yee-haw" echoing down the stairwell.

Thirty minutes later, Weasel swaggered into the saloon and plopped two shiny quarters on the bar, smiling like the canary-eating cat. He ordered two long-neck Lone Star beers and slammed them down, feeling a quick buzz. He then hustled down the front porch stairs and took off for the highway, where he quickly hooked another ride. A man they called Bear was waiting for him in College Station.

• • •

Dennis Goerhing was born on a ranch between San Marcos and New Braunfels in German country. Just down the two-laner were Staples and Zorn and Prairie Lea. Half of the ranch sat on the eastern edge of the Hill Country, and the other half sprawled across the Texas prairie. For years, rains had soaked the pastures. The market prices on goats and cattle soared, and just about everybody felt the pinch of prosperity. Life was good.

The ranches of south central Texas supported a mixture of Anglo, German, and Mexican folks. Everyone got along well, mostly because the Anglos and the Germans loved Mexican food and the Mexicans worshiped football. It seemed that everybody over sixteen drank beer.

Dennis owned a prize-winning grand championship cow that, over a period of four years, won $1,900 at county fair shows. He carried around a wad of money, and in 1951 he wrote a $800 check to his grandfather for his '48 four-door Chevrolet. Many nights were spent tooling up and down Old Spanish Road.

In his early teens Dennis was short and stocky and his arms and chest had yet to develop, even though folks down at the drugstore admired his blocking and tackling and talked about him frequently. He didn't gain much weight because of the long, hard days of ranch work, days that began with the cow-milking at five every morning. He could unload every bale of hay from an eighteen-wheeler and stack it himself without even breathing hard. He was accustomed to the grinding work beneath the blazing sun, and it toughened his hide and his attitude. Even the older boys were afraid to cross him, because Dennis had a mean streak and they couldn't remember the last time he'd been whipped.

Since the third grade, though, he'd been troubled about his left pinky finger that had been smashed in a strange accident. He'd been enduring saxophone lessons one afternoon when the teacher asked him to help roll a piano across the classroom. Pushing with his shoulder and back, he huffed and puffed and managed to tip the piano over. Crushed between

24

the floor and piano was his little finger, which looked like a limp piece of raw meat. The boy didn't cry, though, and his mother took him to the local veterinarian to have it sewed up. The fingernail looked deformed as it grew back and covered the nub of his pinky. Dennis kept his left hand in his pants pocket much of the time, especially with girls around.

Almost ten years later, as he worked the family's ranch one summer day, the scarred finger became tangled in a rawhide rope. Yanking it loose, he saw that the appendage was gnarled and bloody and the end was missing. A few minutes later, he walked into the ranch house with the hand stuffed beneath his right armpit. Dennis calmly fetched the car keys from the kitchen counter and informed his mother that he was going to have the finger fixed once and for all.

"Don't worry. I'll be back for supper."

Dennis drove the Chevy to a doctor's office in New Braunfels where he waved his bloody left hand at the receptionist and was promptly admitted into the examining room.

"Chop it off at the knuckle, Doc. Ain't no reason to save it again. Get your saw."

Grudgingly agreeing to a painkilling shot of Novocain, he watched the doctor go to work with an instrument similar to a miniature hacksaw. Dennis could hear the blade working through the bone and didn't wince when it broke through to the other side, just above the middle knuckle.

"Sew it up tight now, Doc. Someday I might want to use it for a weapon."

For reasons he couldn't explain, the boy loved the hard labor and believed a work ethic had been burned into his genes. He was not among the elite blue-chip football studs recruited around Texas because his weight was stuck at 170 pounds and he just didn't seem big enough for the line. But the Aggies had decided to take a chance on him with a temporary scholarship. Now he faced the task of impressing a new coach. But Dennis had a plan in mind. He was determined to get Bear Bryant's attention, regardless of what it took.

Along with football, Dennis loved ranching—until the drought crept up out of Mexico and began to torch and scar the land. Most ranchers thought it was just another dry spell when the clouds dried up in 1950. That was until it persisted into the next summer, and into the next, and into the next. Thunderheads boiled out of nowhere, made a lot of racket, and then went away. Creeks and rivers began to recede, and a stock tank on the west side of the Goehring ranch became a stagnant mud puddle.

The verdant grass curled up and turned brown and then disappeared altogether. Only the mesquite and live oak and prickly pear survived as the fine dust piled up on rooftops and fence lines.

Old-timers could tell by the summer of '52 that the country was headed for a long and hellish drought. A brownish haze had settled along the horizon as the sun punished the earth day after day. Dust storms kicked up almost every afternoon. Some ranchers compared it to the drought of the thirties that lasted almost five years and practically killed the cow business, bankrupting ranches from Austin to New Mexico. Now, as then, the cattle searched the countryside for something to eat and found nothing but shriveling and often noxious weeds. Their hipbones began to stand out, and their ribs rippled below ragged hides.

A story making the circuit concerned a Texas rancher who died and began his journey to the Pearly Gates through a parched land.

"Saint Peter," he said on reaching his destination. "This looks just like Texas."

The gatekeeper smiled. "I'm not Saint Peter and obviously you don't know where you're at."

Spirits sank as the ranching business marched farther and farther south. If the drought continued—and there was no reason to believe it wouldn't—only the goats would survive. Folks prayed as the land withered.

Now, as he rode onto the ranch atop the big gray gelding, Dennis kept the bulky .45 pistol in the holster by his side. Finding dying cattle sprawled on the dried-up pasture had become all too common. They often were victims of screwworms, a parasitic blowfly that would lay eggs in the sores of the living animals. The screwworms attached themselves to the animal's vital organs and sucked out the life. They sometimes would screw themselves into the brain and then exit through the eyeballs. Dennis left the dead animals for the buzzards or the coyotes to clean up. But all too often the young cowboy discovered animals in the final stages of life, often suffering and crying out for help. That's why he carried the pistol—to point the muzzle into the earlobe and blow away the misery.

Riding the ranch one afternoon, he spotted a pack of turkey buzzards wheeling in the hazy blue sky. They were nasty birds with gnarly red heads and a wingspan of six feet. He figured they were chewing on more dead cattle, but drawing closer, he could see a cow's head flopping in pain on the ground. He kicked the gelding and rode up on a ghastly sight—buzzards chomping on a calf in midbirth. They had devoured everything from the head to the midsection, and as the mother labored to push more of her savaged newborn through the womb they ate that, too. Dennis pulled the pistol and began firing at the giant birds, dropping two and sending the rest flapping straight up. "Get your asses out of here, you sonofabitches. Gawd!" He looked down and saw the last jagged pieces of the bloody calf being born. He turned and retched.

It wasn't long before the FOR SALE sign was posted on the ranch. Then the prize cow sold for only fifty bucks. On the day he was to drive to Texas A&M for the start of preseason football practice, Dennis climbed to the top of the silver water tower. Eighty feet over Texas, as the hot westerly wind burned his face, he could see miles and miles across a land that resembled a flat waffle iron. He could see windmills that didn't turn and barns that needed paint. There were empty cattle pens with gates swinging open. To a rancher, nothing was more depressing than an open gate. It meant there were no cattle to contain.

"We're sellin' everything but the cotton-pickin' goats," his dad told Dennis on the day he left for the start of two-a-days with Bear Bryant at Texas A&M. As he aimed the big Chevy down the two-laner, Dennis was happy to have prospects ahead. He sure as hell had nothing to come back to.

· · ·

Eighteen months before Bryant made his grand entrance at A&M, Aggies assistant coach Willie Zapalac was recruiting boys in West Texas when he stopped at a drugstore in the small town of San Angelo and ordered a fountain drink with a cherry. It was three o'clock in the afternoon, and he had some time to kill. He was fiddling with a handful of toothpicks when he was approached by an Aggie ex-student who recognized the coach from his picture in the game program.

"You're probably here to see the San Angelo game," said Jack Rawlings, extending his hand. Rawlings was a Sears salesman who moonlighted as a high school referee. "Coach, there's this kid playing out in the country you need to see. He's a man among boys. He's playing six-man football. I know those kids don't get much attention from big-time colleges. But if you've got the time, you oughta drive on out."

Willie slurped down his drink and took off. What he discovered about twenty miles down Highway 277 was a wildcatting town that had turned ghostly. There was no one at the drugstore, the domino hall, or the feed store, and even the filling station was closed. Folks in Christoval liked to say on game days, "Last one out of town, turn out the lights." Everybody had gone to see the high school team play in the regional play-offs.

Since the bleachers were no bigger than a hay truck, many fans sat on tractors or lawn chairs in the back of their pickups. The center of their focus was a big redheaded fullback who seemed to score a touchdown every time he touched the ball. As Willie quickly learned, six-man football wasn't much—three men on the line and three in the backfield. All the offensive players, including the center, were eligible to catch passes. But Christoval was quite content to put the ball into the hands of number 32 on just about every play, and he was confounding the defense with his powerful bursts and unpredictable speed. Water Valley didn't have a chance. Jack Pardee had already scored fifty-six touchdowns that season. Fifty-seven went into the books as Willie pulled into the parking lot.

It was true that Southwest Conference teams normally thumbed their noses at six-man footballers, but not this time. The great Jess Neely from Rice had been sending scouts to Christoval most of the year. Jack had his heart set on spending his days walking the beautiful tree-lined campus in Houston and playing for one of the best football programs in the country. But something about Rice and its high-tone attitudes troubled him. He knew he would stick out like a cucumber in a cotton patch among the rich city kids, who wouldn't much care for a roughneck boy from the West Texas desert. Jack had been roustabouting in the oil fields since he was fourteen. You were supposed to be eighteen to occupy one of those dangerous jobs, but Jack was already bigger than most grown men when he turned twelve. By his thirteenth birthday, he was carrying sixty-pound bags of cement and stacking them in a three-foot-high goat shed, day after day. The work put slabs of muscle on his back and arms.

Hard work was expected of him. After the game against Water Valley, he would meet the train at Christoval and unload government hay. West Texas ranchers were suffering from the fiercest droughts anyone could remember, and the federal government was chipping in with freight cars filled with hay that was mostly moldy.

It had gotten so bad around Christoval that banks were calling in loans and some of the ranches were going out of business. Grass no longer grew on the ranches, and trees looked like they had tuberculosis.

Ranchers had turned to feeding their cows the prickly pear—cactus. They would singe the thorns off with a butane torch. Jack drove a green Ford pickup truck that was the family's only transportation. He mounted a butane tank in the bed of the truck, and after turning the valve he'd strike a match to the blowtorch. The cold butane would rush from the fifty-foot hose, shooting a roaring flame long enough to ignite a barn. Jack controlled the flame with a valve. He had to be sure he made a slow gentle pass over the pear. Otherwise, it would melt into a stub.

The cattle were so hungry that they'd eat the pear with the thorns still on it. Jack had seen many cows with bleeding and ruined mouths and many with sores that festered. When he fired up the butane tank, the sound caused the cows to come running from all directions. It was like a dinner bell.

After three years of hard drought, most of the good-paying jobs were in the oil fields, where Jack worked after football practice and on the weekends. He worked because his father, Earl, was suffering from rheumatoid arthritis and had been an invalid for several years. The youngest of six children, Jack became the provider at an early age. Life's hard experiences had made him a humble boy.

Willie Zapalac offered Jack a scholarship thirty minutes after watching him play for the first time. Five months later, Jack graduated with a senior class of six students. By then, he had already changed his mind about Rice. He had only fifty bucks to his name, and that would buy some blue jeans, T-shirts, and maybe a pair of boots. Texas A&M had a uniform to offer, and that meant clothing for nine months out of the year. Little did he know that his destiny was to someday play for Bear Bryant.

Late in the summer of 1953, Jack drove the family pickup more than three hundred miles to College Station. His mother and father also made the trip, and they sat in the truck's cab behind Hart Hall, the athletic dorm, as a blinding rain poured around them. The downpour was the first decent rain they had seen in at least three years. In Jack's lap was a box tied together with string that held all of his worldly belongings, including clothes. That afternoon, he would be issued a uniform and he would be given the first pair of new leather shoes he'd ever owned.

• • •

Twenty miles off the coast of Louisiana, two more Aggies prepared for their first season with Bear Bryant. The wind had been gaining steam since dawn, when the tugboat had pulled away from the Magnolia oil rig and started chugging back to shore with a large chunk of the crew. After the trek to Morgan City, the tug was to return and fetch the remaining riggers, who prayed their ride would arrive in time. Hurricane Audrey was roiling across the Gulf of Mexico less than a hundred miles off the coast.

Soon, the waves were swelling to twenty feet, spraying salty water across the platform. The men were moving drilling pipe from the oil rig to a reconditioned LST, an old navy barge that had seen plenty of action during World War II. The LST had been used to transport thousands of troops to the sands of Omaha Beach at Normandy. The barge was 175 feet long and about 20 feet wide and contained sleeping quarters and a crude kitchen below the deck. It was parked alongside the oil rig platform, and the two were connected by a steel hawser.

Among the crew of twenty men were a couple of college boys—Bebes Stallings and Bobby Drake Keith—who were studying to be petroleum engineers at Texas A&M. They'd spent other summers working for various oil companies, but they'd never tasted this kind of action.

Bebes and Bobby Drake had frantically toiled the last few hours finishing up business atop the oil rig. Now they were stacking the fifty-foot pipes on the long barge that rolled and swayed in the turbulent water. Stallings could sense that all hell—and maybe some heavy equipment— was about to break loose. They had definitely underestimated the power and the proximity of this storm; otherwise everyone would be long gone.

Bobby Drake was a tough boy who had played some hell-for-leather high school football for Joe Kerble, one of the legendary hard-asses in Texas. He was from the small oil-rich town of Breckenridge, where, year after year, the Buckaroos churned out one of the best teams in Texas. Breckenridge was notorious for doing whatever it took to keep West Texas's best players in its school district. High-paying jobs were always available to daddies of blue-chip players. Rivals flatly accused Breckenridge of illegal recruiting. A symbol of the town's lust for black gold was an oil well that pumped day and night just a few yards behind the high school field.

Playing defensive halfback, Bobby Drake had lowered his head to make a tackle in the A&M maroon-and-white spring game a few months earlier and come up spitting blood. His nose was broken and shoved to the right side, and the orbital bones beneath both eyes were shattered. All-conference halfback Joe Boring took one look at Bobby's bloody face and started waving for trainer Smokey Harper.

"I'm not leaving the game!" the injured boy yelled. "I'm OK, dammit."

Bobby Drake figured the best way to win a starting job was to play with pain. So he stayed on the field for two more plays, running on quavering legs until he fainted and landed with a thud flat on his back. Bear Bryant walked onto the field as they loaded the unconscious boy onto a stretcher. "That's one tough sonofabitch," Bryant said to Smokey.

Bryant sensed the same inner strength about Stallings. But he worried that the boy was too skinny to play end for a college team.

"Coach, I'm eatin' second helpings at every meal," Stallings would say. "I'm taking two and three desserts back to my dorm room every night, and I'm eatin' until I'm almost sick. But I can't gain any weight."

Bebes stepped on the locker-room scales every day, and every day his weight was the same—160 pounds. He sewed sheepskin into the lining of his football pants so his bony knees wouldn't bruise.

Every afternoon that spring, Bryant had posted a list of names of boys he was cutting from the team. Stallings sprinted to the locker room after morning classes with his heart stuck in his throat. He prayed his name wouldn't be on the list and that he could keep his uniform. As practice was winding down one afternoon, Bryant approached him and Bebes sensed that something was amiss. So he decided to tell Bryant about a painful ear infection that had bothered him most of his life. Squinting at the bony boy, Bryant said, "Bebes, I want you to see a doctor about having an operation. Maybe all of that infection is draining into your system and that's why you can't gain any weight."

During spring break, Stallings had an operation at Baylor Hospital in Dallas called a mastoidectomy. Two days later, his parents gave him money for the train back to College Station. Since he was a little short on spending money for the spring semester, Bebes decided to save a few dollars by hitchhiking. Standing on the side of the highway with a bandaged ear, Bebes became dizzy and sick and almost passed out from the unseasonable spring heat. As he sat on the suitcase, a man driving a pickup stopped to give him a lift. Bebes slept all the way back to College Station.

Now, months later, Bebes and Bobby Drake were wondering if they would ever see College Station again.

The crew had been fighting the raging wind to raise 20,000 feet of drilling pipe from the floor of the Gulf of Mexico. Men leaned their bodies into the heavy wind and prayed they wouldn't be tossed into the black, rolling water. Bebes peered to the south at the angry clouds and realized that Audrey was upon them. Lightning danced on the coal black horizon. One of the roughnecks shouted above the howling wind, "Schoolboy, stop worryin' about the hurricane! Keep your mind on the pipe! If we don't get this pipe up, this whole thing's gonna tip over anyway!''

Bebes could feel his heart heaving in his chest but tried to appear calm. One of the roughnecks spotted a tugboat chugging toward them across the churning sea. Shouts went up as the workers waved for the captain to pull alongside. The tug had picked up a load of roughnecks from a nearby rig, and the captain, knowing Audrey was closing in, decided to take one pass at the Magnolia platform before heading to shore. Raising a bullhorn to his lips, the captain rasped, ''I'll try to take five or six men back on this trip. That's all we got room for. But we gotta hurry.''

One of the crewmen tossed a heavy line toward the Magnolia rig, and three times it plopped into the water.

''We can't reach you,'' the captain's voice crackled. ''If we keep tryin', this line's gonna end up in my propeller. We're leavin'. Good luck to ya.''

Workers on the Magnolia rig looked at one another in disbelief. ''If I'd had a gun I'd shoot the sonofabitch,'' a man called Cajun Charlie said. Cajun Charlie gave the tugboat captain the finger, ''The law of the sea says the last boat don't pull out until the last man's on board. The sonofabitch just broke the law.'' Turning to Stallings, he said, ''Schoolboy, that was our last hope.''

They still worked like men possessed the next two hours. The roughnecks never spoke as they hoisted drilling pipe from the rough sea and broke it down. Bebes and Bobby Drake hauled the pipe on their shoulders from the oil rig to the LST and stacked it high. As he worked, Bebes studied the face of Cajun Charlie and found nothing there but anger and determination. Charlie was a short but stout man with wide forearms. A thick gray beard covered most of a ruddy face.

Bebes thought about Ruth Ann, his steady girlfriend since the eighth grade back in Paris, Texas. He thought about his mother and father and how proud he was to be their son. He thought about his promising football career and his newfound dream of playing for Bear Bryant. Though Bryant had been a hard-ass during spring practice, Bebes had become mesmerized by his charisma. Now all he could think about was getting off that rig and back to College Station for the start of preseason practices.

Waves were now turning the old navy barge almost vertical, threatening to toss the boys into the tumultuous water. Pipe clanged loudly against the side of the barge as the boys scurried up and down the LST in the blinding rain, securing the pipe with six-foot logs, and fighting to maintain their balance. Then the fifty-five-gallon drums filled with diesel started breaking loose from the thick cable and they created a horrible racket as they rolled from one side to the other. Bebes and Bobby Drake watched in horror as a man was about to be crushed between two rolling drums. They yelled too late. He was violently sandwiched. The boys ran toward the fallen rigger and expected to find a bag of broken bones, but the drums had been virtually empty and he suffered only bruises and a fractured arm.

Charlie ordered the riggers to drop the anchors over both sides of the barge, and Bebes wondered what good it would do. But he helped the other men heave the 500-pound anvils into the water. At the moment, the LST was attached to the oil rig by a single steel hawser. Fear gripped Bebes as he imagined the hawser snapping and the barge surging out of control into the Gulf of Mexico. They'd probably find the dead bodies several hundred miles away, possibly on the sands of Cuba, he thought.

The crew scrambled from the platform and into the bowels of the LST, where they would be out of the wind and, they hoped, safe until the next tugboat arrived. No one spoke as they descended the winding steel stairway into the dimly lit kitchen where the cooks had prepared hot soup and coffee. Many of the men fell quickly to sleep on the hard bunks. But Bebes anxiously paced the floor.

Minutes later, the hawser snapped with the sound of cannon fire.

"We's goners!" Charlie shouted. "Bend over and kiss your asses good-bye, boys!"

The men could feel the rear of the barge surging away from the oil rig. Bebes's stomach turned upside down as held his breath and grabbed the stairway. He wondered in which direction the hurricane would catapult the loose barge. Seconds later, though, the LST crashed to a halt as the crewmen toppled into walls and the lights went out. The only sounds were of the howling wind and clanging pipe.

"Why in the hell'd we stop?" came a voice from the darkness.

Cajun Charlie spoke up. "The anchor. It musta got caught on the leg of the rig."

Cheers erupted. Charlie's explanation made sense. The anchor's steel line would hold for several hours, perhaps even days. It was their first stroke of luck. As the generators kicked the lights back on, Charlie searched the room for his young football player.

"Schoolboy," he said. "Go up top. Stick your head out the door and see if the pipe is still secured."

Charlie, like the other roughnecks, didn't know Bebes was practically deaf in one ear. He didn't realize the boy actually heard him say, "Go out on deck and make sure all the pipe is tied down.'' In spite of his hard-ass ways, Charlie wouldn't have sent Schoolboy walking into an impossible situation. Besides, there was nothing one man could accomplish alone on a rolling barge.

After climbing the stairs and reaching the door, Bebes felt his body being sucked by the wind onto the deck. The hurricane lifted him off his feet and slammed him headfirst into the side of the barge. His right ear began to bleed. Weak and dizzy, he wrapped both arms around the steel pipe and held on for his life. Salty spray stung his face, and breathing became difficult. Letting go, he knew he'd be five hundred yards into the deadly gulf before his body resurfaced. It would be hours before anyone knew he was gone.

''Fight!'' he shouted to himself. ''Fight!''

Then he saw a figure standing near the door from where he'd just been launched. He thought it was a ghost at first.

''Bebes!'' Bobby Drake hollered above the wind. ''Throw yourself this way and I'll catch you!''

Bebes estimated that he was ten feet from the door, but it seemed like two miles. The barge surged from side to side. As it rolled left, he found himself looking down at Bobby Drake. He counted aloud, ''One, two, three,'' and let go.

The men far below could hear his screams. ''Schoolboy's overboard!'' Charlie shouted as he rapidly climbed the ladder. ''Somebody bring some rope.''

Instead of sailing into the drink, though, Bebes had somersaulted through the open door and landed on the stairwell platform. He barfed on Charlie's boots. Bobby Drake and Charlie tried to haul Bebes back downstairs. But he insisted on staying put on the stairwell, where he could suffer his seasickness alone.

For almost twenty hours the men rode out one of the worst hurricanes to ever hit that part of the gulf. Oil company tenders measured the winds at 150 m.p.h. twenty miles offshore and waves associated with the hurricane were monstrous with swells of forty to fifty feet high. It was a miracle that the anchor line remained entangled in the leg of the oil rig. In between shots of warm bourbon, the roughnecks prayed.

Almost twenty-four hours passed before the waves began to recede and the men were able to return to the barge deck in time to see the *Walter E.*, a large and powerful tugboat chugging in the from the west, just a few hours past dawn. On the trip back to Morgan City, Charlie put his arm around Bebes and said, "You're the bravest damn sonofagun that I ever seen. But shit, son, why didn't you tell ol' Charlie that you was half-deaf?"

A crackling radio would reveal to the riggers just how lucky they really were. Most of Cameron, Louisiana had been wiped out and more than five hundred people were dead along the coastline. The final damage estimate would reach $120 million as buildings and houses were destroyed twenty-five miles inland. As the *Walter E.* reached the shore, Bobby Drake turned to his friend. "When my feet hit ground, I'm headin' back to Texas. How about you, Bebes?"

"You know, Bobby Drake, they're still payin' time and a half out there," Bebes said with a crooked smile.

Sure enough, Bobby Drake caught the first train back to College Station and Bebes was back on the Magnolia oil rig a week later. His friends and family members often wondered why he went back.

Cajun Charlie never called him Schoolboy again.

• • •

Sweat glistened from the boy's back and arms. Billy Schroeder grabbed the wooden handles of the wheelbarrow, grunted, and began the 150-foot walk up the steady incline of the asphalt highway toward the bridge that was coming together bucket by bucket. The wheelbarrow was loaded with thick, wet cement that had been hand-mixed in a steel drum by two men. Billy had lost count of the loads he'd toted that hot and sticky afternoon. Muscles in his calves and forearms burned from hauling the heavy goo.

The crew was laboring deep in the woods on Highway 20 that connected Billy's hometown of Lockhart to Seguin. Temperatures soared past one hundred degrees, and the humidity produced hungry mosquitoes. Water moccasins slithered in from the brown water of the San Marcos River and sunbathed on the rocks.

Though he was only nineteen, Billy was a man among hardened men. At six-foot-two and 220 pounds, with a large chest and slim waist, he was perfectly sculpted for backbreaking labor. He'd worked the previous summer unloading sixteen-gallon kegs of beer by himself. His fellow workers had watched him play football for the Aggies as a sophomore in 1953, and they were impressed.

Bubba Dean, the crew foreman, had been verbally jabbing at Billy all day.

"I hear that coach from Kentucky's a rough customer," Bubba said.

"I got a distant cousin who played for him. He said he tore those boys a new asshole every day."

Billy smiled. "It's been my opinion for some time that our football team needs some discipline. I think that Coach Bryant will do us some good."

Billy was not a dumb jock. He'd come from a solid, hardworking family that hadn't hurt for money. He spoke in grammatically correct sentences. But he still couldn't find the words to explain his burning desire to lead the Aggies to the Cotton Bowl on New Year's Day. It would have taken an act of Congress to keep him out of Texas A&M and off the football field. In other parts of the state, young boys grew up dreaming of playing for Baylor, SMU, or Texas. But Lockhart was Aggie country. Billy also had blood ties to Texas A&M. His uncle, Bruno "Pun" Schroeder, had played end for the Aggies in the late thirties and remained Billy's idol.

As he aimed the wheelbarrow toward the bridge, Billy imagined that he was shucking blockers and sacking the quarterback. He could hear the "Aggie War Hymn" playing over and over in his head. In just a few more days, he'd be taking off for the biggest adventure of his life. It was time to meet Bear Bryant head-on.

3

The Journey

In life, you'll have your back up against the wall many times. You might as well get used to it.

—PAUL "BEAR" BRYANT

AUGUST 31, 1954

Bear Bryant wore the scowl of a man who'd eaten spark plugs for breakfast and washed them down with a quart of Tabasco. "We're 10 percent silk and 90 percent sow's ear," he confessed to Pat James. "Half the team is smaller than a monkey's *cojones*. The other half is slower than smoke off shit."

It was a hot and muggy morning when the players returned to College Station and the dark thunderheads rolled up from the Gulf of Mexico. Parked in front of Walton Hall, the football dormitory, were two long diesels with KERRVILLE BUS LINES painted across the sides. The presence of the buses and the sound of their grinding engines caused a stir among the boys, who scurried about like barnyard chickens. Preseason practice had been held for decades a half-mile away. So why, the boys were asking, would they need two buses to travel just down the street?

After completing their summer jobs, many of the players had hitchhiked back to campus. Others had hooked rides with teammates. Few could afford cars or pickups. Some took the train, and others arrived by bus. They toted beat-up suitcases and stringed-up boxes, and their football shoes were tied together by the laces and draped over one shoulder. Most were deeply tanned from working in the oil fields and on the ranches during the hottest summer any Texan could remember. They were eager yet apprehensive. Most of the players secretly wished that Ray George was still coaching the team, even though his easygoing nature promoted laziness. At least he didn't seem hell-bent on fracturing bones and postholing them into the sun-baked ground. They couldn't remember a player ever being run off by Ray George.

At ten that morning, Bryant gathered the players at the front entrance to Walton Hall. Most were still carrying their gear. Wearing khaki pants and a gray T-shirt, he loomed even larger and more intimidating than they had remembered.

"I suppose you boys are wonderin' what the buses are for," he said in a low rumble. "Well, we're going on a little trip. I want you to take your stuff up to your rooms. There's no need to unpack your bags. Just grab a toothbrush, a blanket, and a pillow. After that, go to the chow hall and grab a baloney sandwich. We'll meet back here in about fifteen minutes. So be ready to go."

As the players dispersed, Bryant spoke up again. "One more thing. Don't call anybody and tell 'em we're leaving campus. No phone calls, understand? When we get to where we're going, you can write a letter to your mamas and your papas."

A raw nervous energy filled the air. Players stepped quickly and awkwardly down the halls toward their dorm rooms, bumping into one another and spilling their belongings. Some felt the energy rush that preceded a hunting or fishing trip into uncharted territory. Others wondered if this trip would be like church camp. But the realists figured that a bus trip with Bear Bryant likely portended some kind of boot camp far from public view. Most of the boys were resigned to a torturous two weeks.

Billy Granberry, a short redheaded running back from Beeville, rolled Bryant's words around in his head and felt nervous. What had he meant by, "There's no need to unpack your bags"? Billy wondered if some players would be returning to campus only to leave again. For good. If there was anyone on the bubble, it was Billy Granberry, and he knew it. Billy was small and slow, and he didn't have a strong stomach for some things the others boys liked. He'd been raised in a country Baptist church where there wasn't much tolerance for fun. On his first trip to College Station, he'd ridden in a '49 Ford with three A&M students from Corpus Christi. They'd stopped in La Grange for gas, and the driver had asked the attendant, "Anything fun to do around this little town?" Spitting a long stream of tobacco, the man said, "Yeah, we got the finest little whorehouse in Texas just down the road." To Billy's utter horror, the Aggie upperclassman aimed his car straight for the Chicken Ranch. The three other boys strolled confidently into the bordello as if they were familiar with its debauchery, Billy stayed in the car and ducked under the dashboard. Soon Miss Mona came out, rapped her knuckles on the windshield, and said, "Don't be afraid, little fella. Set the brake and come on in. My girls will set you free."

Billy didn't move from the floorboard until the others returned.

Now his dorm room seemed to be a mile away—far up the steps on the I Ramp of Walton Hall. Players with the best chances of making the team were on A, B, and C Ramps. His roommates were the type of players Bryant hoped to run off long before the first game of the 1954 season. It was clear to many of the boys that Bryant was planning a grand going-away party before the Aggie alums or the university's administrators could get wind of it. Like most of the other players, Billy rolled up his toothbrush and comb in a blanket, grabbed the pillow from his bunk bed, and then sprinted to the chow hall across the street, hoping to learn that his name hadn't already been scratched from the roster.

Bad news awaited several players even before the buses took off. It was scrawled there on the chow hall chalkboard. Bryant had spent the summer evaluating talent, and many players would be changing positions. Because the Aggies needed bigger boys in the line, Billy Schroeder was moving from end to tackle. Several of the slow running backs were shuttling to guard and tackle. It was easy to spot the players who'd learned they'd be swapping backfield glory for grunt work. Their eyes were glued to the floor. All but Schroeder. "I'll do whatever it takes to help the team," he said to anyone within earshot.

On the sidewalk in front of Walton Hall stood John Crow, a muscular freshman with a fresh flattop and a crooked grin. Bryant had coveted Crow more than any other high school senior, and now he belonged to the Aggies. John Crow smiled broadly because, unlike some boys, he really looked forward to the backbreaking work.

Now, though, it was up to Elmer Smith to break the news to the future All-American with his bags already packed. It was Elmer who'd spent practically every day and night for six months in Springhill, Louisiana, recruiting the hard-nosed runner. Coach Elmer, as the boys liked to call him, had intimated to Crow that the team might be taking a preseason trip to a faraway place. One of Crow's fondest memories of growing up in the backwoods of Louisiana was church camp. He figured that if he signed with A&M he'd get to make the trip.

"John, I've got some bad news for you," Elmer said, putting his arm on the boy's shoulder. "The NC-double-A don't allow freshmen to practice with the varsity. So you won't be making the trip with us this time."

Crow's smile vanished. "You know, Coach Elmer, I really was looking forward to going with the guys."

"Maybe next year."

As the buses pulled away, belching clouds of diesel, Crow waved goodbye to the boys. His face seemed longer than an eighty-yard wind sprint.

Every seat on both buses was occupied, and some players sat in the aisles. Others climbed into the luggage bins and stretched out. Coach Elmer, carrying a clipboard, plopped into a seat next to Bryant and began his report: "My count is a hundred and eleven players. We've got three equipment boys on board. Smokey and Billy are driving out there in Billy's Ford. As a matter of fact, Coach, they should be there already."

Bryant gazed through the morning haze and had a vision. He could see overfed Aggie alums—a passel of weirdos, he thought—wearing Bermuda shorts, sandals, and black socks. Soon, they would be gathering on the sidelines of the practice field, waiting for the team to start fall practice. They would stand there maybe an hour in the searing heat, bitching and wondering where the hell the football team was. Then, around noon, the crusty old groundskeeper would limp across the field.

"Bear took the boys away on two buses," he would say. "I don't know where they're going. He didn't say when they'll be back."

Bryant had started cooking up this secret trip at the end of spring training when he got fed up with the meddling jock sniffers. Willie Zapalac told him about a place on the western edge of the Hill Country, just miles from the jumping-off spot into West Texas, where Texas A&M conducted summer school for incoming freshmen along with courses in hydraulics, surveying, and agriculture research for upper-class Aggies. The Texas A&M Adjunct, as it was called, boasted 411 acres and had twenty screened Quonset huts, a classroom building, a bathhouse, a mess hall, and a physical plant building. The camp was about two miles from downtown Junction, a flyspeck on the Texas map. With a population of about two thousand people, Junction fed off ranching, farming, and low-paying jobs at the cedar-processing plants. Junctionites were often called cedar hackers by the oil-rich folks from neighboring communities.

In July, Bryant had dispatched Zapalac and Phil Cutchin on a fact-finding mission. Cutchin had his reservations about taking the team so far to such a crude place, especially one with so much cacti. But Zapalac was intrigued with the place.

"Coach, it kinda looks like an old army base, even though it's pretty new," he said. "They didn't waste much money slapping it together, but there's a helluva lot of land. And, Coach, you can just look into those rocky bluffs and still see them Comanches charging down the hill in war paint. It's kinda exciting, really."

What sold Bryant was the remote location. It would take weeks for the Aggie leeches to locate Junction, and the staff would have no trouble shooing away local folks who wanted to watch practice. No press would be poking around. Mamas and papas might worry about their boys but wouldn't know where to find them. Bryant could teach the boys to play football his way—or they could hit the highway.

As the buses rolled into the vast countryside and headed southeast on Highway 21, Zapalac stood in the middle of the aisle and held several strips of bus tickets above his head.

"You boys listen up. Any of y'all who want to go back home just see me. I got plenty of bus tickets. Be happy to give you one."

The boys were confused. But only Weasel Watson had the guts to speak up. "Coach," he said, "why you figure us boys would be interested in going home so soon? And where in the hell are we going anyway?"

Zapalac looked at Bryant, who nodded. "We're goin' to a place called Junction."

Not more than a handful of the boys had ever heard of the place or had any idea where it was. If the lead bus seemed quiet before, it was now a tomb. Then Dennis Goehring's gravelly laugh from the back of the bus broke the silence.

"Hell, I've been there. I went to summer school there before my freshman year. It's a dandy little place. Got some pretty girls, too."

Heads swiveled as the boys studied Goehring's face. They knew Dennis well enough to have doubts about his definition of truth. He could be the master of exaggeration. Some of the boys thought him a tad crazy, especially during spring practice, when he picked fights by day and blew up cherry bombs by night. Goehring was small for a lineman but plenty tough.

41

His idea of fun might be wallowing around in the desert, eating cactus for breakfast and spitting out the needles.

"Let me tell you boys about a girl I met out there in Junction—Laverne Johnston," Dennis said. "This girl's so good-lookin' that she won the Miss Wool pageant."

Laughter rippled across the back of the bus. It took no time for Dennis to captivate his audience. Boys from the front of the bus walked down the aisle so they could hear better.

"I know you boys won't believe this," he said. "But to West Texas folks, the Miss Wool pageant is bigger than Christmas morning."

In the fifties, when it came to beauty pageants, Miss Wool was just a cut below Miss Texas. Some pageant experts argued that the prettiest girls all over Texas won the Miss Wool contests and not Miss Texas. The wool industry had invested big money, and with the huge ranches turning huge profits Miss Wool became a big item in society circles in the late forties. A young rancher's dream was having a date with Miss Wool to the Cattle Baron's Ball in Dallas.

"How much wool does Miss Wool have?" Watson asked, igniting more laughter. "Did she let you tickle her wool, Dennis?"

In Junction, no prettier girl breathed the air than Laverne Johnston, who'd just turned nineteen. Some folks said there was no finer plum in the Llano valleys. She had auburn hair, light brown eyes, and a walk that exuded confidence. As they said in ranch land, she was a real rodeo stopper. Her father, Fortran Johnston, was one of the richest men in the county and, among other things, owned the combination bus station/filling station on Main Street. Fortran Johnston was a powerful man, and he acted like it. He scared off a lot of potential suitors, but not a boy named Rob Roy Spiller. Rob Roy's daddy owned a large, successful ranch north of town near Bear Creek, and the Spillers were respected people. That's why it was easy for Laverne to convince her daddy that she should be seen socially with Rob Roy.

In the summer of '53, more than a year before Bear Bryant stormed into Texas, Rob Roy was living on cloud nine. Laverne had become his steady girlfriend, and they spent a lot of time together at the picture show. Working at the bus station had its perks. It meant Rob Roy got to see Laverne when she dropped in to see her daddy. All was well until summer school started at the Texas A&M Adjunct and the Aggie boys started finding their way into town.

One afternoon, while Rob Roy was on lunch break, an Aggie driving a '48 Chevy parked his car along Main Street, walked into the bus station, and made a pass at Laverne. Shockingly, Laverne agreed to a date with the boy, and the two walked four blocks to the Texan theater, where *Red River* with John Wayne was playing. The boy dropped two quarters into the silver tray and they took seats four rows from the back.

The bus station felt a little empty when Rob Roy returned from lunch. He soon realized that he hadn't seen Laverne that day. When Rob Roy asked about her, Fortran Johnston bluntly informed him that she'd gone to the show with a boy from the Adjunct—a big football star. A hollowness crept into Rob Roy's stomach and he felt faint as he stepped outside into the July furnace. As he rushed down the sidewalk past the tractor supply company and the feed store, his eyes burned. At the Junction National Bank, he crossed the street and dashed through the front door of the Texan, yelling to the ticket seller, "I'll just be a minute! Gotta check on somebody." Yanking open the door to the auditorium, he quickly spotted the couple sharing popcorn and holding hands.

He slid into the empty row of seats in front of them, turned, and said, "I thought you were my girl, Laverne?"

She looked at the floor and said nothing.

"What are you doin' here with this boy?" he insisted, followed by a long, "Shhhhhhh."

From the darkness, a male voice intoned, "Pipe down, Rob Roy. We're tryin' to watch the show."

No matter what he said to Laverne, she wouldn't reply. Finally, he looked at her square-jawed date and blurted, "I guess you got a thing about out-of-towners."

Dennis Goehring measured the intruder. "Why don't you go on back to the ranch and eat a frog, Rob Roy?"

Rob Roy had heard about Dennis's reputation. He didn't seem physically imposing, but he was widely hailed as a badass. So Rob Roy decided to leave. His heart felt like it weighed a hundred pounds as he made the long walk back to the bus station.

As the Aggie bus rolled past the tiny towns of Deanville and then Dime Box, Dennis's audience had grown to about thirty boys as he talked about Laverne and all of the beauty queens around Junction. He told them about the Saturday-night dances in town and how the Junction girls had all quit their regular boyfriends and thrown themselves at the Aggies, which caused a lot of fights.

"Boys," Dennis said. "Those Junction girls were a real roll in the hay.

They'd come knockin' on our screen doors in the middle of the night. All but Laverne, that is. There's this little river runnin' back behind the Adjunct and we'd all go skinny-dippin' back there. You had to see those pretty girls runnin' around nekked as jaybirds beneath that full Cherokee moon.''

Bryant was now confused about the noise coming from the back of the bus. The boys had been frightened into silence when the buses pulled away from campus. *Why are they feeling so feisty?* he wondered. *What kind of visions is Dennis filling their heads with?*

It really got loud when Goathead Jones pulled a transistor radio from his blanket and some of the boys started singing along with Toy Caldwell:

"I've been a long time leaving
But I'll be a long time gone."

Through the newfound merriment, Billy Pete Huddleston leveled his eyes at Dennis and said, "I hope you're not just pullin' on our peckers."

Dennis wondered how anyone could doubt him. "Come on, Billy Pete; you're from West Texas. You know what it's like out there. Folks are friendlier and girls are prettier than anyplace in the state."

Huddleston had been born and raised on the Pecos River in a tiny oil-boom town called Iraan. If anyone knew about West Texas and the ways of oilmen and ranchers and women, it was Billy Pete. He had gone to work with grown men in the oil fields at age twelve. Three years later, he was assigned the toughest job in the oil patch—working chains on the floor of a drilling rig. A man who isn't quick with his hands is certain to lose one on the rig floor. In the oil patch, roughnecks are the lowest on the pecking order, along with being the toughest and the hardest on the bottle. Billy Pete grew up working side by side with some of the orneriest and ugliest men in all of Texas.

Saturday night in Iraan, population 912, was not for the faint of heart. The biggest attraction in Iraan was the town square, where folks started gathering shortly after sundown. Challenge night, they called it, and it was a good way to beat the curse of boredom. A man would point at another in the crowd and holler, "Come on, mister, let's get it on!" With the townsfolk gathered in a tight circle, the two men would go to work with bare fists. Blood, sweat, spit, and fists would fly until it became clear that one man was superior to the other. Many times, the combatants were coworkers, or belonged to the same church or were blood relatives. The men would shake hands at the end of the fight and walk away peacefully.

One of the best fistfighters was Acie Ray Huddleston—Billy Pete's daddy. Acie Ray was a big, friendly man with a giant sense of humor. He boasted a lot of close friends around town. But he liked to fight on Saturday nights. It seemed to cleanse the blood, he said. One night, Acie Ray chose Jim Box as his adversary, and a long "oooooooooohhhhhhh" oozed from the crowd. Jim Box was a lay preacher at the First Baptist Church. But he was also a big man with a vicious left-right combination and a real sense for the street game. The hot and dry air turned electric when the men stepped into the makeshift ring.

Acie Ray landed some quick early jabs, but Jim Box, light on his feet and thick in the shoulders, started working inside, drawing first blood. The fighters were soon breathing heavily and bathed in sweat. Jim Box landed a jab to Acie Ray's nose, and his eyes filled with water. A powerful right hand knocked Acie Ray down. He was dizzy as he stood and blood poured from both nostrils. Four men from the crowd stepped into the ring, waving off the fighters before Jim Box could do more damage.

When Acie Ray returned home, Mira Huddleston took one look at her husband's puffy face and said, "You know better than to fight a man like Jim Box. You knew you couldn't whip him."

Acie Ray smiled in spite of the swollen lip. "I knew it. But just think of the prestige if I had."

Iraan was a desert town with a history of enormous oil strikes. On the wall of the Oil and Gas Museum in nearby Midland was a picture of the largest gusher ever capped in North America—near downtown Iraan. Besides Friday-night football and the Saturday-night fights, there wasn't much else to do in Iraan other than wash dust off your car. Young boys were known to get restless. Since there was a lot of oil money in town and most of the teenagers had cars, they'd head east searching for some fun.

"Shoot," Billy Pete said to the boys on the bus. "Iraan was so bad when I was growin' up that we'd go to Junction when we needed a vacation. Dennis is right about one thing. They got some pretty girls there."

The Aggies were so enthralled with the stories and the music that few even noticed that Austin was now in the rearview mirror. The twin diesels rolled through Dripping Springs on the edge of the Hill Country, and Bryant observed a distinct change in the land.

"God, it's starting to get brown out here. We've gone from green grass to brown stubs pretty quick."

Zapalac spoke up. "Yeah, these folks out here have been sufferin' for about four years with the drought. Nobody from Austin to New Mexico's had much rain since early 1950."

Bryant fixed a set of cold eyes on Zapalac. "You didn't tell me anything about a goddamn drought," he said. "Hell, I knew it was pretty dry in Texas. But you didn't tell me all the grass was dyin' west of Austin."

The devilish drought had so parched the land that by 1954 the Texas Panhandle had suffered dust bowl damage on more than four thousand acres. It had begun as just another dry spell that, like the proverbial houseguest, wouldn't go away. Texas suffered more than others during droughts because, in spite of the presence of 3,700 rivers and streams, no river originating from another state flowed into its borders. When the rains stop in Texas, much of the water dives underground. According to meteorological data, the drought had officially begun in 1950. But many parts of West Texas were having dry spells as early as 1948.

Arriving from Kentucky in February, Bryant had thought about virtually nothing beyond football and recruiting. The weather didn't seem abnormal to him because, in spite of the heat, the spring rains had come occasionally to College Station. The humidity blowing up from the Gulf of Mexico could soak a man's shirt before ten in the morning. In many parts of the state, though, folks were suffering tremendous hardships, and in July of 1953 dust was blowing into drifts along the highways of the South Plains around Lubbock and Lamesa. Bulldozers were working overtime to remove dirt piles from the roads and railroad tracks. That same month more than $9 million of government cattle feed had poured into 164 counties already classified as disaster areas. A few meteorologists predicted the drought wouldn't end until 1960.

Bryant watched the parched land whizzing by. "We just passed our fourth straight bridge that didn't have water under it. I haven't seen a half-filled creek or a river or a stock tank since Austin."

Near Fredericksburg, the diesels whined as the buses began climbing into the heart of the Hill Country. In a year with normal rainfall, this would have been one of the most picturesque points in the state. But even the cedar brakes looked pale and the mesquites, which could survive years without water, seemed to twist and angle more acutely toward the earth. The buses were one of the first models equipped with air-conditioning. But the blazing sun raised the temperature to the point that some boys were stripping off their shirts and fanning themselves.

"Wonder how hot it is out there?" Coach Elmer asked.

"Got to be a hundred and ten and rising," Cutchin answered. "Hell, I didn't know it got this hot in the Hill Country."

Silhouetted against the sun, the turkey buzzards with their wingspans of six feet circled and wheeled. Charles Darwin, in *The Voyage of the Beagle,* referred to the turkey vulture as "a disgusting bird, with its bald scarlet head formed to wallow in putridity." The Bible referred to it as "an abomination."

Only a few appeared at first, but dozens soon poured over the rims of hills with their black wings and scarlet heads. An Indian witch doctor in the mid-1800s had predicted the world would end when the sky became blackened by millions of turkey buzzards flying side by side.

"I've never seen so many goddamned birds in my life," Bryant said.

But Dennis Goehring had, and he knew it meant there were carcasses ahead. The vultures had come to dine on carrion, and there had to be an abundance, Dennis thought.

The diesels had geared down, and now they were creeping behind a slow cattle truck. A large white-tailed deer was sprawled by the side of the road, and about twenty buzzards were chewing on its guts. The buses passed close enough for the boys to see the dinner party. Red entrails were sucked into curved and jagged beaks. Some of the buzzards were plunging their heads deep into the body cavity. A quarter-mile later, more scavengers chewed on yet another carcass.

For more than thirty miles the gruesome scenes played out in a land where grass had turned to ash. The birds squatted over the deer and pecked the animals clean. Blood stained the brown earth where the prey had fallen and died. Now hundreds of buzzards were circling in the sky and then diving toward the dead and the dying. Goehring saw a cow being picked apart on a hill a half-mile away. It was about the only cow he'd seen on the singed ranches where only the stubborn goats were left to wander around the rocky hills. He figured the cow had died either of starvation or from eating a poison weed.

Bryant could only stare and wonder about this scorched piece of hell more than two hundred miles from College Station. No one had warned him that the drought had turned most of the Hill Country to dust. The valleys, once lush with tall grass, were now barren and scarred with ruts.

Junction, he knew, sat atop the ninety-ninth meridian on the western edge of the Hill Country. West Texas officially began at the 100th meridian, where the shade trees vanished.

"The farther we go, the hotter and drier it gets," Coach Elmer said. "It just ain't gonna get no better."

At the rear of the bus, where Goehring had been holding forth, the Aggies had grown quiet again, sobered by the apocalyptic scenes. Most of the players still weren't sure where they were going and why it was necessary to abandon their green little campus. As they topped one of the final peaks of the Hill Country, they could see the land just beyond the rocky ridges stretching flatter than a mule's spine. A highway billboard greeted them: "JUNCTION—Front Porch to West Texas."

About two miles east of town, the buses turned right at Flatrock Bridge and crossed the South Llano. The gurgling blue river seemed vibrant as it washed across the white limestone rocks. It seemed confusing that a river could appear so vibrant and bubbly while others in the region had simply dried up and vanished. A man wearing overalls was waiting for the buses as they turned right at the dirt road and rolled through the gray wooden gate into the Adjunct. And there, before their eyes, sprawled the open field—nothing more than a rock yard with cactus and gravel and sandspurs and dust. Grass that had tried to gain a foothold had long ago burned up and blown away. A dry wind kicking up from the west stirred up a brown duster that spun along the edge of the property. One of the boys yelled, "It looks like a baby tornado!" The duster blew itself out quickly and was gone.

They had traveled almost three hundred miles to practice football on a blazing patch of parched land that seemed better suited for hell's front gate. Bryant glared at Zaplac and muttered, "I think I'm gonna puke. Was this your idea, Willie? Or was this just some goddamn prank?"

4

Junction

You never know how a horse will pull until you hook him
to a heavy load.

—PAUL "BEAR" BRYANT

Like most settlements in Texas, Junction was won in blood. The small
town survived Indian raids, droughts, drownings, floods, bedroll rattlesnakes and even white renegades masquerading as red ones. On a warm
Sunday afternoon in 1934, a man and a woman approached the home of
Marge Turman Livingston. They inquired about camping on the Livingston's river bank about twenty miles from Junction. Having seen their
pictures on the front page of the local newspaper, she quickly identified
them. She directed the couple to a nearby campsite without tipping her
hand.

An hour later, Bonnie Parker and Clyde Barrow had built their campfire
and were settling in for the night when they sensed trouble. Law officers
opened fire, but the duo made a quick getaway in their powerful gray Ford.
Months later, Bonnie and Clyde were gunned down in Louisiana by law-
man Frank Hamer and five other men. Hamer, the famous Texas Ranger,
had been born near Junction, learning to ride, rope, and shoot on a Kimble
County ranch.

The rocky ridges and grassy valleys around Junction had for centuries attracted painted warriors and white frontiersmen. After the Civil War, when the warring Comanches were driven north onto the reservations, Kimble County began to settle down as a ranching and logging region. But thanks to the abundance of thick cedar brakes, the shinoak hills, dense vegetation, and rough terrain, outlaws had infested the region. The cutthroats weren't happy just to hide. They drove the settlers crazy by stealing horses and pigs. It took the Texas Rangers years to round up all the thieves and they were chained to large pecan and live oak trees down by the river, where district court was held.

The following item appeared in the *Galveston Daily News* on September 27, 1918. "Livestock in fine condition. Grass knee high. Everything quiet. No Indians. All these things show a good degree of prosperity and happiness for Kimble County. Immigrants are moving in faster than ever and boast of our good lands, water, etc. Our new courthouse is nearing completion and its neatness will be an honor to our county. Tell those lawyers who visited us while our courts were held in a blacksmith shop or under a live oak tree to come back in the fall term of the court, and they will be able to hear their voices ring in a two-story courthouse."

Junction City, as it was originally called, sat in a broad grassy valley of several square miles at the fork of the North and South Llano Rivers. It was named for the junction of the two rivers. The town was originally surveyed in 1876; when it became incorporated in 1927, the name was shortened to Junction.

San Antonio, the closest major city, is about one hundred miles east, and the border town of Del Rio is one hundred miles to the south. The three cities form a triangle.

By the time the Texas Aggie football team arrived during the searing drought of 1954, Junction had birthed along Main Street two feed stores, six gas stations, seven motels, three restaurants, a café, two saloons, a bank, a bus station, a grocery store, an infirmary, and a department store called McKinney's.

R. B. McKinney was an original thinker who regularly made the three-hundred-mile trek to Dallas to buy for his customers the newest apparel and the latest clothing fashion. R. B. even offered some dry goods in the store. His showroom window was the talk of the town. During deer season, he would outfit a mannequin in hunting fatigues, a fur-lined hat with earflaps, and a rifle. During Easter, he dressed them in bonnets and white shoes. Christmas inspired the best Santa Claus/reindeer display west of San Antonio.

Junction was an easygoing town that rarely inspired crime, or even divorce for that matter. But the place had fallen upon some hard economic times in 1954 when Bryant's boys came to town. Most citizens were baffled to hear that a big-time college team would come to their dried-up outpost to train for the upcoming season. A small article appeared in the *Junction Eagle* noting that the new coach from Kentucky had decided to take his team off campus for unspecified reasons. The natives figured that something must have gone terribly wrong at Texas A&M.

The area had been battered mercilessly by the drought. The North Llano River, lacking for rainfall, had disappeared underground two years earlier. Jordan Cunningham, one of the town's truly benevolent men and the president of Junction National Bank, had been calling in loans from ranchers and farmers and refusing to extend credit to others. Cunningham hated breaking the news to his debtors, and it often depressed him. Even the ever-smiling R. B. McKinney was forced to cut back on credit to customers he'd been dealing with for decades. The sad reality was that many citizens had to either leave Junction or face the prospect of financial ruin.

Men who held great pride in their huge ranches were chopping them up and selling off large chunks. The lease operators were not as lucky. They were going out of business every day—walking away from decades of sweat and blood. Most locals flatly refused anything smacking of charity because they didn't believe in federal aid, regardless of the hardships. They quickly washed their hands of government hay and feed.

Some of the most trusted men in the county were skipping town without paying off debts. Many ranchers were moving their livestock to the grassy Arkansas hills where it still rained occasionally. It was a confusing time, and Junction had become a confusing place.

Now, as the twin diesels rolled through the dusty Adjunct, the boys groaned at the sight of the rugged brown field where only cacti grew. When the buses pulled into the back of the property, though, they found a grove of live oaks, pecan trees, cedars, and some mesquite. Tall weeds still grew in parts of the dense shade. What really confounded Bryant, and everyone else, was the presence of the South Llano still plugging along. In fact, the river widened a bit behind the Adjunct, and some of the boys thought it was a creek. In reality, it was a sixty-mile river that was flourishing while the others in the county were dead or dying. The magic of its existence

51

was the Seven Hundred Springs, where Bonnie and Clyde had tried to camp.

The South Llano flowed from an underground fountainhead that forced millions of gallons into the mouth of the river. The water gurgled up from the table rock, breaking from its rocky prison and then gushing down the face of a huge bluff. While the North Llano depended solely on rainwater, the South Llano flowed from nature's own superpump—a source that wouldn't dry up even if the sky didn't pee a drop for several decades. As the Aggies set up camp on their new training grounds, they could peer to the east and see desolation stretching for hundreds of sun-scorched acres. To the west, though, they saw a kind of shady paradise with a creek and a canopy of trees that reminded them of days of summer youth camp. Maybe this would be a little vacation after all.

The boys had no more dropped their belongings into the Quonset huts when they were peeling off blue jeans and running toward the water.

"Hey! Wait just a goddamn minute!" Zapalac hollered at the boys. But Bryant stopped him. "Let the little peckerheads go. Let 'em have their fun. They'll be too tired tomorrow to fart."

Their hearts had been tied to a roller coaster that day. The desolate landscape and vivid death scenes had seriously damaged any hopes the boys had for a fun trip. Seeing the rock-infested field and feeling the torchlike heat confirmed their fears. As the buses pulled through the Adjunct gates, Don Watson had turned to Bebes Stallings and said, "He's gonna try to cook us in this oven."

But their spirits had soared again when they saw a water hole in their new backyard.

"See, I told you boys!" Dennis Goehring hollered. "This place is gonna be fun. Just wait till the girls find out we're here."

Leaping from a tall, flat rock, Goehring tucked into a cannonball and sprayed water far onto the bank. He was followed into the river by Bebes Stallings, Bobby Drake Keith, and Bobby Jack Lockett. Joe Boring sailed into the water and felt his left foot crash into the rocky bottom. His knee seemed to collapse beneath the weight of his body, and Boring felt it pop. He'd been struggling all summer with a sprained and swollen knee. He pulled himself out of the water and sat on the edge of the rock but didn't tell the other players of his pain. His knee felt as if it had been stabbed by a hot poker.

Soon, most of the team was in the river, splashing, wrestling, and making enough noise for the girls to hear them two miles away. Fred Broussard, the big center from southern Louisiana, let the running backs stand on his shoulders. Sophomore guard Lloyd Hale located a couple of canoes on the bank, and the races were on.

Watching his boys playing in the river, Bryant leaned against a tall live oak and tapped an unfiltered Chesterfield against the silver lighter. He inhaled deeply and thought about how dry the air felt. A summer's day had never caused his skin to sting in such a way.

He mumbled to himself, "If it's this hot at three o'clock in the shade, think about how hot that dern field will feel tomorrow in full pads!"

Goathead Jones had propped up his transistor radio against a rock, and Hank Williams was wailing into the hot afternoon:

"Somebody else stood by your side
And you looked so satisfied
I can't help it
If I'm still in love with you."

The boys knew that Jack Pardee was afraid of nothing. Most were not aware, however, that he could walk into a den of snakes and never flinch. In West Texas, he was known to handle rattlesnakes with his bare hands. Pardee, in turn, knew that Bob Easley was scared shitless of reptiles. The two boys had just spent three months in the Sinton oil fields, and Pardee had constantly teased Easley. One night he left a garden snake in Easley's bedsheets.

Pardee found a nonpoisonous blacksnake, about four feet long, napping next to a rock. He grabbed it just below the head and whipped it toward Easley, never expecting to hit the target. But the snake landed on Easley's left shoulder, wrapping itself around his neck.

The big fullback squealed and started running. After about ten yards, the snake slithered off his back and flopped on the ground. But Easley was too busy to notice. He kept running and running and didn't stop for more than a mile.

Bryant heard the yelling but thought it was just boys having fun. He returned to his Quonset hut and found three student managers removing two bunk beds and opening a card table in the middle of the room. The huts, which had been purchased from the army, had served as barracks during World War II. They were twenty feet by eighteen feet with concrete slabs for floors. The lower half of the walls was constructed of corrugated asbestos siding. The upper half contained a screen that could be covered at night by canvas flaps. The roof was constructed of corrugated steel, and the entire building was held together with steel and pipe framing.

Bryant knew there would be no reason, even at night, to roll down the canvas flaps over the windows. Any kind of breeze would be welcomed in the these large ovens.

"Coach, I think I might be able to rustle up a fan for you," said a student manager who had an athletic build in spite of weighing only 145 pounds. Bryant considered the offer and decided that if everyone else was going to rough it, he was going to rough it, too.

"M.G.R.," he said, using the abbreviation for manager, "I need you and the boys to do some serious plowin' for me. In fact, I wish we'd brought some mules. I need you go into that godforsaken rock patch out there and clear us off a place to practice football. Don't worry about drawing chalk lines or any of that shit. Just clear the rocks and pull up some cactus and make it as smooth as you can. I know it won't be easy."

Troy Summerlin took one look at the unforgiving patch of land and realized they'd be clearing it until long after dark. As the boys raked and pulled and loaded wheelbarrows, their skin sizzled and soon they were soaked in sweat. They realized how state prisoners must feel, working the rock yard. No one had thought about bringing a thermometer to Junction. It would have revealed at three-thirty on that first day atop the ninety-ninth meridian that the temperature had soared to 114 degrees.

After Bear unpacked, he was sitting at the card table, surveying his schedule for the first day of practice, when a pickup truck came bouncing along the dirt road toward the huts. Three businessmen from Junction were anxious to meet the new Texas A&M coach. They were Squirt Newby, Buckshot James, and R. B. McKinney.

Perhaps in another time, at another place, Bear Bryant would have enjoyed making their acquaintance. Indeed, these were fun-loving men with a taste for drink, an eye for adventure, and an ear for a good joke. Folks around town thought of them as the Three Stooges because they were always entertaining. The three pranksters had recently pulled a real laugher on Old Man Smith during his last trip into town. They knew that Old Man Smith liked to stop for a quick whiz behind the tailor shop as he strolled down Main Street. A temporary urinal had been discreetly stationed there so a man could quickly relieve himself and then move on about his business. Old Man Smith was, as always, nattily attired and moving quite gracefully as he eased to the urinal and unzipped. Squirt, Buckshot, and R. B. were watching the scene through peepholes in the tailor shop. They had hooked a car battery to the urinal. As Old Man Smith's stream of urine struck the pan, Squirt flipped a switch that sent a bolt of electricity streaming into the metal container. Old Man Smith suddenly felt a fire raging in his genitals but was uncertain of what had zapped him. He zipped and quickly left the makeshift rest room. He walked quickly around the corner and headed up the sidewalk toward the doctor's office and then disappeared through the doorway.

The town's comics howled with laughter.

Now Squirt, Buckshot, and R. B. were standing at Bryant's door. He greeted the men and welcomed them into the cabin. Buckshot James was the first to speak.

"Coach, we came out here to propose a barbecue. We could cook up some steaks and hamburgers and maybe even roast a pig. Of course, we'd have all the trimmins and co-colas you boys could drink. We'd like to invite some of the townsfolk and, well, have a big time."

Bryant stared impatiently at the floor. In a monotone as flat as Lubbock, he said, "We didn't come out here to eat. We came out here to practice football."

The long silence that followed was broken by the screen door slamming behind them. The three men were close to a trot when they reached the pickup. Before leaving, though, R. B. McKinney made one last-ditch offer.

"You know, Coach," he yelled, "it ain't gonna get any cooler or wetter out here! Heck fire, Coach, we're in the middle of a dang drought. As president of the chamber, I'd like to offer to bring some Cokes out here after practice for the boys."

Bryant glared at the man and said, "We didn't come out here to drink Cokes, either."

He watched the truck boiling up dust as it pulled away. Then his eyes settled on the student managers pulling up rocks and cacti. He felt depressed and wondered why he had bothered to bring his team all the way to Junction. Unluckily for Willie Zapalac, he walked past Bryant's cabin at that very moment.

"Hey, Willie, thanks for bringing us all the way to hell's little acre. Please remind me to let you pick the property for my next house."

"But, Coach, I—"

"Just keep quiet, Willie. I don't want anyone knowin' I'm pissed off. Just carry on like everything's all right. We'll do the best we can with what we got."

If they had come four years earlier, the Aggies would have discovered a lush green practice field with deer grazing all over the valley. They would have witnessed cattle roaming in verdant pastures with knee-high grass. Rivers and streams would have flowed within a few feet of their banks. Now, they'd need to keep a constant lookout for rattlesnakes. They would hear hungry coyotes baying at night. No telling how many bus tickets Willie would be passing out to boys wanting the hell out of Junction.

Little did the boys know what awaited them with tomorrow's sunrise. Now they were in great spirits, laughing and slapping one another on the back as they lined up in the mess hall for supper. They could smell the steaks cooking. The family-style selection included mashed potatoes, green beans, carrots, okra, spinach, and enough biscuits to bloat an army. Bryant had brought the cooks from A&M's Sbisa Hall to ensure the meals would be first-class. The boys needed proper fuel to practice football.

"We never had food like this back at campus," Jack Pardee said, filling a plate. "Looks like everything out here's going to be a real picnic."

Card games were on that night inside the Quonset huts. With six bunk beds per barrack, the boys were packed twelve to a room. Laughter echoed across the grounds until Bryant strolled into a cabin where Stallings, Lockett, Sid Theriot, and a few others were playing spades. He approached the table and rapped it with his knuckles. "Lights are goin' out in fifteen minutes. There'll be no more card games and no more splashin' in the water."

The boys didn't breathe until Bryant left the cabin and was beyond earshot.

"I guess, boys, this party is over," Theriot said.

5

Hell

Sacrifice. Work. Self-discipline. I teach these things, and
my boys don't forget them when they leave.

—PAUL "BEAR" BRYANT

SEPTEMBER 1, 1954

It was the kind of deep silence you can feel on a dew-covered morning
in the Virginia backwoods, or on a snowy mountaintop, or in the Texas
Hill Country in the middle of the night when even the crickets have dozed
off.

That stillness was shattered at 4:00 A.M. when Troy Summerlin sprinted
through the first Quonset hut shining a flashlight and blowing a coach's
whistle. Behind him rambled Billy Pickard, banging together two cook
pots. The noise could have woken a dead man.

"Get your no-good asses outta here!" shouted bleary-eyed fullback
Bob Easley, kicking at the two student assistants from his lower bunk.
"Don't ever bring that bullshit back in here again."

The screeching whistle and clanging pots signaled the beginning of
preseason camp. The boys knew it was coming but didn't expect this.
Football season in the 1950s didn't begin until mid-September. So the boys

would have to run through hell and a brier patch before that first game was played in almost three weeks.

"What time is it anyway?" asked Elwood Kettler, wiping sleep from his eyes. "Shoot, it seems like midnight."

Bear Bryant liked to get an early jump on the day. Within minutes, the Aggies' football camp was busier than a duck pond covered with June bugs. When Pickard and Summerlin had finished their rounds, Smokey Harper started spreading his normal daily cheer.

"You fellers look like dogshit in the morning," he said, distributing orange juice, salt tablets, and a thick brown Unicap vitamin to each.

"You ain't exactly an oil paintin' yourself in the mornin'," Dennis Goehring barked back. "You old fart. Where the hell's my goddamn breakfast?"

Smokey smiled broadly. "Coach Bryant says there ain't gonna be no breakfast. He's gonna work you fellers till you puke. Says he don't want a bunch of eggs, bacon, and grits all over the field. So get up, take your vitamins, drink your orange juice, take your salt pills, shut the hell up, and get ready to vomit."

Summerlin and student assistant Jack Littman began assembling rows and rows of shoulder pads and helmets outside each Quonset hut. Smokey and Billy were soon busy taping ankles in the trainers' barracks. The assistant coaches, led by Jim Owens, barked orders like marine drill sergeants.

"The last one of you peckerheads to the practice field is gonna be runnin' wind sprints till Christmas," Owens promised.

With one eye barely open, Weasel Watson cracked the screen door. "What are we gonna do, Coach Owens? Practice in the dark?"

"Nah," Owens said, spitting a stream of tobacco. "But we're gonna practice until it gets dark, dumbshit."

Just the process of herding 111 boys from the barracks onto the rock-hard practice field each day was going to be a massive chore. A training staff of two—Smokey and Billy—had to tape all of the ankles, along with eventually attending to injuries. Bryant had brought only three student managers, and they would wrestle with enough equipment to outfit more than two NFL teams on a Sunday afternoon. The only nonstudent on staff was Smokey. At age sixty-one, he seemed almost too old to remember college, and wasn't much help anyway.

Still half-asleep and stumbling around in the dark, the players tried on shoulder pads and helmets and argued over the best equipment. For the first time at A&M, players would be wearing face masks—Plexiglas wrap-around shields.

"Y'all sure look silly with those stupid face masks on," Smokey said, laughing. "Y'all look like a bunch of sissy girls gettin' ready for the prom." Smokey shrugged. "But I guess I won't have to fix as many busted-up noses this year."

More than an hour later, with players now fitted with helmets and uniforms, they began lining up for calisthenics on the rugged field that had been partially cleaned but was still littered with rocks, cacti, and sandspurs. Not once could the boys remember practicing football in the dark, or having to dodge cactus, for that matter. The moment that Bryant's barracks door shot open, though, the sun popped over the tall, craggy hill covered with cedar brakes, mesquite, and shinoak. It was an eerie sight—a man appearing from the darkness just as the sun rose over his head and beyond the rocky hilltop where a wooden white cross stood. "I wonder if he's come to teach us about the fishes and the loaves," Weasel Watson said in a low voice. Nobody laughed.

What Bryant saw in the first light of morning were ten rows of players wearing five different colored jerseys. Maroon was for the first team, white for the second, blue for third, orange for fourth, and yellow for the fifth-teamers and anyone else without a designation. From day one, Bryant wanted his players to understand exactly where they stood in the team's pecking order. The different colors created tension among the troops, and Bryant liked that.

They were a ragtag bunch of skinny boys with drooping pants and scarred-up helmets. Not once in his coaching or playing career had Bryant seen more pathetic equipment. The inner suspension of several helmets had either frayed or broken through. Heads would be cracking against the hard plastic. Many of the Plexiglas face masks didn't fit properly and wobbled when the boys ran down the field. In spite of the stifling heat, players wore long-sleeve jerseys. Somebody had forgotten to pack the short-sleeve ones.

It was written into Bryant's contract that the football budget would quadruple by 1955. So he knew the equipment would improve. But none of the meddling alums or A&M power brokers could promise him better players. That would come with hard work, grit, and some cash under the table. Just the sight of these sorry Aggies put him in a foul mood.

Striding up to the calisthenics lines, the coach cleared his throat. "Boys, I've brought y'all a long way out here—away from your mamas and papas, girlfriends and wives—for good reasons. First, I'm going to whip your butts into shape. Second, I want you to become a team. We're gonna turn this love boat around. You boys been fartin' upwind too long. Just to show you I ain't kidding, I want you boys to form one line over by that pile of rocks. We're gonna start this beautiful mornin' off with a few gassers. Coach Owens, line 'em up.''

The sun had climbed far into the pale blue sky and the gravel pit known as the practice field was dotted with orange juice stains when the eighty-yard wind sprints, also known as gassers, finally ended. More than twenty times the boys had chugged to the other end of the field, taken a short break, and then wobbled back, stirring up clouds of thick dust. Just as Bryant predicted, the boys were vomiting everything in their stomachs— the orange juice, vitamins, and salt tablets. Bryant seemed happy to see the boys bent over and puking so early in the morning.

A big part of the master plan was to shock their systems and separate the quitters from the keepers. Meanwhile, the Man would also demonstrate how he organized and executed precision practices. When he sounded a whistle, the boys would break up into eight groups to participate in different drills. The assistant coaches—Louis Carribo, Phil Cutchin, Elmer Smith, Willie Zapalac, Tom Tipps, Jerry Claiborne, Pat James, and Jim Owens—carried clipboards and were in charge of leading the drills while Bryant moved from station to station, riding herd. Only a handful of coaches around the country ran such regimented practices. Bryant patterned part of his plan after Frank Leahy, the legendary coach who'd just retired from Notre Dame. At the sound of Bryant's whistle, players moved like clockwork to different drills. Bryant had already gained a reputation as a brutal taskmaster. But at least he was systematically brutal.

He wore a gray T-shirt, khaki pants rolled up at the ankles, black coaching shoes, and a baseball cap with a *T* on the front. Assistant coaches had donned the same shirts and hats along with unpadded football pants.

Standing with his hands on his hips, monitoring a drill run by Zapalac, Bryant began to holler, ''No, Willie! Get the sonofabitch into a stance like this and bring the forearm up like this.'' Shoving Zapalac aside, Bryant hiked his pants and dropped into a three-point stance. Charging forward, he thrust a forearm into the sternum of unwitting center Richard Vick, lifting him a foot off the ground. The breath could be heard whooshing from Vick's lungs as he landed with a thud on his back. Bryant smiled. He was just getting warmed up.

Minutes later, Bryant watched a two-on-one blocking drill that was getting the best of Henry Clark, a tall and broad-shouldered tackle with jet-black hair and a thick nose. Clark's objective was to penetrate the wall of blockers and tackle the running back. Henry was failing miserably. As he gasped for air, Bryant could see his legs wobbling from near-exhaustion. With each snap, Henry was engaged by a fresh set of blockers, and each time he was knocked backward and pancaked to the ground by both men. Henry's body was raising a dust cloud almost waist-high every time he landed flat on his back.

Bryant grabbed the big tackle by the shoulder pads and shouted, "What is your name, son?"

Breathing heavily, the boy said, "H-Henry Clark."

Bryant released the boy and blew his whistle. "I want all of you sonsabitches on this practice field to stop and listen up, because this boy tells me his name is H-Henry Clark. Now I want you to see how a fart blossom named H-Henry Clark handles himself."

The players could see Henry's legs trembling as he dropped into his stance. A small running back named Charles Hall spoke up. "How can we all stand here while this man abuses our teammate like this?"

"Shut up, fool," Elwood Kettler said, "or you'll be next."

Again Clark crumpled beneath the weight of two blockers. He was dragging himself to his feet when Bryant grabbed the boy's jersey and spun him around. Seizing the inner part of his shoulder pads with both hands, Bryant pulled Henry's face close to his. "You ain't worth tits on a boar hog. And you call yourself a Texas Aggie football player."

The man with the leather exterior had rehearsed in his mind this little theater that would teach all of the boys a lesson in toughness. He ripped Henry's helmet from his head and grabbed the back of the boy's head with two meaty hands. "Now I'm gonna show you how to do this goddamn drill." Bryant then butted Henry in the nose with his forehead. He yanked his head forward again and again, bashing his skull into Henry's nose, lips, and eyes. Blood poured down Henry's neck and began to soak his white jersey. Even from forty yards away, players could hear the sickening thud as Bryant's forehead slammed into the boy's face. Finally, Henry fell like a sack of potatoes onto the hard ground.

Stumbling forward, blood smeared across his forehead, Bryant breathed heavily as he turned toward the team. "Trainers! Get your butts over here and fix this boy's broken nose." The coach had three cuts on his forehead.

Henry's shattered nose had been shoved an inch to the right. Blood flowed from his gashed lips. Soon his eyes would be swollen shut.

First, though, Smokey Harper had to wake him up. Snapping an ammonia capsule, Smokey crammed it into one of Henry's blood-caked nostrils. "Stand back," Smokey said, acting as if he'd lit a firecracker. "He'll be shakin' and rattlin' any minute." But Henry couldn't inhale the harsh ammonia for the coagulated blood. So Billy Pickard pulled a large swath of cotton from his bag and began clearing the breathing passage. Billy snapped another capsule about an inch from Henry's nose, and he jerked awake.

Standing a few feet away, Bryant said, "Billy, fix his nose and tape him up. Give him a little break. But I want him back on the field before this practice is over."

Moments later, the sounds of bodies and helmets colliding could be heard echoing across the practice field. This pleased Bryant. He walked past a spirited blocking drill where a small but scrappy sophomore guard was opening huge holes for running backs who were darting to daylight. Months earlier, Bryant had filed some notes about this sawed-off boy from the oil boomtown of Iraan. His name was Lloyd Hale. The boy had been an all-state center and even moonlighted at quarterback in high school. He'd been the top scorer on the Iraan High School basketball team and might have been the best all-around athlete to come out of West Texas. But his specialty was the scramble block, which he was demonstrating to near perfection this morning in Junction. Firing off on the snap count, staying low to the ground, the squat guard aimed his head and shoulders toward the defender's knees and, with catlike quickness, he entangled himself in the player's knees. Nobody could get away from him.

Bryant blew his whistle. "Get the hell out of my way," he said, pointing toward Hale. "I'm gonna show ya how to stop this little fella."

The coach whipped off his baseball cap and dropped into a three-point stance in front of Hale, his head inches from the guard's helmet. As signals were barked, Lloyd whispered to his coach, "There ain't no forty-year-old man who can stop me." On the snap count, Bryant grabbed the back of Lloyd's shoulder pads with one hand and the back of his helmet with the other, halting the boy in his tracks. He toyed with Lloyd for several seconds before slamming him face-first into the ground.

Watching the boy scramble to his feet, Bryant smiled and asked, "How old are you, boy?"

"Nineteen," said Hale.

"I'll give you a few more years and maybe you can whip this old man."

Across the field, Coach Elmer laughed and slapped Willie Zapalac on the back. "Will you look at that? Coach is knockin' 'em down faster than good scotch."

Bryant noticed several players vigorously shaking their hands and picking at objects stuck to their skin. Many had bleeding fingers. Along with heat and the parched land, players found another nemesis to be the goatheads, named for their prickly curved thorns that seemed to blanket the ground. As they dropped into a three-point stance, planting one hand on the ground, players would grimace as the goatheads pricked their fingers. The grass had long since curled up and died. But the goatheads were flourishing in the sun-baked sand. They would cling to anything contacting the ground—hands, jerseys, socks, and even footballs. Bryant, curious about the pain-producing little objects, hollered for Billy Pickard, who was putting finishing touches on Henry's nose.

"Where the hell did all these gnarly little stickers come from?"

"Coach. These are the orneriest buggers I've ever seen. I was talking to Elmer Parrot, who runs this place. And he says the darn goatheads are so big as to puncture tractor tires. He tried draggin' the field with burlap sacks. But all of his tractor tires are gone flat from these sharp little devils."

By eight-thirty that morning the temperature had risen to ninety degrees and the boys began to wonder when the first water break would come. Tongues stuck to the roofs of mouths, a condition known as "cottonmouth" because it caused saliva to dry up. The boys felt like they were eating peanut butter and washing it down with sand.

"I'm so thirsty," Jack Pardee said, "that I can't even make spit."

Bryant believed the fastest way to whip a team into shape was to deny the boys water, even in the brutal heat. He had withheld water during practices at Kentucky and Maryland, and those teams seemed to grow stronger in the fourth quarter. The team doctor even agreed with Bryant's harsh methods. Back in College Station, Dr. R. H. Harrison had told him, "A stomach that is full of water can cause the blood flow to increase to the spleen. That, in turn, could cause a ruptured spleen."

Smokey Harper summed it up in a manner that pleased Bryant: "Hell, you never pour ice water into a car's hot radiator. So why pour ice water into a hot boy?" Oddly, Bryant trusted many of Smokey's cockeyed opinions. Bryant could care less that virtually no research had accompanied these theories. He was aware, though, that one Texas high school player and another one at SMU had already died that year from heatstrokes. The four-year drought had caused the average temperature to rise by more than ten degrees across the state. But the Aggie coach considered the unmerciful conditions to be one more conditioning tool at his disposal.

Bryant had been around football long enough to know that some injuries should be treated seriously. But he also subscribed to the old gridiron adage that a pampered boy will never play with pain. Like most coaches of that era, Bryant didn't cry over spilt blood. The NCAA had no restrictions on the number of high school recruits you could sign to football scholarships so most football powers brought in more than a hundred freshmen each year. Why should a coach worry about injuries when he had so many players on his roster?

For most of his life, Bryant had received mixed messages about pain and healing. When he was growing up in the Arkansas creek bottoms, his family so fervently believed in the strict teachings of the Church of God that they thought it sinful to seek medical treatment. His father suffered with a mysterious illness for fifteen years and never received a doctor's care. Wilson Monroe Bryant died in 1931, and even though Bear thought his father had suffered and died needlessly, he still seemed callused years later toward injuries and illness.

In some respects, Bryant's thinking was a byproduct of the times. College football's tough image had mushroomed in the years following World War II. Several players had returned from military duty to complete their college eligibility and, having been toughened by their experiences, the GIs brought a combative edge to the game.

In the forties and early fifties, the general public regarded football as only a cut above pro wrestling. That was before television cast a sympathetic eye on the game. Coaches were generally an unshaven lot who drank and cussed and weren't concerned with the aesthetics of the game. They believed football was strictly won in the trenches, with hard-nosed blocking, tackling, and a lot of bleeding.

Bryant, though, was a walking contradiction. He liked being on the cutting edge and considered himself a masterful strategist. An insatiable student of the game, he studied game films and playbooks from all over the country, places likes USC, Michigan State, and Florida, even though those schools weren't on his schedule. Ironically, his favorite all-time player had been a swift and graceful receiver for the Green Bay Packers named Don Hutson, who led the NFL in receiving for eight of his eleven seasons. Bryant, who was Hutson's teammate at Alabama, admired the receiver's skills. Conversely, though, Bryant was not yet ready to make room for a Don Hutson on his own team. He was looking for hard-asses.

To further the contradiction, Bryant dressed in expensive suits, wore shined shoes, went to the barbershop once a week, shaved every morning, and discarded the foul language when the situation warranted it. He was no stranger to church. Away from public scrutiny, though, he drank heavily, smoked, cussed, and often butchered the language. It seemed he could change his personality by simply changing clothes.

Now, almost three hours into the first practice, several players felt dizzy from the heat and lack of water. Some stumbled around on wobbly legs. Bryant couldn't fathom how healthy young boys who'd worked three months in the broiling summer heat could toss their cookies in his first practice. Finally, calling the team together, he told the boys to take a knee.

"Boys, this mornin' was a total disaster. I thought about lining y'all up to run gassers again. But you can't even get off the damn ball together. So I changed my mind."

Bryant turned as if to walk away, and it appeared that the first practice was finally over. Then he spun and yelled, "So line up over there for punt drills! I want to see if y'all are smart enough to cover kicks."

For thirty more minutes they ran up and down the field, throwing up and chasing the bouncing ball.

• • •

Dennis Goehring grimaced as he sat on the edge of the makeshift table inside the Quonset hut otherwise known as the trainers' room. His neck throbbed where two bulging disks rubbed together. That morning, Dennis had picked two fights and wasn't sure if he'd won either one. His left eye was swollen, and he had a fat lower lip. But he'd accomplished his goal of catching the eye of Coach Bryant, who'd ordered him to run five extra gassers at the end of the afternoon practice.

Dennis was desperately trying to hang onto his roster spot. He knew that Bryant didn't really care for him. Bryant had told Smokey to "run that Goehring boy off." Smokey had said it wouldn't be a problem.

The old trainer sauntered into the training room with his hearing aid hanging by a shoestring. Nipping from a bottle of I. W. Harper, he looked Dennis square in the black eye and said, "Coach Bryant wants you outta here, boy. We both knows you's ain't worf a shit. I knew you weren't worf a shit when I first laid eyes on you. So why don't you catch the next bus back home?"

Dennis rubbed the back of his neck. "Yeah, you ol' stupid geezer. You tell Bryant one thing for me. You tell him I was here before both of you peckerwoods got here, and I'll be here when both of y'all are gone.''

Smokey turned so Dennis couldn't see him smiling. ''Yeah, I'll tell the boss man that. I'll tell him just as soon as I see him.''

Goehring knew the next two weeks would be hell on earth. By the time buses pulled out of Junction, players would be broken mentally and physically. But he had no interest in walking away. Besides, there was no reason to go home since the ranch back in San Marcos had sold. It was clear that the odds of surviving Bryant's boot camp were stacked against him. He was a fifth-string guard with a temporary scholarship that was due to expire at the end of the fall semester, and his college degree depended on his football survival.

As Smokey walked by, Dennis yanked the whiskey bottle from his hip pocket, ripped off the cap, and took a long, soothing drink.

''Thief!'' Smokey yelped. ''You by God better hope I don't tell Coach Bryant about this.''

Dennis rarely drank and never had a shot of whiskey this early in the day. But there was a sharp pain in his neck and, besides, he didn't feel like eating. The brutal morning practice had killed his appetite. The whiskey burned as it passed into his empty stomach.

After the boys showered and changed out of their sweat-soaked uniforms, a heavy southern-style breakfast was served in the chow hall—eggs, bacon, sausage, ham, grits, hash browns, biscuits, and cream gravy. Most of the boys felt queasy just looking at the food. Still fresh on their minds were the early-morning gassers and the heaving. Just the smell of the food made some boys sick again, inspiring mad dashes to the toilets.

That didn't stop Bryant, his coaches, and Smokey Harper from socking away the greasy fare. Bryant sopped his biscuits in the thick gravy and polished off five eggs with bacon and sausage. Smokey and the assistant coaches returned for more helpings.

After breakfast, most of the boys stumbled back to the barracks and fell heavily into the hard bunks. There would be no boat races or water fights or card playing. In a matter of minutes, most were sound asleep and snoring. No longer would they dream of swimming in the moonlight with naked girls. Dennis had even stopped thinking about Laverne Johnston.

One player, however, had something on his mind before sacking out. Bob Easley wanted to clear the air about some rumors he'd been hearing about his Quonset hut mate Fred Broussard, the big all-conference center who occupied a bunk just a few feet away.

Easley was a hard-running fullback who feared nothing but snakes. Coming out of Houston's John Reagan High School, he was one of the nation's top blue-chip recruits. But his dream of playing college football had been put on hold by NCAA investigators who'd learned he'd taken an illegal recruiting trip to College Station. So Easley did an end run on the NCAA, enrolling for one year at Baylor in Waco and then transferring to Texas A&M.

Coaches loved players like Easley—tough kids who lived with pain and never whined. For years he'd played on a surgically repaired knee that ached with his every step. Doctors warned that he would limp the rest of his life if he didn't give up the game. But football was his passion. Pain was just part of football.

Just to show how tough he was, Easley had insisted on a painkilling shot of Novocain before the annual maroon-and-white spring game a few months earlier back in College Station. Smokey and the doctors had gotten a little carried away with the Novocain when they prepared the syringe.

"Smokey," Easley said as he dressed for the game. "You put so much damn painkiller in that needle that I can't feel the left side of my body. As a matter of fact, I can't even feel my left ear."

That didn't stop Easley from scoring a touchdown and ripping off some big runs. It also won him even more respect from teammates and coaches.

Now, as the boys began to doze off, Easley walked toward the bunk that was occupied by Broussard. "Hey, Fred, I gotta ask ya something. Why do folks call you a Red Bone?"

Before Easley could finish, Fred had vaulted from his bunk and was hovering red-faced over the fullback, pointing a large finger at his face. Someone was mockingly called Red Bone in southern Louisiana if he had a mixture of French Cajun and Negro blood.

"Where the hell did you hear that?" Fred demanded.

"Just heard it."

"Well, you better stop hearin' it and sayin' it because I ain't. Next time you say it, I'll kick your goddamn ass."

Easley laughed and fell into his bunk.

Broussard brooded for an hour. He lay wide-eyed on his bunk, wondering why the boys had been picking on him so much lately and why football was no longer fun. He hated this hard-ass coach who had come from Kentucky. Fred had been one of the SWC's most decorated players a year earlier. Now he was in the deepest depression of his life.

. . .

Darkness fell on Junction as Bebes Stallings and Goehring were the last to trudge off the field. After the team had run gassers, Bebes and Dennis ran ten more apiece as punishment for breaking rules. Bebes was five seconds late to the afternoon practice. His chin strap had broken, and he'd sprinted back to the barracks to fetch a new one. Dennis had gotten into two more fights during the afternoon practice. Bryant hated to punish boys who had the gumption to use their fists. But the Goehring boy was acting a little crazy, he thought.

"Hell, Bebes," Dennis muttered as they walked with heavy legs toward the shower room. "Ain't no way that old man is gonna run me off."

As Bryant strolled toward the coaches' barracks, Smokey walked quickly toward his boss and could hold his tongue no longer.

"Coach. I tried to run that Goehring boy off, and you know what he says? He says he's here before us and he'd be here when we's gone."

Bryant turned in time to see the stumpy guard with the mud-caked face round the corner and walk into the shower room. Pulling a cigarette from his pocket, he lit it and took a long, deep draw. The smoke seemed to stay inside him.

Bryant turned to Smokey. "Looks like we might have found ourselves a football player after all," he said.

6

Wounded Duck

I can reach a kid who doesn't have any ability as long as he doesn't know it.

—PAUL "BEAR" BRYANT

SEPTEMBER 2, 1954

Not long after he observed Elwood Kettler throwing a football for the first time, Bear Bryant knew the Aggies had their quarterback. He turned to Coach Elmer and said, "That boy looks like he's trying to sling shit off his hand."

The hard truth was that Bryant didn't want a fancy quarterback who could throw tight spirals or rifle the ball forty yards on a fence rail. He didn't long for the services of someone like ex-TCU quarterback Davey O'Brien, who'd won the Heisman Trophy in 1938 with 1,457 passing yards—a college high-water mark for ten straight seasons. Bryant wasn't searching for Slingin' Sammy Baugh, another TCU All-American who went to on to become the NFL's best all-round player in the forties.

Nor was Bryant fantasizing about the golden arms of George Blanda or Sweet Babe Parilli, his quarterbacks at Kentucky. He wanted Elwood Kettler, by God.

They had met face-to-face for the first time the previous April as the team prepared for spring drills. Learning that Bryant wanted him to move from halfback to quarterback, Kettler had shrugged and said, "Coach, I can't throw a lick. Everybody'll tell you I tackle better'n I pass."

"Boy, you don't mind running the ball thirty times a game, do ya? That's what I'm looking for—a tough sonofabitch to carry the mail."

Mostly, Bryant was looking for a leader. Breathing life into the deflated Texas A&M football program wasn't going to be easy because of one cold truth—the talent was slimmer than a drought-starved jackrabbit. The Aggies would need a hard edge if they were to win any games in the 1954 season. Elwood would have to lead them—regardless of his shit-slinging arm—and he would have to be tough. Bryant knew that Kettler had little natural talent, but he was a hard-nosed boy who didn't mind playing with knots on his head and a few welts on his body.

Bryant studied Kettler and said, "I can see it in your eyes that you got guts in your body."

Like Bryant, Elwood had taken a long, hard look at himself that morning—in the locker-room mirror. He looked bony and wiry, in need of a chicken-fried steak with a vast side of mashed potatoes and creamed gravy. He stripped off his shirt and stepped onto the locker-room scales, still wearing his football shoes and pants that were stuffed with knee pads, thigh pads, and hip pads. The needle climbed all the way to 171 pounds. He figured he was wearing at least ten pounds of shoes and equipment, and he found it hard to imagine that he was cut out to be the Aggies' quarterback.

Kettler had been a high school quarterback/linebacker thirty miles down the two-laner from College Station in the quiet little town of Brenham. In three straight high school seasons, he never missed one second of playing time. He also punted, kicked off, kicked field goals and extra points, and returned punts and kickoffs. He played through several broken noses, a fractured jaw, and cracked knuckles. His run-to-pass ratio was about five-to-one. Grit, not talent, had won him the scholarship to Texas A&M.

Elwood had grown up both tough and dirt-poor in a family that had weathered the depression. His mother and father didn't make it past the third grade because farmwork demanded their daily attention. Times were so tough that Elwood's oldest brother had been dispatched to a depression work camp in Oregon. Another brother was raised by an uncle, and still another was brought up by grandparents. Elwood, the youngest son, could never remember the family owning a car. But he did remember going to the First Baptist Church almost every time they opened the doors.

While the family scratched out a living near the hamlet of Berline, a German settlement, Elwood attended a two-room elementary school. The family's move to Brenham was a stroke of luck for Elwood since Berline had no organized football teams. He started playing on the seventh-grade team in Brenham, and it wasn't long before he started dreaming about leaving the farm.

That dream was brought into sharper focus during the Saturday afternoons in the fall when he sat beside the radio and listened to broadcasts of both the Notre Dame and Army games. His first heroes were Doc Blanchard and Glenn Davis—Mr. Inside and Mr. Outside. Elwood also sat glued to the radio during the 1947 season as Johnny Lujack quarterbacked Notre Dame to the A.P. national championship. Lujack, like the Army halfbacks, won the Heisman Trophy.

Because the family couldn't afford the short trip to College Station, much less tickets to a game, Elwood played in the first college game he ever saw. By his junior season in 1953 he had moved into the starting lineup. But the promotion was based more on timing than talent. That year, the one-platoon system returned to college football, meaning players would play both offense and defense. Kettler was neither the best offensive nor the best defensive halfback. In fact, he'd been listed as a third-stringer on offense. But since coach Ray George was looking for the best two-way player, he chose Kettler over several other more talented boys.

Elwood almost fainted when the starting lineups were announced. He looked at his best friend, Joe Boring, and said, "Never in my wildest dreams . . ." Then he felt dizzy and had to lean on Joe's shoulder to keep from falling. Not only had one-platoon football elevated Elwood to the first string; the system converted him into a sixty-minute player. He and Boring would play side by side both offensively and defensively for the entire season.

Ironically, Texas A&M's opening game of the 1953 season was played against Bryant's Kentucky Wildcats. The Aggies won 7–6 in spite of being badly overmatched by a Kentucky team that would finish the season with a 7-2-1 record, good enough to be ranked number sixteen in the final A.P. poll.

As the A&M players boarded the buses that night after the victory, they could still see the stadium lights shining brightly. They could hear bodies colliding down on the field. Bryant was so exasperated with the defeat that he'd ordered a midnight scrimmage to begin at the same spot where the game had ended. He marked the ball and blew his whistle, and the Kentucky Wildcats went to work—until four in the morning.

Aggie running back Charles Hall shook his head as the Aggie buses rolled into the Lexington night. "Boys, how'd you like to play for a son-ofabitch like that? Those fellas are gonna be sick and sore in the morning."

Six months later, Bryant's plane was landing in College Station.

When the annual maroon-and-white game kicked off six weeks later at Kyle Field, it seemed that every ex-student and Aggie follower ever born had come to see the controversial new coach. They also wanted to know why he'd chosen a weak-armed buzztop from Brenham to lead the team.

Answers came quickly. It was clear there would be nothing artistic about Bryant's offense. From the Split-T formation the Aggies ran off-tackle bursts and countertraps and quarterback sneaks and power sweeps. Kettler carried the ball several times on the quarterback sweep for some decent gains. Postwar college football had been dull, but lately it had been acceptable to exercise a little razzle-dazzle. Granted, wide receivers were still several years from becoming trendy. But several collegiate teams were using a split end or a wingback on passing downs, and even Notre Dame legend Frank Leahy had given in to the passing game before retiring. But not Bryant. He'd forgotten about the passing game when he left Lexington. He'd come to Texas to by-God run the football.

That's why Elwood Kettler seemed so appealing the first time Bryant laid eyes on him. He compared Kettler's soft and wobbly passes to "a wounded bird trying to get to the tree."

It wasn't so much that Bryant didn't want a quarterback who could light up the scoreboard. God knows, he'd appreciated the great Babe Parilli when he led Kentucky to its first SEC championship ever in 1950. Sweet Babe had the smoothest release in all of college football, and he could throw strikes in the face of a full-out blitz. Bryant actually had converted Parilli from a single-wing high school halfback to a quarterback. College football knew no better passing quarterback during Parilli's 1949 and '50 seasons at Kentucky. Bryant had seen George Blanda work the same kind of magic during the '48 season and loved every second of it.

When Bryant turned his eyes on Texas A&M, he envisioned a team rising to national prominence because of two crucial elements—a jaw-breaking defense and a powerful running game. That's why he shunned Dave Smith, the team's best passer and a quarterback many coaches would have coveted. Bryant wanted a boy like Kettler, who could run around and through tacklers and who could play hurt.

Two months after arriving at Texas A&M, Bryant had smiled upon Kettler's fine work in the annual spring game until he broke free on a bootleg and was tackled ten yards downfield by center/linebacker Fred Broussard. As Kettler fell, he felt a horrible pain ripping through his ribs and lower back. Broussard's knees had landed squarely on Kettler's lower back. Air gushed from his body, and as he lay motionless on the ground he thought at first his back was broken.

Thirty minutes later, Kettler still lay on the trainers' table at halftime when Bryant marched into the room. Steely eyes stared daggers into the quarterback. "Looks to me you ain't my quarterback after all," he growled. "I don't need a boy who's gonna get hurt. My quarterback has gotta be a tough sonofabitch."

"Coach," Kettler groaned, "I'm sorry. But I can't even raise my right leg right now. It's numb."

"You mean you ain't gonna play in the second half?"

"Yes, sir. No, I guess I won't. But I'd like to."

Bryant thought about Joe Drach, his quarterback at Maryland during his first season ever as a college head coach in 1945. Drach had broken a bone in his right hand in the first half against West Virginia. The hand was twisted grotesquely into the shape of a question mark and throbbed horribly. Bryant told the trainers to "tape it up" at halftime. Drach was close to tears, and his jaw dropped as he said, "Tape it up?"

In a rage, Bryant grabbed the quarterback's arm and pressed the hand against the locker-room wall. The bone popped back into place, and Drach fainted from the pain. Drach came to after a trainer snapped an ammonia capsule under his nose, and he played the entire second half.

Kettler stayed in the trainers' room. Doctors discovered that he'd broken four bones in his lower back known as transverse processes. Two ribs had been torn completely loose from his sternum. Several days would pass before Kettler could even walk again. Breathing was next to impossible. But Bryant still couldn't fathom why his quarterback hadn't at least tried to play in the second half.

"I really felt like I let Coach down," a despondent Kettler told Smokey Harper a few days later.

"You did all right. Even I can't make a boy play who can't walk."

Now, on the second day in Junction, Kettler again was leading the first-string offense, and Fred Broussard was lined up at linebacker. Four months had passed since Elwood was pounded into the ground by Big Fred, and most of the soreness in his back and ribs was gone.

Again Bryant cussed and ranted about the offensive screwups. Kettler already had dislocated two fingers that day taking misdirected snaps from the inexperienced centers. One of the fingers, dislocated at the middle knuckle, turned at a ninety-degree angle. Smokey laughed as he snapped the finger back into place.

Carrying the ball on an end sweep, Kettler broke into the secondary but could feel somebody breathing down his neck. Broussard grabbed the quarterback's face mask and they fell together in a cloud of dust. In a flashback to the spring game, Broussard jammed both knees into the quarterback's lower back, falling with his full weight on Kettler. Bryant could hear his quarterback's painful howls more than fifty yards away.

"That goddamn girl!" Bryant yelled at Smokey Harper. "Get him off the field and outta my sight."

Numbness was returning to Kettler's right leg as the student trainers carried his limp body from the field on a stretcher. Bryant yelled at Billy Pickard, "If he ain't well enough to practice this afternoon, just send his butt on back to College Station!"

Elwood was hardly being singled out by Bryant, whose wrath had befallen just about every boy on the rugged practice grounds of Junction. During a drill called eye-openers, Bryant stomped around angrily as running back Charles Hall was tackled behind the line of scrimmage. As Hall rose to his feet and pounded the dust off his pants, Bryant stormed toward the small running back. Bryant had learned weeks earlier that Hall had gotten married and was still angry about it. "You know what's wrong with you, you little turd? All of your football is runnin' straight out the end of your dick."

Bryant turned and blew his whistle. The collisions stopped and the practice field grew silent as he prepared to speak.

"I want y'all boys to know that I'm worried about little Charlie here. Seems that getting married has screwed up his football playin'. I don't want to hear about any more of you boys gettin' married. If you want to get married, go join the band, or try out for cheerleader."

Several boys had gotten married over the summer. It was now their secret.

In just three practices, Bryant thought he had witnessed more fumbles and botched snaps and busted fingers than he'd seen in eight full seasons of coaching. Players spent more time shaking goatheads from their hands than blocking and tackling. The coaching staff figured that the heat and hard labor would trigger several fights. Instead, the players seemed more interested in avoiding one another.

Smokey sighed and said, "You know, these boys here are curious. Back in Kentucky, those boys were fightin' every other play. These boys just stand around and look at each other—kind of curious-like."

Smokey, of course, wasn't talking about Dennis Goehring, who would do anything to grab the coaches' attention. He was picking fights with whoever crossed his path, and his number-one adversary was Marvin Tate, the senior guard from Abilene who had what Dennis wanted—a starting job.

Bryant was beginning to appreciate Goehring's gumption and would order the coaches not to interfere in his fights: "Let 'em go! Let 'em go! They ain't gonna hit nobody no way. Don't worry about getting your hands dirty." The truth was, he wanted to see if Dennis could whip the other boy.

After the morning practice ended, the coaches ran the boys until their tongues hung out. Two fell face-first into the thick dust and, although they were conscious, still lacked the strength to crawl from the field. Bryant finally ordered the student assistants to drag the boys off the field by their heels.

The only hospital within fifty miles was located in downtown Junction. It was a small wood-frame infirmary that once had been a three-bedroom home with a long front porch just off Main Street. Elwood was driven there by Billy Pickard after Broussard fell on his back. He was examined by Dr. John E. Wiedeman, a bald, dignified man who wore a coat and tie and seemed out of step with the rough-edged town. *This is no small-town doctor,* Billy thought. He noted how confidently Wiedeman worked and how he moved so gracefully around the examining room. The doctor asked about Elwood's history of back problems and was told about the broken bones in his back and the ribs that had been unfastened from the sternum a few months earlier. Wiedeman nodded. After x-raying Elwood's back, Dr. Wiedeman asked one of the nurses to prepare a room for the Aggie quarterback.

"Oh, no, no," Billy said nervously. "Doc, if we don't get back pretty quick, Coach will be plenty pissed. He didn't want Elwood getting hurt in the first place."

Removing his glasses, Wiedeman looked puzzled. "Well, this young man is hurt. There isn't much we can do unless he stays overnight. If he were Superman, he could go on back to the Adjunct and practice football. But I see no *S* on his cape.''

''No, Doc. You just don't know our coach. He don't believe in players gettin' hurt.''

Billy grabbed Elwood's hand and, amid some heavy breathing and deep groans, pulled him up from the table. Elwood stumbled across the room and banged into a wall. He coughed and his face turned crimson.

Billy wrapped his arm around the quarterback's waist. ''Elwood, you're just gonna have to straighten up and fly right. Coach is waiting for us back at camp.''

Wiedeman watched the boys scrambling toward the car and shook his head. Like most citizens in Junction, Wiedeman had wondered what was taking place at the Adjunct. No one had been allowed within a mile of the place since the team started practicing.

''I'll have the X rays back soon!'' the doctor yelled to Billy. ''Maybe I'll take a little ride out to the Adjunct this afternoon and tell you how they turned out.''

With Elwood lying in the backseat of the Ford, Billy drove back to camp just as practice was ending. Crossing Flatrock Bridge, Billy found himself deep in thought. He worried that Elwood's football career was coming to an end. As he parked the Ford next to the chow hall, Elwood let out another painful groan.

''What am I gonna tell Coach?'' Billy muttered to himself.

. . .

Survival was now on the mind of every boy who'd had come to Junction. When the buses had pulled out of College Station two days earlier, none of the 111 players had given Billy Granberry much of a shot to make the team.

''You know, Granberry,'' Don Watson said, ''you're small. But you're also pretty dad-gum slow.''

Soaking wet, he weighed 155 pounds. Even worse, he stood only five-foot-seven and had freckles all over his body. He'd been mistaken many times for the water boy. From all indications, Billy figured his number was up. Bryant seemed always to be in a foul mood around him. What Billy didn't know, though, was that he'd actually made a good first impression on the unforgiving coach.

Of all the players in Junction, only Billy had received a nickname from Bryant—Redbird. This was in deference to the boy's flaming red hair. It was also a sign that Bear liked him. Players would learn in the weeks, months, and years ahead that earning a moniker from the Man was a good thing.

Redbird had impressed Bryant with a bell-ringing lick he'd delivered on punt coverage during the spring game just months earlier. Flying down the field, he jackhammered the return man a split second after the ball arrived. There was a thunderous crash and a fumble. But Redbird didn't rise quickly, thanks to a severe dislocation of his left shoulder. He walked slowly to the sideline, his arm flopping like a rooster wing.

Redbird walked within a few feet of Bryant, who actually felt sorry for the injured boy. Billy Pickard instructed Redbird to lie on the grass. Pickard jammed his right foot into the boy's armpit, grabbed his left hand, and yanked his arm until the shoulder snapped back into the socket. There was a loud pop and, quite amazingly, most of the pain subsided. Pickard suggested that he sit the rest of the game out, but since he was feeling OK, Redbird assumed a place on the sideline next to Bryant and said, "Coach, I'm ready to go back in . . . I think."

"Redbird," Bryant softly drawled. "Why don't you go sit down before you get yourself hurt again?"

As the team watched the game film the next day, Bryant showed Redbird's injury several times, running the projector back and forth.

"Redbird, this is where you hurt your funny bone," Bryant said, cracking a rare smile. A smattering of laughter made Redbird feel uncomfortable. It seemed that Bryant was mocking the boy when, in fact, he was giving him a macho hug.

Now, in just two days of practice in Junction, Redbird already had dislocated the shoulder three times. Twice Pickard had placed his foot in the armpit and yanked it back into place. Redbird had also discovered he could fix the shoulder himself by placing a balled fist in his armpit and forcing his arm downward.

The team had scrimmaged for more than two hours when Redbird, playing linebacker, found himself in a scary predicament. Fullback Jack Pardee, the toughest man in camp, had rumbled through a large hole off left guard and now was barreling down on him. Redbird did what any red-blooded overmatched linebacker would do as he closed his eyes, ducked his head, gritted his teeth, and hit Big Jack as hard as he could. The helmet-to-helmet wreck sounded like a freight train colliding with an eighteen-wheeler. Pardee did fall, but not before ripping Redbird's shoulder out of its socket again. With the arm dangling loosely at his side, Redbird trotted to the sideline and was looking for Billy Pickard when he ran into Smokey Harper. The old trainer grinned and grabbed the injured boy by the face mask.

"You know, Redbird, when you was in high school you was a boy among boys. Now, you's a boy among men."

The dislocations had seemed bearable until now. Redbird would just grit his teeth and cope with the pain until the shoulder was popped back into place. But this one felt as though there was a fire in the socket. Grimacing and pulling away from Smokey, Redbird said, "Where's Billy?"

"Don't worry, little feller; I know how to fix your dad-gum shoulder. Been doin' it for years. So lay down, boy."

Instead of sticking his foot beneath the armpit, Smokey placed it on the back of Redbird's shoulder and, before he could protest, Smokey began to yank his arm the wrong way. Standing about twenty yards away, attending to another player, Billy suddenly could see that Smokey was about to rip the arm right off Redbird's shoulder. Sprinting toward them, Billy yelled, "Whoa! Stop! Whoa! Stop, you dumb sucker!"

Luckily for Redbird, Smokey's hearing aid was on. He heard Billy yelling and stopped pulling before he could inflict more damage. "Smokey, let me handle this," Billy said. "You're doin' it backward."

Watching as Billy placed his foot in Redbird's armpit, slowly pulling the shoulder back into place, Smokey shrugged. "You know, if ol' Redbird was worf a shit, he wouldn't be gettin' hurt all the time. We wouldn't have to be fixin' the boy every other play."

As Billy completed his work, he could see a car boiling up dust in the distance. He placed a hand over his forehead to shade his eyes from the blazing sun. At first, he wondered if it were merely an illusion, a shimmering mirage on the desert's horizon. No one had dared come into the Adjunct in more than three days since Bryant had scared the bejeebers out of the last three visitors.

The car moved slowly down the dirt road and, sure enough, headed directly toward the football camp. More shocking than its presence was the type of car headed their way—a large white ambulance with an orange top.

Walking toward the road, Billy couldn't imagine what this unannounced visit was all about. But he was determined to find out. He waved and the driver stopped a few feet away.

"May we help ya?" Billy asked.

The driver had dark hair and thick sideburns and wore large, round sunglasses. "We come to pick up your boy with the broken back," he said. "Doc Wiedeman says he's got four broken bones. He needs to come on back to the hospital. We'll get a stretcher and load him up."

"Won't need to do that."

"Why not?"

"Because the boy with the broken back is out there on the practice field right now, quarterbackin' our offense." Billy pointed toward Elwood. "Besides, you walk out on that field with that stretcher, you might just find it shoved up your ass. Bear Bryant is pretty good at shovin' things."

His mouth agape, the driver shifted gears and steered the ambulance back onto the dirt road. Billy watched the ambulance blowing dust and could tell it was gaining speed all the way to the highway. Hours would pass before the dust returned to earth.

Billy shook his head. "Folks around here've gotta lot to learn," he said. "They surely do."

7

Pain

I don't care how much talent a team has—if the boys
don't think tough, practice tough, and live tough, how can
they play tough on Saturday?

PAUL "BEAR" BRYANT

SEPTEMBER 3, 1954

Only the gentle clacking of typewriter keys could be heard across the
sleepy football camp.

That morning, the players had scrimmaged and run gassers in the searing heat and then picked at their scrambled eggs and fallen asleep in their
hard bunks. The night before, ten players had fled into the darkness.

Fatigue had brought some peace to the hell camp. If not for reporter
Mickey Herskowitz's typing from his screened-in barracks, the place
would have seemed deathly silent. It was early afternoon, and Herskowitz
sat on the edge of his bed and pecked at the portable Royal keyboard. This
was the nineteen-year-old's first official sports "beat" for the *Houston
Post.* He'd covered a lot of high school football and Little League baseball.
But now he'd been assigned to cover this radical football camp. Though
he lacked hard experience and was younger than most of the players, Herskowitz recognized that something had gone wrong in Junction.

80

For years, Mickey had listened to other sportswriters talking about pre-season football camps, and he knew the first couple of days normally were reserved for lightweight stuff like physical exams, photographs, and brief practices in shorts and T-shirts. Other college coaches maintained tough practice standards, too, but didn't start camp with two-hour scrimmages and eye-opener drills. Mickey had never heard of players throwing up before the coaches called roll.

A day earlier, he had filed a three-page story about the backbreaking labor in the dust bowl almost three hundred miles from College Station. He'd written about bodies crunching and bones mangling. Then he'd been driven by public relations director Jones Ramsey forty miles across some twisting two-lane Hill Country roads to Kerrville, where the closest Western Union teletype was located.

That morning, Mickey had called the sports desk at the *Houston Post* to see how they had liked his story. "What story?" fellow reporter Jack Gallagher asked. "Hell, Mickey, we thought you were out there takin' some vacation time." As it turned out, Western Union had closed early and his story didn't make it onto the wire.

So Mickey decided to rework yesterday's piece and spice it up. Nothing in the last twenty-four hours had changed his mind about a camp that, to him, resembled the Bataan Death March. Bryant was running some players into the ground and others off. Folks back in Houston, where many Texas A&M ex-students lived, would consider this big news. Mickey couldn't wait for the story to hit the morning editions.

Mickey decided against the drive back to the Western Union office in Kerrville. So, he grabbed his copy and walked outside to the closest pay phone, fastened to a wooden pole about ten feet behind Bryant's barracks. In a few minutes, the entire coaching staff would convene for its daily meeting, and already Mickey could hear some arguing and spirited discussions emanating from the Quonset hut, which was the norm this time of the day. Bryant hated dull staff meetings.

Mickey dialed the sports desk in Houston and Gallagher answered. "Jack," Mickey said. "Give me a byline and a dateline and spell it capital *J-U-N-C-T-I-O-N.* Let's begin: 'For decades, the Texas Aggies have been known for fighting wars all over the world. The last five days, they've been going to war for new coach Paul Bear Bryant.' Period. New paragraph.

" 'In probably the toughest and most brutal fall camp ever, Bryant has literally been running players into the ground here in Junction.' "

Mickey made references to "helmets colliding" and "bones mangling" and "blood flowing from the nose of one player." He told of Bryant chasing two players off the practice field during the first workout. He described the coach's T-shirt as splattered with blood at the end of one practice. Twenty minutes later, as he hung up, he turned to see student manager Troy Summerlin standing a few feet away.

"Uh, Mr. Herskowitz," Troy said, his face turning red. "Coach Bryant would like to see you in his office. Pretty quick, in fact."

Mickey had felt self-conscious about dictating his story and worried that someone might be eavesdropping. Reading your own words over the phone to another person who is typing can be unnerving. The sportswriter wiped sweat from his brow. He thought to himself, *How loud was I talking?*

Walking past his Quonset hut, Mickey whispered to Ramsey through the screen, "Did Coach hear me dictating?" Ramsey didn't speak but nervously tapped his index finger against his thumb. Mickey knew this old nervous habit signaled that Ramsey was worried. Now Mickey was really nervous.

The day before, Mickey and Bryant had spoken briefly, but the coach had offered few explanations for traveling to Junction. Mickey knew that Bear had mixed feelings about his own presence there. Sure, Bryant wanted the publicity because it could eventually help in recruiting high school players, but Bryant didn't want the world to know so quickly of the torturous workouts or that players were already fleeing camp to get away from him. The reporter was both a help and a hindrance. Furthermore, Mickey was about seven inches shorter and sixty pounds lighter than Bryant, who cast both a physical and psychological shadow over anyone he encountered. Mickey hardly felt like going one-on-one with the man they called Bear.

Summerlin opened the screen door to Bryant's barracks and motioned for Mickey to enter. He swallowed hard as he saw Bryant sitting behind a table where ashtrays and sheets of paper were strewn. Two coaches were drawing plays on a chalkboard behind Bryant, who turned and said flatly, "Go get me some iced tea at the chow hall. Come back in about ten minutes." Jim Owens and Willie Zapalac gave the reporter furtive looks and then bumped into each other as they hurried toward the back door.

"Mickey, sit down," Bryant said in a low rumble. "Let's visit awhile."

Bryant tapped a Chesterfield against the silver lighter. "Mickey, I couldn't help but overhear what you were dictating back to your office. Seems that you were pretty graphic about some of the things you were saying."

"Yes, sir."

"Well, Mickey, why don't you tell me about your little article."

"Coach, I was just trying to get across that you were running a pretty tough camp out here. I've seen some practices and I know that you're not foolin' around."

Bryant drew deeply on the cigarette and seemed in deep thought. Lines creased his forehead. "Mickey, what bothers me are some of the words you used, like 'bodies crunching.' Did you say something about bones getting mangled? Mickey, what do you think the mamas and the papas in Houston, and all over Texas, are gonna think when they read that?"

It was clear now that Bryant had been listening closely, perhaps had even taken notes. Mickey felt trapped. He certainly couldn't deny that he'd written those phrases. *Holy shit! I've made him mad,* Mickey thought.

"Coach, I don't know what to say."

"Let's try this," Bryant said. "What can we do to make this whole thing a little easier on both of us?"

Through the years, Bryant had become a master psychologist, and one of his favorite tricks was tossing the problem into the other person's lap. Bryant knew that people naturally felt better about the solution if they helped solve the problem. Bryant often used this ploy with assistant coaches, saying, "Now what would you do if the opposition was in a five-man front and we needed three yards on third down from their fourteen-yard line?" Bryant, of course, had the answer but liked for others to participate. That way, they would feel part of the problem-solving.

"Coach, I've got some thoughts. I see there is more to the story than I thought. Perhaps I could do some editing."

A smile creased Bryant's lips. "Tell you what—I'll give you a few quotes to use." The sportswriter would need to fill some space when he started editing the controversial phrases. While Mickey scribbled into his notebook, Bryant talked about players who'd already impressed him—like Bobby Drake Keith, Bebes Stallings, Jack Pardee, and even Dennis Goehring.

"Hold, on," Bryant said. "Edit out that stuff about Goehring. I don't want him thinkin' I like him. Yet."

An hour later, Mickey called the sports desk again and, to his chagrin, the cynical Gallagher answered.

"Well, hell, Mickey, what's goin' on out there? I hear Bear Bryant's a turd. He got you on the run?"

"No. I just missed some things, Jack, that's all."

• • •

Hammering could be heard from the barracks that had come to be known as the trainers' room. Smokey Harper was tacking a sign to the screen door that he'd scrawled that afternoon. It read: BE GOOD OR BE GONE.

The first customer that afternoon was Elwood Kettler, who'd received the blessing of Bryant to spend an hour each day soaking his sore back in the whirlpool. Elwood had continued to practice in spite of his injury. But as he walked slowly into the training room, he was bent over like an old man. He saw Smokey lift a fifth of Jim Beam and swallow hard.

Smokey was wearing the crude hearing aid. The volume control was located on the front of the square metal device. Elwood noticed that Smokey had the volume turned to low.

Elwood lip-synched several words without uttering a sound. Smokey reached for the button on his hearing aid and turned the volume to high.

"What'd you say?" Smokey said.

Elwood shouted, "I was just wondering if you were deaf, you ol' sumbitch!"

Smokey covered his ears with both hands and yelled, "You can take the boy out of high school, but you can't take the high school out of the boy!"

From the first day of camp, Kettler had been bunking with ten other players in one of the southernmost Quonset huts. He'd discovered on awakening that morning that each one had vanished. After holding a secret meeting following supper, they had decided to sneak away just past midnight without telling anyone. They couldn't summon the courage to tell Bryant or even Elwood, for that matter.

Elwood informed Smokey of the mass escape. "Where'd you figure they go?"

"Don't know. I just hope the coyotes didn't eat 'em."

Elwood tested the hot, swirling water with his right foot. "You surprised those boys would be leavin' without tellin' Coach?"

"Nah. Boys is curious around here. Besides, Coach Bryant is trying to run the curious ones off."

Curious was one of Smokey's favorite words. Instead of saying "odd"

or "strange" or "funny" or "wacky," he would say, "The boy is curious." Smokey was eating Tex-Mex food one afternoon across the main
drag from campus when he said, "Those tacos sure look curious."

Settling his body into the hot water, Elwood noticed Smokey taking
another pull from the Jim Beam. Elwood had enjoyed a few beers in his
lifetime, but never whiskey—much less straight whiskey on a day when
the temperature had risen to over one hundred degrees.

"Tell me," Elwood said, pointing at the bottle. "How does that whiskey feel when it hits the bottom of your gut?"

Smokey licked his lips. "Let me tell ya a little secret about hard whiskey. You might go a few rounds with ol' John Barleycorn. And you might
win a couple. But pretty soon, if you don't stop, ol' John Barleycorn's
gonna whip your ass."

Smokey had been known to go long stretches without drinking and had
tried unsuccessfully several times to quit completely. His two favorite
coaches of all time—Bear Bryant and Red Sanders—drank frequently, and
Smokey enjoyed tipping the bottle with those men. Sanders, who had been
Smokey's boss ten years earlier at Vanderbilt, was now the head coach at
UCLA.

Both Sanders and Bryant were fully aware that Smokey was not a
competent athletic trainer according to anyone's standards. But big-time
college football programs rarely provided day-to-day treatment for athletes
beyond the taping of ankles or the whirlpool. Players were expected to
play with pain and heal quickly on their own.

Because Smokey was afraid of flying, Sanders would send him to away
games several days ahead on the train. Smokey would typically leave
Nashville on Tuesday and spend the entire trip in the club car. Upon arriving at the site of the game, he would spend a day sobering up before
setting up the team's training room.

What appealed to Bryant and Sanders was that Smokey understood the
nature of people. Smokey had an eye to quickly determine if a boy had
football ability just by watching how he handled himself. After years of
working with athletes, he didn't need a stopwatch or a set of scales to
measure one. Bryant kept notes and files on things Smokey said about
players, although few people knew it.

Elwood knew Smokey had plenty of data socked away in his head.
He'd been anxious to ask Smokey what he thought about the prospects for
the 1954 season. Elwood found his opening, as they were now alone.

"Do you think we can win many games this season with this bunch?"

Smokey frowned. "We got too many narrow-assed people playing for us. We got too many boys saying 'excuse me' instead of gettin' into fights. We got too many lazy-asses like Fred Broussard stinkin' up the joint. Besides that, I think we could win one or two games this year."

Just then, the screen door slammed and in walked a scowling Dennis Goehring. He rubbed his neck. "You gonna do somethin' about my pain, you old geezer?"

In the corner of the training room was a contraption that resembled a hangman's noose. Smokey shooed Dennis in that direction, instructing him to sit down, shut up, and wrap the straps under his chin.

"I thought you and Bryant were gonna kill me. But now I know for sure."

"Well, if you were worf a shit, it'd be different. But I'm gonna try and fix your neck anyway. Then maybe I can run your ass off."

For several months Goehring had suffered a shooting pain in his neck where two protruding disks rubbed together. Smokey's sling suspended Dennis's head and allowed the neck to stretch. Hour upon hour each day, he would sit in the corner, looking as if he'd hung himself. The little contraption helped separate the disks, and soon the pain would subside.

With Elwood in the whirlpool and Dennis in the neck sling, the trainers' room began to fill up. The hard days in Junction were taking a physical toll. That morning, center Lloyd Hale had tried to trap-block Bobby Jack Lockett. The big defensive end threw a haymaker into Hale's helmet, breaking it in half. As the helmet shattered, one of the jagged edges gashed the top of Hale's head. Lockett's right hand swelled like a cantaloupe and both boys were carted off to the infirmary, where Dr. Wiedeman put fifteen stitches in Hale's head and a cast on Lockett's broken hand. Now the two boys were in the trainers' room.

"Smokey," Bobby Jack said. "Lloyd and I were wonderin' if we had to practice today. The Doc says we both should sit out a few days."

The old trainer looked at the boys and nodded. "I'll tell Coach Bryant that you boys ain't got no business practicin' this afternoon. I'll clear it with boss man, you can be sure."

Limping into the training room and barely able to put weight on his right foot was Joe Boring, the all-conference back whom most players considered the best all-round athlete on the team. Boring had been examined over the summer by an orthopedic specialist who insisted that he operate on the badly damaged knee. But Boring opted to wait with the hope that he could make it through the football season. But the knee wobbled as he ran and had popped out of place four times during the Junction practices. On two occasions, Boring had become sick to his stomach after popping the knee back into the socket. Now the knee had swelled to twice its normal size and needed draining, but there were no doctors around to perform the task.

"I just can't go this afternoon," Boring told Smokey. "I would if I could, but I can't. If I can just get the dang thing drained—"

"Don't sweat it," Smokey interrupted. "I'll get Billy to run you over to the infirmary." He turned toward the whirlpool and yelled, "Elwood, get out of there, boy! You been in there an hour. Let Joe get some hot water on his leg."

Over the next thirty minutes, Smokey informed five more players that they wouldn't be participating in the afternoon action. Their injuries ranged from a serious hip pointer to what appeared to be a fractured ankle. Smokey instructed Billy Pickard to drive four of the boys, including Boring, to the Junction Infirmary for examinations. Kettler and Goehring, however, would suit up in spite of their injuries. They feared the wrath of Bryant if they didn't.

Fifteen minutes before the start of practice, Smokey spotted Bryant heading toward the training room. He met the head coach at the screen door, and they talked outside for about five minutes.

"All of these boys need some time off," Smokey said. "Some got some bad injuries in there, Coach. Joe Boring can barely walk with that bum knee, and another boy looks like he's got a fractured ankle."

Bryant nodded and said nothing. Then he swung open the screen door and marched into the trainers' room. He jabbed at the air with his index finger and shouted, "You, you, you, you, you, you, and you! Get your butts dressed for practice. Be on the field in ten minutes. I want no more excuses out of you candy asses!"

Smokey walked in behind Bryant. "Yeah, that's right, Coach. I told them boys they weren't hurt and that they oughta be practicin'. Ain't nothin' wrong with these boys that some hard work won't cure."

Lockett held up the cast that had been fitted that morning. Dr. Wiedeman had told him the cast would stay on six weeks, meaning he'd miss the first four games of the season. Southwest Conference rules prohibited players from wearing casts during games.

"I see your broken hand," Bryant said. "I feel your pain. But, son, I played a game in college with a broken leg once and nobody gave me no pity."

"But I can't play in the games," said Lockett.

"That's all right. You can still suit up and practice."

Even the boys with bad limps hustled out of the trainers' room and began searching for their wet, dirty uniforms. With Bryant still within earshot, Smokey hollered, "I told you sonsabitches you were gonna have to practice today. Told ya!"

. . .

Big Jack Pardee was rapidly becoming Bryant's favorite Aggie player. In fact, Pardee reminded Bryant of some of his great players at Kentucky like All-America tackle Bob Gain and quarterback George Blanda.

Pardee already had lined up at center, end, linebacker, fullback, and defensive halfback. He came to practice thirty minutes early to work with various coaches and stayed late. He was the best ballcarrier and blocker on the team and never seemed to let up. But Bryant hadn't taken the time to notice that Pardee had already lost twenty pounds in less than four days. The boy was a walking case of dehydration.

As the stragglers limped onto the field for the afternoon practice, Bryant turned to Coach Elmer. "That Pardee boy might be the toughest kid I've ever seen."

Elmer nodded. "You gotta take into account where he comes from. His daddy was took down with the arthritis, so Jack had to become the breadwinner of the family at an early age. Hell, Coach, he started doin' roughneck work when he was fourteen. He'd work in the oil fields all night and then do ranch work in the afternoon after football practice. Five years ago, he could stack more hay than ten grown men. And, Coach, I bet you didn't know that he's only nineteen years old."

Pardee had pinkish skin that looked like it had been scrubbed with a coarse rag. His face was covered with freckles, and it was rarely without a smile. He was the all-American boy, and Bryant liked every inch of him.

With a puzzled look, Bryant said, "We just got to figure out where to play him, Elmer. Hell, I wish we could play him at every position on the field."

Peering across the field, Bryant could see Lloyd Hale lining up at first-team right guard. The gash in his head was so painful that he couldn't bear to put on his helmet. Now he was in the midst of a full-scale scrimmage with no headgear. Striding across the field, Bryant blew his whistle. "Lloyd Hale, get your butt over here."

After admonishing him for practicing without a helmet, Bryant ordered the guard to take the rest of the day off. Bryant patted the boy on the shoulder and watched him slowly walk away.

Not a cloud had appeared in the Junction sky since the team arrived. Because the region was extremely dry, the temperature settled into the eighties at night. But the mercury rose past 100 degrees by ten each morning and on this afternoon had climbed to 109. The air shimmered with the heat radiating from the practice field. Bryant stubbornly refused to give the players water or ice breaks. Three or four players had to be dragged off the field after each practice, and Dr. Wiedeman's infirmary had turned busier than an open bar at the local VFW post. Between the players quitting and others entering the infirmary, the coaches could no longer keep tabs on the number of players in camp.

This afternoon, Bryant could sense the energy evaporating from every player. Some stumbled around with a condition called blind wobbles. They had come to Junction smiles and high hopes. Now most were wondering if they would last until the season opener in two weeks against Texas Tech.

About fifty yards away, Bryant spotted Billy Pickard kneeling over a fallen player. The coach placed a meaty paw to his forehead to shade his eyes. He couldn't make out the downed Aggie. As he walked across the field, Bryant could see that Pickard was holding the player's head in his hands.

Pickard soon saw shoes approaching from the corner of his eye, and he quickly recognized the man's gait. Bryant stopped a few feet away. "Billy, what the hell is wrong with that boy? I don't want boys laying down on the field."

"Coach. His head's hot."

"That right. Well, my head's gettin' hotter by the second."

With that, Billy dropped the boy's head and dashed away. Pardee rolled over and scrambled to his feet and then ran the other way. Bryant was surprised to learn that Pardee was the downed player. If he couldn't handle the heat, no one could, the coach thought.

Bryant stood at the same spot for several minutes, staring at the distant hills. Were the boys out of shape? Or was he just driving them too hard? Jack Pardee was in shape. He knew that. So it had to be the heat.

At the sound of the whistle, the players gathered around Bryant on one knee. He ordered them to run only ten gassers and drink plenty of water at the end of practice. The players would have celebrated if they'd had the energy.

An hour later, Mickey Herskowitz and Jones Ramsey were driving down Main Street in Junction, looking for a diner with a good chicken-fried steak and listening to KMBL, the local radio station. At full power, the station soared to all of fifty watts. Earlier that day, Ramsey had recorded a couple of phone interviews with the station manager. Now one of the reports was coming on. "The Texas Aggies practiced today at the Adjunct, and they worked on blocking and tackling," Ramsey said in a voice that sounded like it was coming from the bottom of a tin cup. "Some of the boys tossed their cookies. A few others just walked off and quit."

The two men laughed. "Hell," Ramsey said. "I thought they'd edit out the part about tossing cookies."

Herskowitz laughed. "You know, Jones, you're the only reporter in this car who didn't get edited today."

8

Quitter

The first time you quit, it's hard. The second time, it gets easier. The third time, you don't even have to think about it.

—PAUL "BEAR" BRYANT

SEPTEMBER 4, 1954

It was a typical late-summer evening in Junction. While kids with glass jars chased fireflies in the backyard and the women played canasta, the men gathered on the front porch of the large frame house to smoke hand-rolled cigarettes and to discuss the drought.

As darkness settled over the Hill Country, the Hagood farm was abuzz with kids and dogs and card playing when the storm appeared on the western horizon. The men bolted to their feet with the first streak of lightning. It had been almost six months since a storm had soaked the Llano Valley, and it was hard to remember the last good rain before that.

Luke Hagood was a dryland farmer, and his family lived on the old Kountz place in a two-story house built right after the Civil War. Isaac Kountz was the last Anglo settler in Kimble County to be killed by the Indians in 1870. Ranchers and farmers chased the guilty Comanches out of the county but couldn't catch them.

91

Rain had been so scarce that Luke's oldest daughter, Nancy, had outgrown her yellow slicker without ever wearing it. The raincoat had been passed down to daughter Ann Beth, who was five years younger.

Five men stared at the coal black sky, waiting and hoping for more lightning. Then they silently counted the jagged streaks crisscrossing the sky above the flat country to the west. They sniffed the air for rain, and Luke Hagood licked his right index finger and held it aloft, trying to gauge the wind's direction. Almost an hour had passed since the broiling sun dipped below the horizon, but the wind was still dry and hot.

"Feels like it's blowin' straight out of the west," Luke said. "Not a good sign. I think we'd need a little more southerly wind to blow up a gulley washer."

The card game had stopped, and now the women were surveying the sky through the screened front door. They huddled quietly, waiting to hear what the men had to say. The men listened intently for the sound of thunder.

Lightning danced with spider legs on the horizon and revealed a gathering of low clouds. Chances were now fifty-fifty for a hard rain, something the farmers and ranches thirsted for. The clouds then boiled upward, and as the jagged streamers grew longer Luke could feel his pulse quickening. He told his heart to be calm. There had been too many teasing storms the last four years, too many reasons for bitterness. Hearing the deep boomers, though, they could be sure a thunderhead was taking shape somewhere in the dark sky.

The smell of rain was thick and, as usual, tumbleweeds preceded the storm, scuttling along the crusted ground. When the front slammed into Junction, it dropped the temperature by fifteen degrees in less than three minutes. Winds gusted to forty miles per hour, and dust and sand blew into the men's eyes as they watched intently from the Hagoods' front porch. Finally, thick drops splattered the front yard, raising plumes of dust. Luke Hagood thought about dropping to his knees for a thankful prayer. But he still wasn't convinced that the heavens were opening.

Then the rain stopped and the wind died and the lightning bolts, once so prominent in the western sky, were now streaming toward the east. The storm had been fierce but almost reed thin. It passed almost as quickly as an eighteen-wheeler on the highway. Behind it came a hot and dry west wind and a starry sky.

• • •

The coyotes had awakened Dennis Goehring twice in the early-morning hours with their hungry howls. They had been searching without success for rabbits in the brush around the camp. Lying on his bunk close to the screen, Dennis thought he heard one of the wild dogs with jagged teeth rustling through the trash.

Just the day before he had seen a bobcat, so skinny that his ribs stood out, combing the eastern hill for scraps of food. A starving jackrabbit had been busy stripping bark from the cedar fence posts. As the sun fried the last vestiges of weeds and grass, only the mesquite and the cedar brakes kept a healthy color. Even when the rains were plentiful, those moisture-robbing trees often encroached on the grass. Dennis knew that the cedar brakes could probably take root in an asphalt parking lot and grow to be ten feet tall.

Most of the Hill Country and all of West Texas had gone bone-dry. Many ranchers had turned to raising sheep and goats as their main live-stock. Those animals, in spite of commanding far cheaper prices, were more rugged and needed less water and a lot less to eat.

Even the rattlesnakes seemed smaller and less plentiful. The fire ant colonies were growing, giving the Aggies another reason not to dawdle on the hard ground. Don Watson had come up screaming that morning as a batch of fire ants had crawled into his pants, leaving red welts across his legs and buttocks.

The morning practice had ended as all of the others had—with so many gassers the boys lost count. Goehring felt the blind wobbles creeping into his legs. Now, walking toward the shower room, he could barely control himself and feared he might fall flat on his face. He concentrated on every step. He wasn't so sure he had any friends among the coaching or training staff, and he worried whether anyone would pick him up if he fell. His face was powdered with a pinkish dust, and his mouth felt as sticky as pine tar.

Since the drought's stranglehold on Texas began four years earlier, Dennis had been haunted by the strange-looking raptors called turkey buz-zards. "Beastly," was how his dad had once described the red-headed menaces with the curved and pointed beaks. The vultures had seemed to grow larger as the drought intensified and the carrion became more plen-tiful. They often hissed or uttered guttural noises.

At first, he wasn't sure if it was a mirage or perhaps a trick that Smokey Harper was playing on him, but Dennis blinked his eyes several times and prayed he wasn't seeing this. He realized that dizziness and dehydration could play tricks on one's mind. So exhausted at times were some of the players that they seemed to be talking in tongues. Everything was getting crazier and crazier, and there were times when Dennis couldn't remember what day it was.

That ain't a goddamn turkey buzzard I'm seein', Dennis thought. *That ain't a goddamn turkey buzzard sittin' up there on top of that goddamn shower room.*

He dropped his helmet and scooped rocks from the ground with both hands. He fired projectile after projectile at the vulture, and as they clanged off the steel pipes the buzzard didn't move. The clanging continued until the boys in the shower room rushed outside to find their teammate screaming and cussing. "Get outta here, you goddamn bastard!" he yelled. "I'll *kill* you."

The boys, on hearing the ranting, feared at first that Dennis had attacked Bryant. Now, as he chunked rock after rock, they were seeing the symptoms of madness. The scene became even more confusing when Dennis, still dressed in his football uniform, began trying to shinny up one of the rain gutters. He was now hollering at the top of his lungs.

"What the heck is wrong with him?" asked Jack Pardee, running from the shower room wearing only his football pants.

"He thinks he's trying to kill a bird—I mean a vulture," Paul Kennon said.

Pardee grabbed Dennis by the back of his pants and dragged him down the rain gutter. "Leave me alone, Jack!" Dennis yelled. "I got a damn turkey buzzard to kill."

"There ain't a bird up there," Pardee said. "Dennis, you've gone plumb goofy on us. You're seein' things."

Bryant and Smokey Harper hustled around the corner of the shower room just as Dennis hugged the rain gutter and began to climb again.

"Get him down from there," Bryant said. "What the hell is wrong with that boy anyway?"

"Brain's fried," Smokey said. "We need to get him in the shower and get him some water."

It took five players to drag Dennis into the shower, where he gulped water straight from the shower nozzle. Still wearing his jersey, shoulder pads, pants, and shoes, he then leaned against the wall, gasping for air. Slowly, his body began to slide down the slick tile. For thirty minutes he sat on the cool concrete floor, letting the water pour over his head and body and pads while Kennon stood a few feet away, making sure he didn't fall asleep and drown.

This craziness concerned Bryant. But he wasn't about to cut back on the marathon practices. It was this kind of conditioning that had turned his Kentucky teams into powerhouses. He hadn't brought them to Junction to win a popularity contest.

Walking toward the chow hall, he saw several boys down by the river, floating on the surface in full pads. They were too tired and hot to strip down before wading in. Some were actually drinking the water.

While Bryant, Smokey, and the coaches gorged themselves on biscuits, gravy, ham, bacon, and eggs, the players barely touched their food. Bryant noticed that their appetites had dried up like the parched land. Looking at the old trainer, Bryant said, "Smokey, how're we gonna get these boys to eatin' again?" Smokey shrugged and said, "Give 'em a day off."

"Not a chance."

In many respects, the camp had come to resemble a buzzard wheeling in the high blue sky. With the boys becoming more and more exhausted, the vulture seemed poised to swoop down and pick the carcass clean. Each day, the boys hoped and prayed they could last a little longer. Some already had chosen to escape Bryant's clutches by running off into the night. The quitters, it seemed, could feel the vultures closing in.

Striding across the Adjunct, Bryant spotted a huge turkey buzzard perched on the roof of his Quonset hut. He chunked a large rock that caught it flush in the chest. With wings fluttering madly, the vulture hissed and climbed straight up, soaring away on the south wind. For several minutes Bryant watched dreamily as the raptor with a six-foot wingspan sailed across great blue expanse. It really wasn't such a bad-looking bird at all, he thought, slamming the screen door behind him.

• • •

Buses pulled away from the Adjunct that afternoon, headed for the Junction Fairgrounds. Bryant had grown tired of the blazing rock patch, the cactus, the sandspurs, and the goatheads. It was hard to practice football at a place where players were constantly pulling thorny objects from their bleeding fingers.

Navigating a highway that ran parallel to the South Llano River, the buses prepared to cross a two-lane bridge. Bebes Stallings peered through the window at the deep blue water below. *God, if these buses could just run off the bridge into the water*, he thought. *We'd all drown and be dead and we could escape the misery of having to quit. Back home, they'd say, "Those boys died bravely." What a relief that would be.*

Bebes knew he was only dreaming.

The Junction Fairgrounds was a place where you could punch, punt, and even play the ponies. It was a thoroughbred racetrack, high school football stadium, and rodeo arena rolled into one. More important, it was a social center. The Aggies thought it was prettier than a homecoming queen when they discovered it had been swept for goatheads. A few strands of grass made the place seem almost lush.

The multipurpose facility was actually well kept and far ahead of its time. It was situated in the shadow of Lover's Leap, a tall, craggy hill with high rock bluffs that, according to legend, is where an Indian prince and princess jumped to their suicidal deaths. Not many people around Junction actually believed the story.

Beginning in 1935, the Kimble County Fair Association had begun staging the Hill Country Fair. It was a festive occasion that included six days of horse racing, a rodeo, a dance, and plenty of car sex.

The football field and rodeo grounds were actually situated on the in-field of the five-furlong oval racetrack. The smell of manure was as constant as the summer heat. Thanks to creative design, one grandstand filled the seating needs for three sporting events—racing, rodeo, and football. There were eight sections of bleachers, a high corrugated tin roof, and box seats in front. A peculiar sight during the football season was the Junction High cheerleaders doing cartwheels and back flips on the racetrack near the finish line. Players knocked out of bounds often tumbled into the home stretch. Small boys were known to fill paper drink cups with racetrack dirt and hurl them like footballs at the players.

So it was amid great amusement that the buses arrived at the team's new practice facility.

"Hope none of you boys fall in cow shit," Smokey Harper said as the boys, dressed in full gear, filed off.

Moving to a public facility, Bryant could no longer shoo off the curious Junctionites. Several cowhands dropped what they were doing to watch practice. The driver of a long cattle truck left his livestock mooing restlessly while he took a seat in the grandstand. An exercise rider sat atop a chestnut brown thoroughbred colt, watching the team warm up.

"Which one is Bryant?" asked a leather-faced rancher from his grand-stand seat.

"That one with the scowl on his face," said R. B. McKinney, the owner of the department store on Main Street. McKinney was familiar with Bryant and his bad moods.

"What the hell's got his goat?" the rancher asked.

"A bad football team."

It seemed nothing could lighten the coach's mood. He'd grown sick and tired of this dry and depressing hellscape. Today he was determined to conduct a solid two-hour scrimmage that would weed out some of the losers and push the talented boys to the front. The rancher removed a toothpick from his mouth, spit a stream of tobacco, and said, "That Bryant looks like he either smelled a pile of shit or just stepped in some."

A day earlier, Bryant had demoted most of the starters to second team in the middle of practice. The first-stringers had faced the humiliation of trading their maroon jerseys for white ones. The indignity left some of the players in a fighting mood. But not Fred Broussard, who continued to languish as Bryant's number-one whipping boy.

None of Bryant's psychological tactics had motivated Fred. The coach had even threatened to replace him at center with student manager Troy Summerlin, who'd been used lately to snap on punts and placements.

"Fred," Bryant said. "This boy here weighs a hundred and forty-five pounds. You weigh at least two-thirty. But this student manager is tougher than you."

That, of course, was stretching the truth, although Troy did have a perky attitude that pleased Bryant. Still, it was doubtful Bryant would ever issue Troy a uniform. Most of the players had admired Broussard's work during the 1953 season. Fred's weakness was that he hated practicing. He had quit the team twice, only to return the next day because Ray George always welcomed back his most prized player with open arms.

Since the Aggies rarely lifted weights, it was difficult to rank the strong-est players on the team. One night in the football dorm, though, Fred proved just how strong he was. He'd grown tired of walking down a flight of stairs to buy a ten-cent bottled Coke. So he bear-hugged the massive Coke machine and carried it up the stairs and down the hall to his room, where it produced cold refreshment for more than a week.

Now even the Aggie players were beginning to question Fred's com-mitment, and they could see him shrinking from the hitting drills. Elwood Kettler liked Fred less and less every day, thanks mostly to the lower back injuries inflicted by the large Cajun. But the player who hated him the most was Weasel Watson, who'd walked into Fred's dorm room one afternoon to find that two dogs had pooped on the floor.

"Why don't you clean this shit up, you lazy slob," Weasel had said before bolting through the door. Now, Weasel liked to bark, "Woof, woof, woof," whenever Fred made Bryant mad.

For reasons not explained, Bryant had given Fred back his first-string maroon jersey the previous day. Elwood felt a slight relief. Fred could at least snap the ball. But everyone knew Fred was no longer the great center who had once dominated the SWC. Bryant had psychologically broken him down, piece by piece, and forgotten to put him back together again. On the first play of the scrimmage, linebacker Herb Wolf shot past Broussard and nailed halfback Joe Schero in the backfield, causing a fumble.

Bryant came unglued. "Take that damn maroon jersey off and give it to Wolf. Put on that white jersey and let's see how you like playing second-string linebacker, you sonofabitch."

Fred was bent over, changing his jersey, when Pat James kicked him hard in the butt.

Elwood stepped into the huddle to call another play and felt Bryant standing beside him. "Listen up," Bear said. "We're gonna drive Broussard into the ground. I want every play run right at him. I want you boys to double-and triple-team. Kick his ass!"

Three blockers shoved Fred ten yards downfield, and Schero gained fifteen yards. From the fifteen-yard line, Marvin Tate and Lawrence Winkler double-teamed Fred as Elwood easily scored on an end sweep. Fred was either bulldozed from the play or knocked down on six straight snaps. Bryant then stepped into the huddle and called, "Fake toss right, fullback counter!" Fred bit on Elwood's fake and didn't see Lawrence Winkler coming. He was eighteen-wheeled by the big tackle as fullback Don Kachtik rumbled thirty yards for another score. Buried beneath Winkler's body, Broussard didn't see the touchdown.

Near exhaustion and gasping for air, Fred Broussard gave up. At first, Bryant didn't see the big center sauntering toward the rail fence that separated the football field from the rodeo ground. "Coach," Tate said softly. "I think Broussard is leaving."

Hands on hips, Bryant watched the exasperated boy walking on wobbly legs. The scrimmage stopped and the grounds grew silent. Bryant hollered, "Broussard, if you go over that fence, you'll never come back!"

Fred kept walking.

"Let me repeat myself, Fred," Bryant said, his voice booming across the field and echoing in the grandstand. "If you quit this football team today, you're never coming back."

Fred began climbing the four-rail fence, grunting as he cleared the top rail. Landing on the other side, he found himself in a cattle chute. Head down, he walked past the cattle truck. The cows stared curiously and mooed loudly. The smell of fresh dung almost gagged him.

Bryant turned back to the field and hollered, "All right, get me another linebacker in there for Broussard! Somebody take Wolf's spot at center. Wolf, you come here."

Wolf walked slowly toward the coach, wondering what he'd done wrong. Bryant put his arm around the boy's shoulder pads. "Now, Herb," he whispered. "I want you to walk out to that bus and bring Broussard back. All right?"

"Yes, sir."

Wolf scaled the fence and then held his nose as he dashed past the cattle truck. He found Broussard sitting in the back of the second bus, head bowed.

"Come on, Fred. Coach is tryin' to give you a second chance."

"Go to hell, Wolf."

"Fred. I think I know this man. If you don't come back now, your football-playin' days at Texas A&M are over."

Fred considered the advice and tried to muster new courage.

"Look here, Wolf. I ain't no meat on the hoof and I ain't playin' no more football for that sonofabitch. You tell him that."

"I won't tell him that exactly. But I'll tell him you ain't comin' back."

Bryant seemed to accept the news in stride, and the full-scale scrimmage continued almost until sunset. For the first time since they'd come to Junction, the offense operated in sync and fumbles were held to a minimum.

Bryant sat on the front seat of the second bus on the ride back to the Adjunct. The coach thought little of Broussard, but Fred was thinking of him. By the time the Aggies arrived back at camp, Fred had changed his mind and wanted back on the team. His teammates, of course, were used to Fred's waffling. It wasn't surprising that a meeting of several players took place in Billy Schroeder's Quonset hut where Fred Broussard broke down and cried. Also there were Sid Theriot, Lawrence Winkler, Bennie Sinclair, "Dutch" (Norbert) Ohlendorf, and Marvin Tate.

"One of you guys has gotta convince that bastard to take me back," Fred said, wiping tears from his cheeks. "Without football, I ain't got no chance of graduatin' college."

After they discussed the matter for thirty minutes, it was decided that Marvin Tate would take up the matter with Bryant. Marvin didn't want the job. But since he was a senior and a starter, he was the logical pitchman, the players thought. Besides, Bryant seemed to like the gutty little guard.

Players had been streaming to Bryant's barracks the last few days to tell him they were quitting. So when he heard Tate's timid knock, he figured it was just another good-bye.

"What do you want, Tate?" Bryant said. "Is it time for another pity party?"

"No sir, Coach, I didn't come to quit. In fact, Coach, you'll never see me quitting. But I did come to see if you'll take Fred Broussard back. He's changed his mind—"

"Tell him to kiss my ass. If a boy'll quit on me in practice, he sure as hell'll quit on me in the fourth quarter. We don't need his kind around here."

"In all due respect, Coach, Fred is a two-year starter, made all-conference last year, and lots of the boys think we need him bad—"

"What? Need him bad for what? For a blockin' dummy?"

Tate thought, *Let me get out of here fast. This man's mind is made up.*

Outside, Dutch Ohlendorf and Billy Schroeder were hiding around the corner of a Quonset hut. Bennie Sinclair and Lawrence Winkler had crouched behind Pickard's Ford. Three other boys were hiding against the shower room wall.

Tate was walking at top speed when the screen door slammed behind him. "Forget it, boys; Fred is gone." Tate hustled toward the chow hall like his britches were on fire. "There's no reason to give it another thought. Forget Fred."

Later that evening, Broussard asked Troy Summerlin to drive him into town so he could call his girlfriend. Troy fired up the black sedan that he'd been using quite frequently lately to drive players to the bus station. They rode in silence until Troy found a pay phone near the Junction National Bank.

After dialing the number in Houston, Fred said, "Baby, I've got some news to tell you. I just quit the football team."

There was a long pause. Then she said, "Fred, please say that again."

"Baby, I decided to quit today. I'll be in Houston tomorrow to see you. Ain't that great—"

"If you quit the football team, Fred Broussard, you just quit me." Fred then heard three clicks along the long-distance line and a dial tone. A bad day had taken a turn for the worst.

Back at the camp, five backup centers had come to Bryant's cabin to announce that they were quitting. They didn't receive an ounce of argument. Instead, Bryant stood and shook their hands one by one. Walking down the line, Bryant said, "Good-bye, good-bye, bless your hearts, good-bye."

Troy and Fred rode in silence back to camp. Hoping to catch one last supper, Fred walked slowly into the chow hall with Summerlin a few feet behind. Bryant spotted him as he walked through the door.

Still chewing, the coach wiped his mouth on his napkin, stood, and marched toward the big ex-Aggie. "Fred," Bryant said, his breath smelling of roast beef, "you must be confused. This is where Texas A&M football players eat their meals."

His head bowed, Broussard turned and walked through the door. No one was sure where he went or how he got there. For years, the Aggies wondered if he hitchhiked, rode the bus, or walked all the way back to College Station. Most of them never saw Fred Broussard again.

9

Escape

When you win, there's glory enough for everybody. When you lose, there's glory for none.

—PAUL "BEAR" BRYANT

SEPTEMBER 5, 1954

Rob Roy Spiller aimed the sky blue Chevy pickup down Main Street in the first morning light as Hank Williams wailed about whiskey and misery on the radio. The weatherman was calling for a high of 107 degrees and estimated that the closest rain clouds were somewhere between Edmonton and Nome.

Rob Roy planned to hose down his dusty truck during his lunch break. His first hour at the Kerrville Lines Bus Station/Johnston Texaco Gas Station in downtown Junction would be routinely quiet. He'd sweep the floors and clean the ashtrays and drink a Big Orange, and he might sneak a phone call to his girlfriend, Laverne Johnston. Folks wanting rides to places like San Antonio or El Paso or San Angelo normally started arriving around seven-thirty, when the shiny diesels began to roll in and out of Junction.

Along with writing bus tickets, Rob Roy pumped gas, cleaned windshields, checked oil, changed flat tires, polished mirrors, talked about the

102

drought, and hand-washed cars for fifty cents. Regular gas was selling for twenty-three cents a gallon.

Not since the Aggies' arrival in Junction had he heard from his nemesis, Dennis Goehring, and that was good news. Rob Roy was still courting Laverne—had even forgiven her for going out with Dennis a few times—but knew his heart was due for a bruising. In two weeks he would enroll as a freshman at Texas A&M, and he doubted he could keep the fires burning for very long from three hundred miles away.

Rob Roy and Laverne had joined several other curious townsfolk at the Aggies' practice the previous day when Fred Broussard had quit. Rob Roy had kept a close eye on Laverne, wondering if she were making eyes at Dennis, who seemed more occupied with picking fights than practicing. He doubted that Dennis had even noticed them.

Broussard's escape had surprised many folks in the crowd, but not Rob Roy. Watching the boys leave Junction had become as commonplace as wiping dust from his pickup's dashboard or watching government hay unloaded from freight cars. Now, as the Chevy eased down Main Street, Rob Roy focused on a scene that struck him as both surprising and odd—several boys milling around the front door of the bus station. Most were wearing blue jeans and T-shirts and had buzz haircuts. *Texas A&M football players?* Rob Roy thought. *Nah. Couldn't be.*

As he pulled into the station, though, Rob Roy realized it was the Aggies. *They must have sneaked off from the Adjunct in the middle of the night,* he thought. *Guess they didn't want to wait around to say good-bye to the old man.* Many of the boys appeared to be anxious, and some were pacing. A couple of the boys had rolled-up blankets, but for the most part, they carried nothing but hangdog looks. He noticed that a couple of the boys were chewing on beef jerky.

"Morning, fellas," Rob Roy said, sliding the key into the lock. In silence, they filed into the station as the ticket clerk took his position behind the counter. It was an amazing sight, these boys who had run away from Bryant and then sneaked two miles down the dark highway to make their getaway—like wartime prisoners who had scaled the wall and were on the run from the camp commandant.

Rob Roy noticed a handful of other boys huddling in the shadows on the other side of the bus station, and it was apparent they were hiding from someone.

One of the boys spoke up. "We gotta get out of here before Coach Bryant finds us."

"Where is it you fellas would like to go?" Roy Roy asked.

"We don't care," Billy Jake Perryton said. "Just put us all on the first bus out."

The boys were in luck. The first bus that morning was scheduled for San Antonio, and since Rob Roy surmised they were headed back to the campus, he started writing tickets. The large buses traveled east and west from Junction. The eight-seaters traveled north and south. So there would be plenty of room on the next fifty-seater heading east to San Antonio, where there they could make a connection to College Station.

"I guess you boys are lucky the next bus isn't to El Paso," Rob Roy said, trying not to smile. "Otherwise, you'd be on your way to California."

The boys began digging deep into their pockets and pooling their resources when they learned the tickets would be three dollars. Some had no money, thanks to being whisked away without warning from College Station a few days earlier. Rob Roy had decided he would make loans to those in need, but that wasn't necessary, as they were able to scrape up the cash.

Fear was evident in their eyes, along with a sense of urgency. Otherwise, they would have waited around until the lunch break, filled their stomachs, said good-bye to Bryant, and been given tickets home. Now, unable to face the Man, they were trying to get out of town before anyone noticed they were missing.

The previous night, Marvin Tate and Elwood Kettler had watched from their bunks as the boys fled through the bright moonlight. They thought at first it was a pack of wild dogs chasing a jackrabbit across the Adjunct grounds. Realizing it was their teammates, they called to the escapees, who didn't even turn to acknowledge them. "Where you boys going?" Kettler yelled. "Tell everybody back in College Station we said howdy!" At top speed, the quitters scrambled across the rocky practice field to the dirt road that led to Flatrock Bridge. After crossing the river, they never looked back but still worried that Bryant might track them down like dogs. So they walked in the dark shadows of the bar ditch for the first mile. If they spotted headlights, they were prepared to hightail it into the craggy hills and hide among the cedar brakes like outlaws of the previous century.

As Rob Roy collected the money, he could hold his tongue no longer. Peering at one of the forlorn Aggies, he said, "I gotta ask. Why didn't your-all just wait around for a ride to the station? You know that Coach Zapalac has a bunch of bus tickets to hand out."

The room was silent until Billy Jake spoke. "Me, personally, I didn't want to go through another practice with that sonofabitch Bryant. I think the rest of the boys felt the same way. This football team ain't out here to train for the season. They're out here to get their butts kicked. That man's gonna kill somebody if he don't quit this pretty soon."

One of the boys spotted a green Ford creeping down Main Street. "Everybody duck!" Billy Jake yelled. They dived into the couches and onto the floor. The boys standing outside sprawled onto the asphalt parking lot. Meanwhile, Rob Roy kept an eye on the car.

"Was that Coach Zapalac?" Billy Jake whispered. "It sure looked like Billy Pickard's Ford."

"Hard to tell," Rob Roy said. "But whoever was driving that car sure was looking for something or somebody."

Minutes later, a long gray diesel groaned into the lot and parked next to the gas pumps. Like prisoners on a jailbreak, the boys scrambled for the bus. The driver watched with wide-eyed amusement as they piled aboard, stumbling and climbing over one another. Then they slumped far down into the seats as the driver released the air brake that split the morning with a flatulent sigh. If not for two ladies in the front seats wearing white bonnets, the bus would have appeared empty as it rocked from side to side, coughed diesel smoke, and headed slowly up Main Street. But Rob Roy, after popping the hood on a white pickup, waved good-bye anyway. Then he kept an eye on the main drag for the next thirty minutes, but the green Ford never came back.

. . .

As the black studebaker traveled deeper into the Hill Country, groaning to ascend each ridge, Dave Campbell noticed that the land was becoming drier by the mile. Campbell was the newly appointed sports editor of the *Waco Tribune* and, along with Mark Batterson of the *Austin American-Statesman,* was on his way to Junction for the third stop on the SWC Press Tour.

Three cars were transporting eight sportswriters. The plan, after leaving Austin, was to spend as little time in Junction as possible. Unlike the other stops, the press wouldn't be staying overnight here.

Campbell had heard and read about the effects of the drought on the Hill Country and West Texas but until now didn't know just how deeply the land had been scarred. Even the cedars and the shinoak and the prickly pear seemed to be screaming for a drink of water. Batterson and Campbell stopped for breakfast at the Admiral Nimitz Inn at Fredericksburg, just fifty miles east of Junction.

Delivering coffee, the waitress said, "Yeah, the ranchin's just about dead. So's the water supply. Rivers and lakes are so low that even the catfish got ticks."

Batterson and Campbell laughed loudly until they realized the waitress wasn't even smiling. Drought humor had been funny at first, but, like everything else around there, it had dried up with time.

Returning with scrambled eggs and bacon, the waitress said, "You know my uncle's got five miles of creeks and no water."

Shaking his head, Campbell said, "That's bad."

"I wish it would rain this summer until it's axle deep to a Ferris wheel," she said, "and snow this winter until it's downhill to Denver."

"Amen," the writers said in unison. They struggled not to laugh.

The SWC Press Tour was still in its infancy. So the handful of writers traveled by car from town to town. When they'd all arrived at one of the seven SWC camps, the interviews would begin. Typing and fact-finding occupied their days while whiskey, card games, guitar picking, and singing filled their nights. Cameras, microphones, and tape recorders weren't invited on the tour and wouldn't be for several years.

Since most of them had never heard of Junction, the writers were careful to check their road maps before leaving Austin. They had been treated to barbecue and beer during the first two stops at the Rice Institute and the University of Texas. They wondered if Junction even had a decent hamburger joint.

Rice boasted a tree-lined campus on South Main Street in Houston that attracted squeaky clean rich kids with ultra-high GPAs and board scores. For the writers, it was an entertaining stop, filled with great quotes. The Owls were defending SWC co-champions, having fought Texas to a tie the previous season. They had whipped Alabama in a Cotton Bowl game that featured one of the strangest plays in the history of college football—scatback Dicky Maegle shaking loose on a long run only to have Alabama's Tommy Lewis leave the bench to tackle him. The officials awarded Maegle a ninety-five-yard touchdown, and fans from coast to coast were still talking about it. Lewis's compulsive act had drawn plenty of headlines for the Owls.

For the 1954 season, most of the Owl starters were returning, and Jess Neely's team seemed fresh and filled with energy. They'd been working out in shorts and T-shirts. Neely, a southern gentleman with a velvet drawl, was being interviewed by the *Houston Chronicle*'s Dick Freeman when the writer observed, "Coach, your boys look tanned, rested, and ready."

By the time the three cars headed northeast toward Austin, most of the writers had already mentally logged Rice as their preseason number-one pick in the SWC.

In Austin, they found the Longhorns practicing in the lush Bermuda grass next to Waller Creek. Not far away was a canopy of trees that lined the crystal-clear water. Coeds wore shorts and cotton blouses that, tied at the back, revealed tanned midriffs. Most were barefoot and they leaned against late-model cars, tossing coquettish looks toward the players. Students in shiny convertibles drove by, honking at their heroes, who, like the Rice boys, were practicing in shorts and T-shirts.

The writers noted that the players were basically goofing off—linemen pretending to be quarterbacks throwing passes to other linemen. Many of the players sat on the benches or on overturned water buckets and kept one eye on the girls. Many of the boys had ducktail haircuts.

"Is this football practice or a fraternity party?" Blackie Sherrod of the *Fort Worth Press* asked no one in particular.

Texas had 120 varsity players. One hundred and fifty freshmen were drilling in helmets and pads on the adjoining field. For years, Longhorn coaches had flared out across the state, signing players they knew would never set one foot on the playing field, especially now that one-platoon football had returned. Marginal players were signed to scholarships to keep them off competing rosters at Rice, Baylor, SMU, TCU, Texas A&M, and Arkansas—the other SWC schools. Many players wearing the burnt orange and white would never play enough to earn a letter. Some had no hope of setting foot on the field, and others wondered why they even needed a postgame shower.

Houston Post sportswriter Jack Gallagher leaned down to feel the thick green grass of the Longhorns' practice field.

"Shoot, this is better than the seventeenth fairway at Augusta. Hell, I could hit a five-iron from here to the state capital, and that's two miles away."

Texas had won the SWC title outright in 1952 and then shared it with Rice in 1953. With quarterback Charley Brewer returning, along with most of the starters, the Longhorns could sleepwalk through the schedule and still win eight games. Life would be grand again on a campus that attracted some of the best-looking coeds in the country.

Now, descending on Junction, the sportswriters felt as if they were driving into the desert. Sherrod's brand-new two-door Pontiac coupe had been the best-looking car on the highway the last three-hundred miles. But it had no air-conditioning. His sweaty back stuck to the seat like Brylcreem to a ducktail.

Most of the writers had never met Bryant, but they knew of his hard edge. They'd heard stories of his Kentucky freshmen shinnying down the dormitory drainpipes, trying to flee the preseason training camp. They'd heard about Bryant growing up barefoot and tough in the creek bottoms of Arkansas.

Most of the writers were looking forward to meeting Bryant, though they wondered if they would like him. Some were insulted by what Bryant allegedly once said about sportswriters: "Give 'em a bottle and tell 'em nothing." The quote been passed down for years.

Gallagher had seen red flags waving when fellow *Houston Post* writer Mickey Herskowitz dictated his first story from Junction, then called back with a second version. Wondering if Bryant had intimidated the young reporter, Gallagher had decided to go to Junction to find out for himself.

As the Aggie players started lining up for the team picture, Sherrod parked the light blue car on a gravel field bereft of grass. Herskowitz was running toward him and waving.

"Hey, Mickey," Blackie grumbled, his brow furrowed. "Where the hell is the practice field?"

Mickey chuckled. "Blackie, my friend, you just parked on it."

The writers didn't know that a man in the distance was leaning against a tree, smiling. He had been waiting several days for this visit from the statewide press. Soon they would walk into the web he'd been spinning. They would witness the spartan life and count the missing bodies and wonder in print how the Aggies could possibly survive the 1954 season. Would they win one game or two? Bryant knew the writers would take one look at his team and pick them to finish dead last in the SWC race.

Turning to Phil Cutchin, Bryant said, "I'd give a million dollars to see the faces on those fat-ass Aggie alums when they read tomorrow's paper."

Blackie was busy counting the players as they trudged from the practice field back to the barracks. He had counted more than 120 players at both Rice and Texas and knew the Aggies had brought a number close to that to Junction.

Aggies sports information director Jones Ramsey stuck out a large hand, and Sherrod shook it.

"Jones," the writer said. "I was a little surprised to learn that we're standing on your practice field. Back in Fort Worth, we call these things parking lots.''

Dabbing the air with his right index finger, Blackie started counting again. Turning to Ramsey, he said, ''I'll give you this much. You're the only college sports information director in the country who can type his three-deep roster on an eight-by-ten sheet of paper—sideways.''

The writers were stunned to learn that Broussard, the all-conference center, was among the missing. He had been an SWC first-teamer on all of their ballots the previous season. When the photo session ended, Sherrod sought out Donald Robbins, an end from Breckenridge, a small town about 150 miles west of Fort Worth. The writer had covered a lot of the Buckaroos' games when Robbins's dad was coaching the team.

''I hear you lost a pretty good boy last night,'' Blackie said.

''A pretty good *man*,'' Robbins corrected.

Robbins seemed so disconsolate with the loss of a teammate that Blackie decided to end the questioning there.

Meanwhile, Bryant was waiting for the writers in his Quonset hut. He couldn't wait for them to see the battered huts and recognize the vivid contrast between his hell camp and the ones taking place at Rice and Texas—vacation spots compared to Junction.

Some of the writers had fought in World War II. So they were familiar with the Quonset huts, their steel roofs and screened half-walls.

Blackie had served three years in the South Pacific. As he walked into Bryant's room and looked around, he said, ''I never thought I was going to see one of these things again.''

Bryant leaned back in his chair and smiled. ''Boys, it's been heaven on earth out here. We've been able to separate the quitters from the keepers, the turds from the champions. And we're pretty darn close to being ready for the start of the season.''

Bill Rives of the *Dallas Morning News* coughed nervously. ''We normally start these things with the coach reading off the three-deep roster—''

''Well, I guess you boys are shit out of luck here,'' Bryant interrupted. ''Texas and Rice, well, they've got fourth- and fifth- and sixth-stringers. We've barely got enough for a good scrimmage.''

Bryant lit a cigarette. ''Hope you boys are hungry.'' he said. ''With so many boys down the highway, we got enough food to feed the whole county.''

There was a long silence. Then Campbell asked, ''Coach, is there any chance that you'll bring Fred Broussard back?''

Bryant leveled his eyes at the writer. "Chances are better that it'll come a gulley washer here in about three minutes. If the skies open up and if I get struck by lightning, Fred Broussard can come back and get his suit on."

Gallagher had sat quietly but was poised to strike. He was a salty writer who never backed down. "Hey, Bear," said Gallagher, grinning. "Guess you're aware that John Crow signed conference letters of intent with both LSU and Oklahoma. Until he officially enrolls at A&M, he can change his mind and go elsewhere. What if he finds out you've run off more than half the team? Are you worried he'll hightail it out of College Station?"

Bryant had prepared himself for the question. Gallagher was right. Since there was no national letter of intent, Crow still had time to change his mind. So before leaving College Station, Bryant had ordered Elmer Smith to install an air conditioner in the apartment belonging to John Crow and his wife, Carolyn. Bryant had also assigned one of the freshman coaches to stake out the apartment every day and call if the couple started packing.

Bryant shook his head and narrowed his eyes. "Ain't no chance at all that John Crow will be leavin' me any time soon. Got that?"

Later, as the writers gathered in Ramsey's hut to write their stories, Abb Curtis, the SWC's assistant commissioner, grabbed Gallagher's elbow and pulled him aside. "You silly sonofabitch. Ain't you figured it out yet? Bryant's got John Crow stashed away in one of those Quonset huts out back. He's hiding the boy. No way Oklahoma or LSU are gonna find him before the season starts. No way."

As expected, the newspaper dispatches were filled with despair. Sherrod wrote: "Bear Bryant might have just bought himself a ticket to last place in the Southwest Conference. That is, if he has enough players to start the season." Others wrote with the same sour pen.

By midafternoon, they had piled into the three cars and were on their way back across the Hill Country en route to Waco. The fourth stop would be at Baylor, where the Bears were keeping their good players on board. For the next three hours, the writers couldn't keep their minds off Broussard and Bryant's camp.

Dave Campbell had jumped into the backseat of Blackie's new Pontiac. Campbell, Rives, and Blackie talked nonstop all the way to the little town of Killeen, home to Fort Hood. Though the Korean War had ended a year earlier, Fort Hood was still the largest army base in the world. The heavy artillery could be clearly seen from the highway.

"Wouldn't it be funny if we found Fred Broussard hitchhiking along this highway?" Campbell said.

Rives laughed. "Blackie, pull over at this next culvert. I want to see if Broussard is hiding down there."

The sportswriter ran down the embankment and peered beneath the bridge. There was no water and no Fred Broussard to be found. Rives laughed and threw up his hands.

. . .

Since the boys were up by five and practicing by six each morning, the afternoon naps had become a critical component of survival. By noon, though, any trace of a breeze was gone and the Quonset huts had become large ovens. Bebes Stallings had one of the top bunks, and his nose was parked about three inches from the steel corrugated roof that felt like a griddle at a short-order café.

Around one o'clock, Bebes and Bobby Drake Keith would routinely hear a familiar sound—the water fountain kicking on outside. Two or three boys would take turns drinking water and talking in low voices. They were summoning the courage to knock on the Man's door.

"There's three more of 'em out there," Bebes said. "And they look scared to death."

After rapping on the screen door, they would quietly file into Bryant's barracks. Then the voice like a foghorn could be heard all the way to the river: "M. G. R.! Get the car fired up and drive these boys down to the bus station. This pity party is over."

This day, though, Troy Summerlin was also asleep in a bunk. Previously, it had been his job to collect the bus tickets from Zapalac and haul the boys to Rob Roy. Now, though, Troy was an official member of the Aggies football squad.

Since arriving in Junction, Troy had been alternating between student manager and deep snapper. On hearing his name called by one of the coaches, he'd drop his tool belt and hustle onto the field, lining up at center on punts or placements.

The previous night, Bryant had encountered Summerlin returning from the chow hall. Bear was leading a phalanx of assistant coaches marching shoulder to shoulder a couple of feet behind the coach. Summerlin thought about George Patton and his officers tramping through Europe. The procession halted and Troy felt a knot in the pit of his stomach.

"M. G. R.," Bryant growled. "Get your suit on tomorrow."

"Coach, I don't think you got one small enough to fit me."

"I'm serious, dammit."

"Yes, sir."

Scratching the top of his head, Bryant peered down at the boy and said, "You do have some playin' eligibility left, don't you, son?"

"Yes, sir."

The Aggies had a shortage of centers, and Summerlin, who stood five-foot-eight and weighed 145 pounds, had been drafted in spite of his size. Not since Fair Park High School in Shreveport had he played organized football in pads. But he wasn't afraid to take a hit and was particularly adept at deep-snapping. Not a boy in camp could fire a tight spiral between his legs faster than Troy.

It hadn't occurred to Bryant that he'd just resurrected one of the proudest Aggie traditions—the Twelfth Man.

Having not yet coached his first regular-season game at Texas A&M, Bryant wasn't familiar with the famous legacy born with coach D. X. Bible back on January 1, 1921. That day, the Aggies were playing heavily favored Centre College in the Dixie Classic, a forerunner to the Cotton Bowl in Dallas. Several Aggie players had been injured, and Bible sent a student manager into the stands to summon E. King Gill, a backup tight end who had been excused from the team in December to join the basketball squad.

Bible asked Gill to suit up, and he stood behind the coach as an emergency substitute, watching the Aggies win 22–14. Though Gill didn't enter the game, he became a symbol of the Twelfth Man—an Aggie who'd come out of the stands in an hour of need. Since that day, Aggie students have always stood during the entire game to salute the spirit of King Gill.

•   •   •

As the boys slept and snored, Joe Boring limped across the camp grounds, his right knee aching with every step. The sound of the drinking fountain caught the attention of Stallings and Keith.

"Bebes, I can't believe Joe's about to quit. Shoot, he might be our best player." Along with being an all-conference halfback, Boring had been named the league's best shortstop the previous spring. He was a starting guard on the basketball team. But the pain in his knee had become unbearable for Boring. It seemed to jump out of its socket with every practice.

Two days earlier, Boring had come to Bryant's Quonset hut to suggest that he see a doctor.

"Coach, I hurt the doggone thing during spring drills and it bothered me all the way through summer baseball." The previous summer, Boring had played semipro ball for Taco Ray's in Dallas.

"Coach, it just feels that it's all jumbled up in there. It keeps working its way out of the socket. It doesn't feel right. One doctor's already told me that I need an operation."

Boring unwrapped the Ace bandage to reveal a knee swollen to twice its normal size.

"Joe. I know it doesn't look good. But the season's less than two weeks away. I was plannin' on starting you. You gotta tough it out. Put some tape on it. Get in the whirlpool."

Boring estimated that Smokey had used twenty rolls of tape on his knee since the start of camp. The tape had forced the blood and water to flow into his calf and thigh and made his leg feel like it would explode. Boring now viewed the situation as hopeless.

"Coach, I can't even perform," he said. "I'm afraid I'm just gonna have to quit."

Bryant thought about suggesting that he take a few days off and see a doctor. But he stopped himself short of sympathizing with the boy.

"Joe, you gotta play, or you gotta go."

Joe decided to go. As he left the Quonset hut, the screen door slamming behind him, Boring encountered Bennie Sinclair, who had been summoned by Bobby Drake Keith.

"It's over, Bennie."

"I wish you'd told me before you went in there. Maybe we could have done something. Did you really quit?"

"Yeah."

News spread across the camp, and many of the boys felt sick. Fifteen minutes later, Joe was on his way to the bus station.

Billy Pete Huddleston sat on the edge of his bunk and penned his daily letter back home to his fiancée, Flora. Billy never mentioned the heat or the drought or the marathon days. But he did end each letter by listing the players who had quit.

Darling,

This place is growing emptier by the day. Fifteen more boys ran off in the middle of the night, and I saw three more leaving in the black sedan this afternoon. You won't believe this. But Fred Broussard quit yesterday and Coach Bryant wouldn't let him back on the team. Shooed him right out of the chow hall about an hour later. Here's some really bad news. Joe Boring just left out of here. He's the best athlete I've ever seen. We're in deep trouble now. I haven't been able to count heads, but I'd bet we're down to about forty boys. That means seventy-something have quit. Don't worry, darling. They couldn't run me out of this place with a shotgun. I'll be home soon. I hope.

Love,
Billy Pete

TV commentators Red Grange, Lindsey Nelson, and Bear Bryant discussing an upcoming game against Texas in 1956. Credit: Cushing Library Archives.

Fullback Don Kachtik, wearing a mask to protect his broken nose, scores against Texas in 1954. Other Aggies in white: Dee Powell (76) and Ray Barrett (60). Credit: Cushing Library Archives.

Halfback Billy Pete
Huddleston gains yards
against Rice in 1954.
Credit: Cushing Library Archives.

Fullback Jack Pardee
in 1955.
Credit: Cushing Library Archives.

Tight end Bennie Sinclair catches a pass against Texas in 1954.
Credit: Cushing Library Archives.

1956 Co-captains: Jack Pardee, Gene Stallings, Lloyd Hale.
Credit: Gene Stallings Collection (Laughead Photographers).

1954 Aggie captains.
Norbert Ohlendorf (left),
Bennie Sinclair (right),
and Paul "Bear" Bryant.
Credit: Dutch Ohlendorf Collection.

Aggie tight end Gene Stallings.
Credit: Cushing Library Archives.

Aggie center Lloyd Hale.
Credit: Cushing Library Archives.

ggie running back Don Watson.
Credit: Cushing Library Archives.

Coach Paul "Bear" Bryant in 1954.
Credit: Cushing Library Archives.

Aggie tight end Bobby Drake Keith.
Credit: Cushing Library Archives.

Aggie guard Dennis Goehring.
Credit: Cushing Library Archives.

Four Aggies clown around after 1955 upset of TCU. Bottom: Jack Powell and Charlie Krueger. Top: Billy Dedney and Don Watson. Credit: Cushing Library Archives.

Coach Paul "Bear" Bryant admires the Junction ring presented to him at the 1979 reunion. Credit: Don Watson Collection.

Coach Paul "Bear" Bryant wears the Junction ring presented to him at the 1979 reunion. Credit: Don Watson Collection.

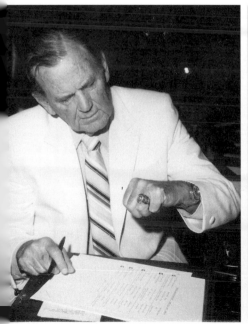

1979 reunion of Junction Boys. Marvin Tate at lectern. Right to left. Paul "Be Bryant, Dennis Goehring, Paul Kennon, Lawrence Winkler, and James Burkhart.
Credit: Marvin Tate Collection.

Aggie players. Bottom: Gene Stallings and Lloyd Hale. Top: Jack Powell, Jack Pardee, and John David Crow. Credit: Cushing Library Archives.

10

Death's Door

Winning isn't imperative, but getting tougher in the fourth quarter is.

—PAUL "BEAR" BRYANT

SEPTEMBER 6, 1954

A dust storm kicked up around noon, and by four o'clock the sun looked like a copper ball hanging in the sky. The air was tinted orange when the boys tugged on the wet and stinking uniforms and began the dreaded march back to the rock patch for the second practice of the day.

Bryant's plan of busing the team back to the fairgrounds was preempted by a rodeo. Just as well. It was time to push the boys to the breaking point, and today he wanted no witnesses. People were already talking too much. His desk drawer was filled with worrisome letters from mamas and papas, and newspaper accounts across Texas the last twenty-four hours had described the brutal practices, the shrinking numbers, and the warlike conditions. Pretty soon, Texas A&M chancellor Dr. Thomas Harrington would call and demand Bryant knock it off. The clock was ticking on the hell camp.

Bryant didn't need a doctor to tell him that the thick dust hanging in clouds over Junction posed a hazard to his players' health.

Along with the heat and the drought, dust had become another menace. It was so thick in the Panhandle town of Borger that the streetlights kicked on at midday and, during the peak of the storm, it began to rain—mud.

As the players trudged back to work, a Texas duster danced across the eastern edge of the Adjunct. A duster is a thin brown twister that appears from nowhere, often on a cloudless day, and travels about twenty miles per hour. This one spun along the parched ground the length of a football field and blew out.

Fatigue had made cowards of many of the boys, who'd run off in the moonlit nights without even saying good-bye. Now there were forty-one left, but only twenty-eight were able to practice. In spite of the near-exhaustion, the survivors seemed more determined than ever to stick it out.

The night before, in the darkness of his screened-in barracks, Jack Pardee had considered his own plight. "I'd die before I'd quit," he said to his two remaining roommates. "What the hell am I going to do? Go back to the ranch in Christoval? Hell, we lost the ranch years ago. I got nothin' to go back to."

This march into the land of pain had shaken even the cocksure boys like Bob Easley. He'd awakened from a nightmare the previous morning in a pool of sweat. The camp was playing tricks on his mind. Thinking a rattlesnake had crawled into his bunk, Easley kicked and screamed until Don Kachtik shook him from his sleep.

A day earlier, Easley had made a dreaded phone call back to Houston.

"Dad, this guy is killing everybody. We don't have more than three dozen players left and we got here with over a hundred."

Robert Easley Sr., a plumber and pipe-fitter and man of few frills, said, "Boy, I never figured you a quitter. But if you're a quitter, then do what you gotta to do."

Easley hung up and decided he wouldn't quit even if Bryant held a .45 to his head.

Both pride and scholarships were on the line. Redbird Granberry's dad worked for the chamber of commerce back in Beeville and made enough money to put food on the table and gas in the car. College tuition was out of the question. Redbird's shoulder had become so loose that it popped out when he combed his hair. But quitting was unthinkable.

Back in the central Texas hamlet of Rogers Ranch, Dutch Ohlendorf had attended a three-room school that was heated by a potbelly stove. Since the school had no indoor plumbing, drinking water was pumped from a cistern and the kids went to the bathroom in outhouses. They didn't ride buses to school in Rogers Ranch. They rode their horses, which were stabled in a barn built by the school district. Making the huge leap to Texas A&M and earning a football scholarship had been a lifetime dream, one that Dutch wasn't giving up without a bloody fight.

At night, when the practices and the gassers and the skull sessions were over, the survivors prayed the camp would end because none wanted to be as impulsive as Broussard, who they knew was sitting somewhere back in College Station, regretting his decision to climb that fence. Some feared they would snap like a dry twig under the tremendous mental and physical duress.

There were so many reasons to leave, yet so many to stay.

Weasel Watson knew he wasn't going anywhere. Just the thought of showing his face in a one-horse town like Franklin after quitting almost made him sick. They'd gossip him out of town.

Charles Hall was a shy and introverted boy who was tortured by the taunts and the cussing. But without a football scholarship, he could forget about Texas A&M and the prospects for veterinary school.

After the ranch had been sold in San Marcos, Dennis Goehring's folks had taken low-paying jobs. Dennis's temporary scholarship now meant everything. Bear Bryant and Smokey Harper would need a ton of dynamite to run him off.

Bennie Sinclair, the ultimate team player, had dreamed about being an Aggie captain for four years. Now, as a senior, he'd grown into a team leader and liked it. Besides, he'd been preaching to the other boys that they shouldn't quit. How could he possibly even consider it?

Quitting never entered Bebes Stallings's mind for reasons that had everything to do with pride but also transcended his scholarship. Bailing out meant his coaching dream would vanish. Oddly, in spite of the brutal practices, Bebes found himself drawn to Bryant and was awestruck by his charisma.

"Why are so many boys quitting?" Bebes had asked Bobby Drake Keith a few days earlier. "Heck, they couldn't run me with off with a hot cattle prod."

In spite of the fatigue and the dwindling numbers, Bebes and Bobby Drake would lie in their bunks at night making plans for the Cotton Bowl. Now, more than ever, they believed it would happen.

Billy Schroeder was a stout-hearted boy, and nothing was going to waylay his dream. He would rather die than tell Texas A&M good-bye. Billy had been hardened both physically and mentally a season earlier by an assistant coach named Mike Michalsky, who could have been a Bryant disciple. Michalsky had a jaw more square than a deck of cards. He played guard for the Green Bay Packers from 1929 through the '37 season. After practice, when the so-called skilled players had called it a day, Michalsky led the linemen in more gassers and several trips around the quarter-mile track. That's why the linemen were the best-conditioned players and why so many had survived Bryant's preseason training. Eighteen of the boys still in Junction were interior linemen.

The players knew that Billy Schroeder would walk three miles over hot coals to wear the Aggie uniform. Now, after six days of heat, dust, drought, and no water breaks, Billy felt weak. Dehydration had cost him fifteen pounds and sapped much of his strength. Pants that fit snugly a few days earlier now bagged at the waist and they had slid all the way to his knees during the morning practice.

At four o'clock, the boys were lined up for calisthenics when Bryant placed the ball down near the middle of the field, blew his whistle, and hollered, "First-team offense versus second-team defense!" Minutes later, about fifty yards away, the second-team offense was scrimmaging against the first-team defense. Since there were only twenty-eight players in uniform, each unit was short a few bodies. The second offense, in fact, had only six players, and former manager Troy Summerlin was the center.

Bryant surveyed the chaos and turned to Jim Owens. "The boys in the press would love to see this, wouldn't they?"

Stallings thought he heard Bryant calling his name and ran toward the coach. "Yes, sir," Stallings said.

"Get away from me, Stallings!" Bryant yelled into the boy's good ear. "I've seen enough of your shit today."

For more than ninety minutes, helmets collided and bodies crashed to the rock-hard earth and more than ever, the boys suffered from the absence of water. With every play, Schroeder found it harder and harder to push himself up from the ground. He could feel the dust caking in his nostrils and throat. He was no longer blocking the man in front of him. He was merely leaning into Henry Clark, and the coaches were cussing him for it.

"Billy Schroeder, you couldn't block your mama like that!" Zapalac yelled. "Your mama's a better football player than you are."

Breaking the huddle, fullback Don Kachtik felt his wobbling right leg give up. He dropped to one knee. Pat James landed a shoe to Kachtik's rear end. He then stood and felt his left leg collapse. Now he was down on both knees. He tumbled forward until the crown of his helmet rested in the soft dust. Billy Pickard dashed onto the field and snapped an ammonia capsule under Kachtik's nose. He stood and then toppled backward as Pickard saw his eyes roll back into his head.

"Heat exhaustion," Pickard said to Bryant. "We need to get him to Doc Wiedeman."

Pickard stuffed Kachtik, shoulder pads and all, into the black sedan and told one of the assistants to drive him to the infirmary and then hurry back. It wasn't long before three more boys were loaded into the back of a pickup truck and hauled to the doctor. *If he doesn't stop, he's going to kill one of us*, Charles Hall thought. *Maybe I should just haul my ass off the field just like Fred Droussard did.* Instead, Hall stood there shaking, wanting to cry. He wanted to leave but couldn't force his legs to start walking.

Bryant blew his whistle and signaled for the start of the dreaded punt drills, the conditioning phase of practice. To the players, it was pure torture. They would run up the field, chasing a ball that had been punted about forty yards and then they would run back. As players fell out from heat exhaustion, they would either crawl to the sideline or be dragged off the field by student assistants.

Between kicks, players bent forward in the huddle with hands on knees, sucking the dust-filled air into their aching lungs. Jack Pardee peered into the sky and saw the sun begin to spin wildly. He wondered if the other boys saw the same thing.

The last thing Billy Schroeder remembered was breaking from the huddle and dropping into a three-point stance. He stumbled down the field through darkness. Billy didn't know where he was or where he was going. The others didn't know that he was out on his feet and his body was operating on some kind of automatic pilot. Bryant noticed his legs wobbling and his feet floundering but said nothing.

As the team broke the huddle again, Billy tripped and toppled face-first into the crusty field. Clouds of dust were raised almost waist-high, and his right shoulder landed on Jack Pardee's left foot. Not a muscle in Billy's body twitched as a pall fell over the field. The next sound was the voice of Bryant: "Get this goddamn big ox off the field and out of my sight. Where the hell is Billy Pickard?" Bryant marched toward the fallen boy and swung a right shoe into a motionless left leg. The hard smack could be heard more than fifty yards away where quarterback Dave Smith was standing. Smith yelled, "What the hell is he doing?" and then ran full-speed toward his fallen friend—the boy he'd known since childhood. Schroeder and Smith had been football teammates in Lockhart.

Smith and Pickard arrived at the same time and quickly flipped Billy over. His face was turning blue, and his breathing was heavy. Pickard checked his pulse and found it to be somewhere between 250 and 300 beats per minute. "He's dying," Pickard said frantically. "We gotta get him to Doc Wiedeman. Somebody fetch my Ford!"

No longer concerned with what Bryant might think, Hall ripped off his helmet and sprinted toward the car. Meanwhile, players stood over their fallen teammate, watching his face turning purple and gray.

"Is he alive?" Pardee asked.

"Yeah," Pickard said. "But his heart's about to bust."

Three players and Pickard lifted Billy and placed him in the backseat. His body was too long, and his feet were sticking out of a door that wouldn't close.

"To hell with it," Pickard said, jumping behind the wheel. "Let the door flop open. This boy's gonna die if we don't get him to the infirmary."

Hall leaped into the front passenger seat, turned, and looked at Billy's face. "He's getting bluer," Hall said. "Drive fast."

Pickard said a prayer as the Ford kicked up dust and raced toward the front gate. Crossing Flatrock Bridge with a door propped open was going to be tricky. "I hope to God nobody's coming the other way when we get to the bridge. We won't be able to cross."

His prayer was answered. But Pickard slowed the Ford to make sure the door didn't slam into the abutment. Billy Schroeder was in enough pain and didn't need two broken ankles.

"Hold tight to him," Pickard said, worried that Billy might slide out of the car. He wheeled the Ford sharply from the gravel road onto the main highway as tires squealed and dirt flew. Three minutes later the car screeched to a halt in front of the infirmary. Pickard and Hall placed Billy on a stretcher and rolled him into the lobby, where Don Kachtik sat with an ice pack on his head. Billy was regurgitating every two seconds, the vomit leaping from his mouth. It looked like a coffeepot percolating. Kachtik almost threw up himself just watching it.

They placed Billy on an examining table, and Pickard noticed that his own hands were shaking. Doc Wiedeman, meanwhile, moved about calmly. He placed a thumb on Billy's left jugular and, while surveying his watch, checked the boy's pulse rate. No emotion registered on Wiedeman's face, even though Billy's heart was flying. The doctor was tranquil and seemed almost cold as he strolled into the other room and spoke to a nurse.

Doc Wiedeman was again wearing a neatly pressed suit, white shirt, and tie. In another setting, he could have been a banker or a lawyer. He rarely spoke, but the air of confidence was unmistakable.

God, this man has ice water in his veins, Billy thought. Wiedeman had dealt with many emergencies as a rural doctor. He once swam across a swollen river to deliver a baby. Highway slaughter was a frequent occurrence, especially on the road to Mexico.

For several days the doctor had been preparing for the crisis that now lay before him. Several deliveries had been made from the local icehouse. The ice had been chopped and bagged and stored in a long deep freezer situated in one of the back rooms. He'd shaken his head in disbelief when he'd learned that Bryant wasn't giving the boys water breaks because he knew that heat plus drought plus long days in the sun without water equaled heatstroke and possibly death.

Pickard could stand the silence no longer. "Doc Wiedeman, do you think Billy here's gonna die?"

"No," he said in a casual voice without looking up.

"Why is his face turning so purple then?"

"Heatstroke."

Two nurses began packing Billy in ice. The first ice bags were placed along his ribs. Chopped ice was then piled onto his chest and stomach and secured with several thick towels. Smaller bags were placed around his neck and shoulders. Another bag balanced on his forehead.

Billy started to feel himself floating above his body. He gazed down at the nurses, who were applying more ice and towels. The bald-headed doctor with glasses stood next to the table with arms crossed. A light mist permeated the room. There was a sharp glare from a hot white light, and Billy could see Pickard sitting with his head bowed. Standing in the doorway was Charles Hall, wearing a sweat-stained T-shirt and football pants covered with dirt and bloodstains. Billy wondered why Charlie looked so worried.

"Hey, everybody!" Billy yelled. But no one heard him. Floating higher, he bounced lightly like a balloon off the ceiling.

What are they doing down there to me? Billy thought. *Why is my face purple?*

The pain in his ribs and chest was sharp at first. Then he realized that he was lying on a snowy mountaintop, snow beginning to melt around

121

him, and he felt someone wrapping a clothlike material around his midsection. He felt suddenly refreshed and decided to inhale the cold air deeply.

"Doctor, he's coming to," one of the nurses said.

Wiedeman placed a hand on Billy's chest and could feel rhythmic breathing return. No longer was his heart pounding like a jackhammer. His face had faded to a pinkish red. Never opening his eyes, Billy blurted, "I'm sorry, Coach Bryant. God, I'm really sorry."

. . .

This time, Billy Pickard needed almost an hour to convince Dr. Wiedeman that he should drive both Schroeder and Kachtik back to the Adjunct. Schroeder was awake but groggy.

"Coach Bryant is gonna be plenty mad if these boys don't eat and sleep in camp tonight."

Wiedeman had frowned. "You tell Coach Bryant that I'll be out there pretty soon to have a talk with him."

After he'd parked his car at the Adjunct, Pickard ushered the two boys to Bryant's Quonset hut. Bryant gazed at Kachtik and Schroeder, who could barely hold his eyes open. "You boys take a few days off and make sure you drink plenty of water. But when you get to feelin' better, I want you back at practice. No faking, OK?"

At the training barracks, Billy Pickard found Smokey polishing off a pint of Old Charter. They talked about Schroeder and how close he'd come to death.

"Smokey," Pickard said. "That doctor was as smooth as banana pudding. I've never seen anything like it. He never got flustered. He just had his nurses pack Schroeder in ice and it worked. Shoot, I've never seen so much ice in my life."

Smokey took a swig and wiped his mouth with his sleeve. "Good thing I didn't have to treat him. Only ice I got around here is for my John Barleycorn."

Though they were shaken by the sight of Schroeder's purple face, the boys didn't discuss the heatstroke during dinner. One player, however, was still too rattled to eat. Dave Smith slipped away from the chow hall and located the pay phone fastened to the pole just behind Bryant's barracks. He dialed the home of Maggie and Bill Schroeder Sr. back in Lockhart.

"Mr. Schroeder," Dave began. "Something bad happened here in Junction today. You need to know about it. That's why I'm calling."

For fifteen minutes Smith described how Billy Schroeder had collapsed on the field and was kicked by Bryant and how he had been rushed to the infirmary and treated for a heatstroke.

"Mr. Smith," the boy said. "Billy barely survived."

"Where is my son right now?" Bill Schroeder Sr. asked.

"He's in the barracks, sir."

"Tell him that me and his mother will be there in the morning. I need to know more about this."

Bill Schroeder Sr. and his wife, Maggie, drove most of the night from Lockhart to reach the football camp. Traversing the last hundred miles in the dark through the twisting two-laners of the Hill Country had been grueling. They pulled up to the practice field around six-thirty in the morning to find the Aggies snorting and grunting through a full-scale scrimmage. They were told by Smokey Harper that Billy was resting back at the Quonset hut.

For more than an hour Bill and Maggie Schroeder tried to convince their son to pack up and return to Lockhart. Like his son, Bill Schroeder Sr. was a large man with rugged features.

"Quite frankly, Son, this whole scene scares me. You're out here in the middle of nowhere and this man, Bryant, has no one looking over him. If you were workin' this hard back at campus it'd be a different matter. But somebody could keel over and die out here and the parents wouldn't know for days."

"Mom, Dad. I'm not going back with you. I've seen too many of the boys quit and I'm not a quitter. Right now, this is the biggest thing in my life. Coach Bryant is really doin' the right thing. We need a disciplinarian."

"Son. You've had self-discipline all your life."

"I'm not talking about me. I'm talking about the whole team. If we'd had a good coach last year, I honestly think we would have won every game. Coach Bryant is a winner."

"A winner!" Maggie said incredulously. "That man's out there driving his team into the ground and the sun's barely up."

"It's been tough," Billy said. "But I'm not blaming Coach Bryant for what happened to me. I just think that I got tired, that's all."

Maggie and Bill Schroeder knew they were wasting their breath.

They'd spent the last twenty years instilling pride and ambition in their son, and now they were asking him to change. A determined man is hard to stop, especially when he's your son.

About an hour later, the dirty and overworked players began returning to their barracks. Bill Schroeder Sr. stood near the door of Bryant's barracks and watched several boys, still dressed in full pads, wade straight into the South Llano River. He decided to hang around to discuss his son's condition with the man they called Bear. Little did he know that Bryant had been tipped off. Smokey Harper had caught up with the coach as he was striding from the practice field.

"Billy Schroeder's parents are here and they don't look happy."

"Great." Bryant kept walking.

From afar, he saw Bill Schroeder. Bryant owed no one an apology or an explanation, he thought. He'd come to Texas A&M to run this football team his way, and if they didn't like it they could take their boy home. Bill Schroeder watched as Bryant took a hard right turn, striding in the other direction. Bill knew the coach was avoiding him, and that gave him some satisfaction. Maggie was greatly relieved when her husband returned to the car and drove out of the Adjunct. But she knew deep in her heart that she wouldn't stop worrying until the boys were back in College Station.

. . .

With the sun setting over Junction, the players huffed and puffed through the last few gassers. Before practice, many of the boys had checked on Billy to see just how close he'd come to death. Lying in the oven-like Quonset hut wasn't the best rehabilitation for a heatstroke. But Billy had decided to ride it out.

Near the end of practice, Bebes Stallings was chugging down the rocky field when he spotted Billy sitting under an oak tree, sucking on a piece of ice. His mouth drier than a West Texas sandstorm, Stallings deeply thirsted for anything wet. He felt a little jealous of the boy sitting in the shade.

"Hey, Billy!" Bebes yelled hoarsely. "Tell me how I can get me one of those heatstrokes."

11

Whiskey River

I'm just a simple plowhand from Arkansas, but I have learned over the years how to hold a team together. How to lift some men up, how to calm others down, until finally they've got one heartbeat, together, a team.

—PAUL "BEAR" BRYANT

SEPTEMBER 6, 1954

The utter stillness was broken by the sounds of croaking bullfrogs down by the river and snoring boys from the screened-in barracks. Around midnight, Bryant stood by the table and stared into the hot summer night as lines of perspiration streaked his tanned and furrowed forehead. A thin, naked bulb hanging on a limp black cord cast long shadows across the four half-screened walls. The hut smelled of sweat-stained clothes, cigarette butts, and whiskey. Lifting a fifth of Jim Beam from the table littered with team rosters and ashtrays, he could see dozens of names crossed from the list, names that had been part of the Aggie roster when the team left College Station just a few days earlier. Now those boys were far down the highway, hoping to land jobs in the oil fields or on burned-out ranches or to catch on with another college team.

"Got any ice over there?" Bear asked Smokey Harper, who shook his head. "Never mind. Just pour a little of that co-cola over my bourbon."

The old trainer lifted a twelve-ounce bottle from a wooden case and popped the cap with a metal opener that had been engraved with the words: LONE STAR BEER. He slowly poured the warm, fizzing liquid into the coach's cup. "You know," Bryant said slowly, his head tilting forward, "at least a few of those quitters had the guts to come in here and tell me they were haulin' ass. When they did, we gave those boys a bus ticket, a ride down to the station, and a peanut butter and jelly sandwich for the trip. The others were so chickenhearted that they ran out of here at three in the morning like it was some kind of goddamn jailbreak.

"Smokey, we got so many damn players quittin' that I can't keep track. When I walk on the field in the morning, I don't know who's in the starting lineup."

A screen door slammed in the distance, and they could see yet another shadowy figure running off through the moonlit night. "Look at the little jackass run," Smokey cackled in delight. "Shit, son, I didn't know we had any boys with that kind of speed."

The broiling Texas sun had deepened the craggy lines around Smokey's eyes. His face was like an old football left to dry up for several days on a sun-baked field. The eyes, however, were steely and clear. Years of working with football men and tending to their pain had given Smokey a keen perspective on why some succeeded while others ran off into the night.

"Why do you figure," Smokey asked, chomping on a thick cigar, "that those peckerwoods ain't even got the guts to face ya? Why do you figure that boy just lit out without so much as a good-bye?"

"Lack of respect," Bear said, slamming the warm bourbon and Coke down his gullet without a trace of expression.

"Nah."

"Then what is it, Smokey?"

"Fear. If a boy ain't got the guts to stick it out, he sure as heck ain't gonna walk in here and tell ya why. By God, Coach, those boys snoring in their bunk beds tonight are scared to death of ya. They're runnin' out of here like flatlanders two steps ahead of a tidal wave. Hell, they walk around you out on the practice field like you're some kind of smelly swamp. They don't even want to sit near you in the mess hall. They don't know who you are, and they sure don't know where you came from. Hell, I've known you for almost twenty years and I don't know everything about you. But those kids—face it. They're scared to death of ya."

Bear walked toward the screen door, turned, and jabbed a finger at the old man. "Then what in the hell am I supposed to do?"

Smokey pulled hard from the uncapped bottle, smacked his lips, and exhaled. "Have you ever sat down and wondered why the hell you gotta be the meanest damn sumbitch in the valley?"

Bear didn't answer and Smokey could see deep thinking in those far-away eyes.

It wasn't easy being somebody in the Arkansas backwoods of Moro Bottom, where a boy could hardly see past the gravel streets of downtown Fordyce. Six families were scattered along three miles of the creek bottoms where the land was cheap and unforgiving and unpredictable as summer rain. Paul Bryant was born the eleventh of twelve children to Wilson Monroe Bryant and Ida Mae Kilgore. Some called the Bryant home a shotgun house, although it was really a leaky shack, with four rooms, no electricity, no running water, no indoor plumbing, and a floor that threatened to collapse with the next heavy foot. The children slept three and four to a bed.

By the time Paul Bryant was three, his father fell ill and was rendered a semi-invalid. Since the family's religion didn't allow for doctors, it never was known what struck down poor old Monroe. Seeking medical care then was considered a sin among the Bryants. Whispers along the creek bottom were that his problems were not purely physical. Miss Ida, as she was called in Moro Bottom, found Monroe one night wallowing around in a huge mud puddle following a blinding rainstorm. Monroe couldn't explain why he'd risen from his warm bed in the middle of the winter night and taken a seat in the middle of a muddy road.

There was talk along the bottoms that he was too lazy to work, and the Bryant family left it at that. Miss Ida, a devoutly religious woman with the will of six mules, took charge of the family and managed to keep food on the table. She had to lean heavily on a young boy who wore dusty overalls and had no shoes. Paul Bryant grew up fast.

An hour before the first light, young Paul would feed the mules and then hitch them to the wagon. He'd drive the team three miles to the one-room schoolhouse. Paul and his two sisters had to cross Moro Creek, which often froze on winter mornings. Coaxing the mules across the icy water was tricky business, but Paul was strong enough, even as a kid, to handle the hardheaded animals. On those frigid mornings, the children would heat bricks in the fireplace and sit on them as they rode the wagon to school.

Saturdays in the fall and spring were really the hard days. Paul and his mother would load up with butter, milk, eggs, and fresh vegetables and head for nearby Fordyce to peddle the homegrown products for pennies from door to door. In the early 1920s, Fordyce was a town of about three thousand people and, in spite of being just a cut above a country village, was sophisticated compared to where the Bryants lived. Folks in Fordyce treated farmers from Moro Bottom like so much plowed dirt. Riding into town, Paul and Miss Ida passed the movie theater, a hotel, a dry goods store, and the train station. Invariably, they'd pass the schoolhouse just as it was letting out at noon. In those days, kids went to school half a day on Saturday, and when the Fordyce "city slickers" saw Paul in his worn overalls and bare feet they hollered things that sliced to the bone. "Hey, country idiot, where'd you get those old mules? Can't you afford a pair of shoes, country idiot?"

. . .

Mashing an unfiltered cigarette into the butt-filled ashtray, Bryant peered across the table at his old friend who was mixing two more cups of bourbon with Coke. He raised his hand to make a point, and a long, thin shadow slashed across the far wall. He broke a long silence. "Smokey, I don't know what it is. You know, I grew up so far out in the country I had to go toward town to hunt. When I was a kid, I had biscuits and a few beans in my belly. I was so country I could barely carry on a decent conversation. They paid me fifty cents a day to work fourteen-hour days pickin' cotton. Hell, you know why I didn't shine my shoes? Because I didn't have any damn shoes most of the time. I didn't own a pair of new shoes until I was thirteen. I smelled so bad that my fifth-grade teacher moved me from the front of the class to the back row. Mother and I'd drive that mule team into Fordyce and those kids would laugh their asses off at me."

Smokey sipped the warm bourbon. "So you thought you were never gonna amount to nothin'?"

"Yeah, and it scared me. I never had a lick of hope until I got to growin' and those kids stopped pickin' on me."

. . .

By the time the carnival barker rode into Fordyce in the summer of 1926 with a bear in the back of his wagon, Paul Bryant was cutting a large path across Fordyce. He was a package of lean muscle, a little over six-foot, and his ankles and wrists had long been liberated from the worn flour-sack shirts and jeans. He was still so clumsy that he'd walk into tables, sending the salt and pepper shakers spilling onto the floor, and his cousins had started calling him thunderbutt. There wasn't much to do around Fordyce, other than watching movies or playing football. In the days of silent films, folks often packed the Lyric theater for only a dime to see the Tom Mix western movies. Some nights, bluegrass bands would take the stage with fiddles wailing and spoons tapping.

When the fourteen-year-old boy learned that a carnival man was willing to pay a dollar to anyone who'd wrestle a bear onstage, he was the first and the last boy in line. "I'll do it, and I'll do it good," he told the man, who'd led a wagon train of carnies into town. The kid was growing up tough and a little mean. A year earlier, he'd beaten up a grown man who refused to pay him for some groceries he'd delivered. Not a seat was empty when Paul took the stage opposite the bear. The objective was to wrestle the animal for one full minute and then collect the dollar. Young Paul figured the promoter had plenty of money in his pocket since he'd packed the house at ten cents a head.

Paul's strategy was to pull the animal to the floor and hold him down for sixty seconds, but about halfway into the main event the muzzle slipped off and the bear bit off a chunk of skin behind the boy's right ear. With blood smeared on the right side of his face and soaking his shirt, Paul vaulted from the stage and landed with a heavy thud in the front-row seats about ten feet below.

"Smokey," Bear said, plopping both shoes on the table. "Take a look at these shins." He rolled down his socks to reveal long red scars along the shinbones of both legs. "This is what happened when I landed in that row of seats. Hell, it took the skin off both legs. I was so damned embarrassed that I just took off running up the aisle. And you know what the carnival man did? He skedaddled out the back door of the movie house with his dad-gum bear and I never saw him again. I never even got my dollar."

Blowing a smoke ring across the room, Smokey grinned. "But you got a nickname and that's all that matters."

"Hell, no. And you know damn well that my coaches don't call me

Bear, my players don't call me Bear, my wife doesn't call me Bear, and my friends don't call me Bear.''

''What about the sportswriters and the fans?''

''That's fine. Let 'em write it. Let 'em say it. Just don't call me Bear to my face and expect to be my friend.''

It was obvious now to Smokey that the frustration of inheriting such a lousy football team at Texas A&M was eating a hole in his boss's stomach. A man who'd overcome so much and then grown accustomed to winning big couldn't fathom the thought of a losing season. Fear of failure had always driven him, and now it was traveling at a blinding speed. Some of those boys who were sleeping in bunk beds scattered across the Adjunct grounds were the worst damn football players he'd ever seen.

What had happened at Kentucky was a miracle. Winning four bowl games and then a SEC championship was virtually unthinkable before Bear rolled into Lexington in 1946. His 7-3 record that first season was the school's best since 1912, which was the year before he was born. He should have been the hottest coaching commodity in the entire country, but his timing couldn't have been any worse when he got mad and quit in February. The major football powers were already committed to their head coaches, who'd been out recruiting for more than two months.

When the Adolph Rupp situation became unbearable, Bryant had called his old friend John Barnhill, the athletic director at the University of Arkansas, where he'd been offered the head coaching job twice before. Bryant practically begged for the job, but Barnhill said he was quite happy with his current coach, Bowden Wyatt.

Fate had dealt Bryant a bad hand the first time the Arkansas job was offered to him. The date was December 6, 1941. The next day, hours after Pres. Franklin Roosevelt declared war on Japan, Bryant enlisted in the navy, and he was soon sailing to North Africa.

Ten years later, he turned down an offer from Barnhill because he was winning so many games at Kentucky.

Now he was stuck with a tattered bunch of Aggies and two-thirds of the team had already quit. Smokey lit another cigar and swilled the last bit of bourbon from the bottom of the Jim Beam bottle.

''Now look what you done gone and did, Smokey,'' Bryant said, his face crunching into a deep frown. ''I'll be damned if I'll ever drink with you again.''

The old trainer chuckled as gray plumes of smoke rose from the deepest recesses of his lungs and floated through his nostrils. "Never fear, my friend." Smokey reached into his boot and pulled out a fresh pint of George Dickle. From the other boot he retrieved a pint of moonshine whiskey that he'd been saving since leaving Kentucky.

"Is that the same shit we used to drink in Lexington?"

"Yep," Smokey said with a sly grin.

"Then uncap that sucker and pour me a big drink and forget the cocola." Bryant smiled.

The two men drank heavily and listened for more players fleeing into the night. They heard coyotes baying and June bugs banging against the screen doors and boys snoring. Bryant thought about hijacking a Chevy pickup that was parked next to the mess hall and driving to the bus station to reclaim the night's escapees. He could picture those quitters standing outside Fortran Johnston's place, waiting for the sunrise and the first bus out of town. By God, they'd be praying he didn't come looking for them.

"How much longer we gonna stay out here among the cacti and them howlin' dogs?" Smokey asked, gazing toward the open field now bathed in moonlight.

"Don't know. But if they keep quitting, we won't have enough to play Tech in the opener. Guess I'd better change my ways and heed your lecture here tonight. I'd better be nicer to these boys, or they'll sure as hell run me out of coaching." Smokey didn't need to look at Bryant to know he was rolling his eyes.

The old trainer pulled a worn bandanna from his back pocket and wiped sweat from his forehead. "Ain't nobody giving you no advice. But you do need to rethink what the hell you're doing."

Bryant grunted and walked toward his cot in the corner of the room.

"Maybe I will. Maybe I won't. But don't drink all of that whiskey up. We ain't going home just yet."

12

Christian Soldiers

You have to be willing to outcondition your opponents.

—PAUL "BEAR" BRYANT

SEPTEMBER 8, 1954

TEXAS AGGIES was stenciled in broad maroon letters on the front of his wrinkled gray T-shirt. At sundown, as the screen door slammed, the coach strode slowly to the front of the classroom where the Aggie players had assembled for the evening meeting. Gone were the hawkish eyes and the scowl he'd worn since camp started and Bryant seemed slightly pensive as he dropped a stack of notebooks on the wooden desktop and took a seat on the corner.

He surveyed the room, quietly counting heads while taking mental notes. It didn't surprise him that the players wore exhaustion on their faces like a five-day growth, but it was worrisome that he could read the fear so evident in their eyes.

The night before, he'd listened to Smokey through the whiskey haze. They'd talked into the wee hours, and Bryant had decided it was time to show a little mercy. Otherwise, he might wake up one morning and find the barracks cleaned out.

Bear stood, cleared his throat, and placed his right hand firmly on the side of the desk. For the first time the boys could remember, he dropped his chin and examined the floor. Normally, his eyes burned through them like the West Texas sun.

"Boys, I'm going to have to level with y'all. I know that I drug you away from your homes, took you away from your mamas and your papas, your girlfriends and wives, and I'm responsible for bringing you out to this godforsaken place in the middle of nowhere and this whole thing probably doesn't make a lot of sense to ya. There ain't a lot of people too happy back in College Station to hear that I've run two-thirds of y'all off. They think I'm a madman and maybe I am.

"So why am I here and why am I doing this? Because for years and years the coaches of this football team were too dad-gum soft, and I could see that in the game films. You played like a bunch of pansies. A lot of y'all are still wonderin' why I let ol' Fred Broussard walk out of here a few days ago. I think that most of y'all thought he was some kind of god. Well, he wasn't. He was a quitter before he got here, and he's a quitter still. When a boy quits on me during practice, I know he'll lay down on me in the fourth quarter. And I don't think that anybody in this room wants that.

"But that's all beside the point. A couple of y'all have come to my cabin to express some concerns about the way I'm runnin' this camp. Hell, I don't want to see any more players quit. God knows we had to move Troy Summerlin to center and he came out here to be a manager. So maybe I need to change some things."

The coach paused and gazed around the room. He could sense a shift in the collective mood. The players studied his face even more closely and, for the first time, detected a trace of compassion in his eyes. They had heard him utter the word *change*. They all wondered if he really meant it.

Bryant had dragged them without warning almost three hundred miles away from their campus, and now they were stuck in the middle of a rock patch with nobody but coaches monitoring the proceedings. Sure, there was a cub reporter from Houston hanging around and asking questions, but they sensed he was as intimidated by Bryant as they were. Even the local townsfolk had been shooed away like so many dumb chickens. Bryant had demanded that the players have no contact with the outside world— no letters and no phone calls. Now some of the boys who had promised they would never quit were wondering if the quitters were right after all. This whole mess was getting more and more confusing.

The night before, as he'd stirred restlessly in his bunk, big Sid Theriot had gazed across the room at Bebes Stallings.

"You know what?" Sid said.

"What?"

"Ain't gonna be no more Sid round here after Turkey Day."

In spite of sore ribs, Bebes managed a chuckle. Sid, a senior, was saying that he wasn't planning to stick around after the Aggies' traditional Thanksgiving game against Texas, always the last one of the season.

Now, as he studied Bryant's expression, Sid was as curious as the rest of the boys about this sudden change of heart. A half-smile creased the coach's face as he slapped the desktop with an open palm.

"I tell you what I'm gonna do." His voice was rising. "Tomorrow's Sunday. How many of you boys'd like to go to church in the mornin'?"

Heads began to turn as the players looked at one another, and hands shot up. A trip to church would mean a cancellation of the morning practice. They had visions of sleeping until seven o'clock, eating a big country breakfast, and then loading the buses for a trip to town. Most of the boys wouldn't have gone to church on their own. But they'd walk ten miles through cactus to church if it meant they didn't have to pull on those cold and soggy uniforms before daybreak.

Bryant studied their eyes. Instead of fear, he could see rays of hope. Fatigue no longer tugged at their faces, and he could feel a surge of human energy generating through the room. Boys who had slumped in their seats from exhaustion were now sitting up straight.

"Hey, Pat!" he hollered at assistant coach Pat James. "I want you to get a notebook and write down the names of all of these boys who want to go to church. Make sure you get all the names because we'll be going to church in the mornin'." Bryant now spoke in the lilting tongue of a man in the pulpit. The boys wouldn't have been surprised if he'd climbed upon the desk and shouted, "Have you found Jeeee-zus?"

As James recorded the names, Bryant strolled to the chalkboard where he would deliver the evening address on defense. He began drawing *X*s and *O*s on the board, dragging the screeching chalk across the blackboard. He quickly diagrammed a defense that the Aggies had been working on during the morning practice.

"Yes sir, boys," he almost sang as he drew. "We'll be goin' to church in the mornin'. That's right. To church we'll all be going. Right *after* the morning practice.''

In unison, forty boys stopped breathing.

• • •

His thick face was smudged with chalky dust as Dennis Goehring struggled just to place one heavy foot in front of the other. Another three-hour practice without water breaks had included a bloody ninety-minute scrimmage. Nobody had bothered to count the gassers. Many of the boys were left sprawled on the field, their chests heaving and lungs begging for air. It was only nine o'clock, but the sun was frying the earth like Mama's Sunday chicken.

"I told you that sonofabitch ain't runnin' me off!" Goehring hollered as he limped past Smokey Harper.

"You still ain't worf a shit," the old trainer half-spit, cocking his right eyebrow. "Whoever gave you that damn scholarship ought to have to pay for it hisself."

Bryant didn't like to see the boys laid out like roadkill. So the stragglers were given some help. The student managers started dragging players off the field. Some of the boys were determined not to be hauled across the hard, stubby earth on their backsides. So they crawled the final thirty yards on hands and knees to the shower room, where they collapsed again on the cool concrete floor and dry-heaved into the drains. The boys would lie there on their backs, mouths agape, hoping to catch cool spray from the spigots.

Others who had the strength to wobble into the shower room turned on the water full blast and placed their lips over the nozzles. They'd been repeatedly warned by Bryant and the coaches not to guzzle the water. But they were parched after three hours of eating nothing but sand and dust. Mudballs caked beneath their tongues.

"I think I swallowed enough dirt that I'm starting to gain weight," said Bobby Drake Keith, hanging onto a showerhead. His face was so dirty that his eyeballs looked like two marbles peeking through a mud pie.

Walking past the shower room, Bryant could hear the slurping and the gurgling. "Get away from those damn shower nozzles!" he hollered. "You're gonna be cramped up. You ain't gonna be able to walk."

The warning came too late. Their stomachs had been filled so rapidly that the leg cramps were already coming on. Paul Kennon and Theriot fell to the floor screaming in agony. Large lumps appeared beneath the skin of their lower legs as the calf muscles balled up like baseballs. They tried to work out the heavy knots with their fingers, but as one relaxed, another muscle would contract. Players flopped around on the shower room floor like marlin on the back of a chartered fishing rig. Their painful sobs could be heard all the way to the river.

"Grab your big toe and pull back," came the command from the doorway. Smokey barked out the instructions as he walked along the row of fallen players. He grabbed the toe of Clark's right shoe and pulled it toward his shin. "Like this. Pull it backward like this." Thanks to years of experience, Smokey had become an expert on dehydration and cramps. He knew that the human body did funny things when it totally dried out.

Bryant could still hear the players' painful howls as he walked toward his barracks. He turned and gazed at the dry, jagged hills as the student trainers dragged the last limp body off the practice field and deposited him at the door of the shower room. A plume of gray smoke rose from one of the distant ranches. Bryant thought about a cowboy burning the prickly pear off a cactus with a butane torch so a starving steer could eat. He thought about the boys guzzling water out of the showers and wondered if they were just like dried-out West Texas cattle.

• • •

Two buses rolled away from the barracks a little before eleven for the short ride into town, where the First Baptist Church was situated on Third Avenue. Bebes Stallings took a window seat on the third row and slumped into the corner. He could feel his young bones creaking and knew that it was going to take a lot more than prayer to make his body feel whole again. Bebes wondered if old people felt this bad.

It had been nine days since the boys had seen anything beyond the barracks and the practice field and the rugged hills and the stubborn South Llano River. From the first row of the bus Bebes could hear Bryant and Pat James talking about the river that wouldn't die.

"It's still amazing to me," Bryant said, "that the South Llano keeps rollin' and the North Llano died over a year ago!"

James eyes widened. "Let me tell you somethin' really amazing, Coach," he said. "Right before the North Llano dried up and went under the gravel a couple of years ago, folks around here waded into the river and saved a lot of the fish. You'll appreciate what they did. They went out into the river with nets and scooped up most of the live fish and put 'em in the South Llano. If that's not the dangedest thing you've ever heard.''

Bear pulled a cigarette from his shirt pocket and lit it with a wooden match. "Folks around here must have a lot more gumption than I thought. I wish I had a few of their boys on my team.'' The stillness was broken by the roar of the two diesels as the buses rolled along the narrow ribbon of a highway into town. Bebes thought about a quick nap but was jerked awake by Weasel Watson punching him in the sore ribs.

"Lookie there, Bebes,'' Watson said, pointing to gravestones that stood in the front yard of one of the houses. The gravestones were marked with names of the deceased, along with dates of birth and death. They'd been standing in the yards for years because the families of the deceased didn't have money to pay the stone makers. Oddly, the proprietors regularly mowed and trimmed the grass around them, just like they were trees or bird feeders. But they stubbornly refused to sell them on a pay-as-you-go basis, because if the buyers were deadbeats, the stones would have to be repossessed from the graveyard.

"Bebes, I think I saw my name on one of them grave markers,'' Watson said.

"Yeah, I think I saw it, too.'' Stallings watched Weasel's face turn the color of cow's milk. "Watson, if you don't get in control of your mind, you're gonna wind up crazier than a loon.''

The First Baptist Church had been constructed on a hill between the rivers in 1911. The lower half of the walls was built with brown rock and the other half with wood. Potluck suppers were served on Tuesday and Sunday nights. A large bell hung in a steel-encased spire above the roof. Fourteen gray steps led to the front door.

None of the townsfolk had expected the Aggie footballers to show up for the eleven o'clock service. These curious folks were now mystified by the sight of the weary boys wearing T-shirts and blue jeans as they filed into church. Rumors about the hell camp had been flying. The locals wondered why the boys stood outside the bus station every morning. The players now quietly took their seats in the final three pews. Bryant lingered on the front steps, nodding at the Baptists who strolled toward the door. He wanted to be the last one into church, and he wanted to finish one last Chesterfield before he went in.

A few minutes later, as the voices of the choir filled the sanctuary, he slowly opened the front door and strolled in. Every head turned as the Baptists stared.

Redbird Granberry was familiar with the spell this man cast over people. He elbowed Ray Barrett in his thick arm and whispered, "Can you believe how these people are looking at him? They look like they've seen a ghost."

"They ain't seen nothin'," Barrett whispered.

Bear nodded and smiled at the preacher as he took a seat in front of the players. A large ceiling fan clacked and clattered. The fierce morning sun was kept at bay by the stained glass. For the first time in several days, the boys were now sitting in a dark, cool place with a fan kicking a nice breeze into their faces.

The music director stood and directed the congregation to turn to page 121 of the hymnal and join in the singing. A woman with gray hair tied in a neat bun bobbed her head twice like a chicken pecking the barnyard for feed. Her fingers then moved gracefully over the yellowed piano keys, and the church came alive with spirited voices.

"Rock of ages, cleft for thee,
Let me hide myself in thee.
Let the water and the blood,
From thy wounded side that flowed.
Rock of ages, cleft for thee,
Let me hide myself in thee."

Bryant never opened his hymnal. But he surprised the folks in front of him with his fine bass voice. Church was not his passion, even though he'd gone to worship there many Sundays in his life. A fervently religious mother had at least started him on the righteous path, and that's why he knew most of the hymnal by heart.

As he returned the songbook to the pew cradle, he turned to check on the boys behind him. What he saw were forty heads, each resting on the shoulder of the boy to the right. The soothing music and cool air had worked a kind of magic. Some of the boys were snoring.

Turning toward the pulpit, Bryant realized that every eye in the congregation was now focused on his sleeping team. He could only imagine what the Baptists would be saying as they gathered around the Sunday dinner table for collards, turnip greens, black-eyed peas, fried okra, mashed potatoes, and fried chicken. They would prate on about the Aggie camp and the locked gates and the boys standing around the bus station, and they would wonder if Satan was loose in Junction. The very thought of it made him smile.

13

Last Dance

Football changes and so do people.

—PAUL "BEAR" BRYANT

SEPTEMBER 9, 1954

The knock came softly and Bryant figured that another quitter had darkened his door. He was busy mapping a game plan for the season opener against Texas Tech and was in no mood to hear another sob story.

A heavy fist then rattled the door's hinges. Craning his neck, he peered around the chalkboard to see a neatly dressed bald gentlemen standing at the screen door with a medical bag in hand. It didn't take a brain surgeon to know that Dr. John E. Wiedeman had come calling.

Bryant could barely keep a straight face as he cracked the creaking door and welcomed the visitor. "Hell, I didn't know doctors made house calls out here. Why, come on in, Doc Wiedeman."

Dr. Wiedeman didn't smile and it was quickly apparent he was in no mood to shake hands or to chitchat. A grave and serious matter had brought him to the football camp. Bryant wasn't surprised that Wiedeman had come and, in truth, had expected him earlier. He figured the doctor to be baffled

139

by all of the bleeding, battered, bruised, and dehydrated boys tossed his way like so many smoking hot potatoes.

Bryant had briefly visited Wiedeman's infirmary five days earlier, and the doctor had greeted him by saying, "Why, Coach, it appears that I have as many of your players as you do." It was close to the truth.

As Wiedeman moved toward a seat on the other side of the desk, Bryant said, "I guess you came out here to see where we buried the bodies."

No reply.

Bryant would have sworn that the temperature dropped by ten degrees when Wiedeman sat down.

"I've come out here to check on Billy Schroeder and I feel certain you won't deny me this. And, Paul, they're some other things we need to discuss."

"Shoot," he said.

Wiedeman removed his glasses and cleaned them with a white handkerchief. He set a hard gaze on the coach. "I don't need to tell you that you're putting the boys at great risk. Every day you continue to practice in this brutal heat with no water breaks, you're putting lives on the line. I don't know if you realize this, but Billy almost died before we got him cooled down."

"Billy Pickard told me something about that."

"Well, sir, I must insist that if you continue to live in these ovenlike Quonset huts Billy Schroeder must come back and stay at the infirmary. The odds of having a second heatstroke are dramatically increased after the first one."

"Somebody told me something about that."

"Sir, I don't know what it was like back in Kentucky. But here in Junction, we're in the midst of one of the worst droughts in our history. And there have been some bad ones, mind you. Just look around and you'll see that our rivers and creeks have dried up. Our cattle have withered to bones. Not many living things have been able to survive. I'll never understand why you coaches won't give the boys water and ice breaks."

Bryant rolled the word *madness* around in his head. He didn't like it. He didn't consider himself crazy—just a hard man who believed in work and dedication. But in his heart, he'd been bothered by Billy Schroeder's heatstroke and by his own calloused reaction. The memory of seeing the boy turning blue made his stomach sour.

He tapped a pencil on the desktop. "Doc, we start the season in eight days. We gotta get out of here pretty quick. Now, I don't want to broadcast this all over the countryside. But I'll bet we'll be gone before you know it. Billy'll stay with us until we leave.''

Though he clearly didn't trust Bryant, Wiedeman felt his point had been made. He forced a slight grin as he opened the screen door. ''Best of luck, Coach. We'll be listening to your games on the radio. You've got a lot of fans out here.''

Wiedeman realized that if Bryant wasn't smart enough to recognize his dilemma, he was bound to cut his own throat. That, in turn, would get him fired. For the next thirty minutes the doctor examined Schroeder from head to toe, making certain his life wasn't at risk. Wiedeman warned the boy to stay away from the practice field and drink as much water as his stomach could handle. He turned the ignition on the blue Ford and headed down the dusty road. He peered through the rearview mirror and hoped he'd never again see the Aggies in Kimble County—not under these conditions, anyway.

Driving slowly past the bus station, he spotted a young man wearing blue jeans and a T-shirt boarding a bus bound for San Antonio. Wiedeman hoped he would be the last one to flee Junction.

. . .

Striding toward the meeting room, Bryant saw his quarterback walking a few feet ahead of him.

''Elwood, let me speak to you for a minute,'' he said, placing his hand on the boy's shoulder.

''Sure, Coach. What's on your mind?''

''Well, you remember the talks we had back in College Station?''

''Yessir, Coach.''

''I told you that you were gonna have to be a tough sumbitch to quarterback this football team.''

''Yessir, Coach.''

He gazed at his shoelaces and then shifted the cap to the back of his head. ''Well, son, I've come to tell you that I'm sorry.''

Swallowing hard, Kettler paused and felt blood rushing to his face. ''What for, Coach?''

''For making you play with those damn broken bones in your back. I should have never done somethin' like that.''

''Ah, Coach. I'll make it through the season OK. I just need a few more rounds in the whirlpool. Smokey'll keep me propped up.''

Bryant rubbed the boy's head, which felt like an onion. "I've been too rough on you, son, and most of the boys, too. I want you to know that we're gonna be out of here soon and that everything's gonna be all right."

Striding to the front of the meeting room, Bryant could hear the floor creaking through the silence. He sensed the boys were completely out of gas. Many of the faces were badly sunburned. No one had thought to bring a set of scales to Junction, but it seemed that each boy had dropped at least twenty pounds. Much of the loss was water weight and could be recovered through starchy meals, Coke floats, and long nights of cool sleep in the athletic dormitory back in College Station.

In the last ten days, Jack Pardee had lined up at six different positions. Now he looked like a man who'd fought most of the Korean War by himself. Henry Clark still had a black and swollen nose. Somehow, Redbird Granberry seemed even smaller. Weasel Watson's cocky grin had disappeared. Even the scowl on Dennis Goehring's face had faded with fatigue.

Bryant cleared his throat. "We've got one more little piece of business to take care of now that every center in camp has quit. We're down to Troy Summerlin. Have we got any volunteers in this room?"

A cherub-faced boy with a flattop began waving his right arm.

"Coach, I'll do it!" shouted Lloyd Hale. "Yessir, I'll be your center."

"All right, then. This meeting here is adjourned. You boys get a good night's sleep and be ready for practice tomorrow."

The boys filed slowly into the darkness. Weasel Watson could feel every muscle in his body aching. He thought about taking a dip in the South Llano but figured he might drown. What he really wanted was to lie down and sleep for two days.

Watson turned to Bebes Stallings. "You know why I never quit?"

"Nah."

"For one thing, I ain't got the guts to face him. Second, I ain't got the energy to walk to the bus station. Third, they'd throw me out of Texas."

"Good reasons."

• • •

A gray light with streaks of orange was streaming across the camp when Dennis Goehring snapped awake and realized that something had gone wonderfully wrong. There had been no predawn whistles or potclanging and no Smokey Harper standing over him shoving vitamins and orange juice in his face.

Wiping sleep from his eyes, Goehring raised his head from the hard bunk and spotted Smokey through the screens twenty feet away in the trainers' room. The old man was smoking a cheap cigar, packing rolls of tape into brown boxes, and humming off-key.

"Hey, you white-haired geezer!" Goehring yelled. "You oversleep?"

"Nah."

"Then what the hell am I doin' still in bed? And what the hell's the sun doin' risin' over that goddamn hill yonder?"

"Shut up and get packed. We're goin' home."

Home. The word seemed to race through the valleys and down the river before sailing over the rocky bluffs. For days and days no one had dared to utter the word for fear they would never see it again. Bodies lurched from the hard beds, and war whoops rang out across the camp. Goehring was wearing only skivvies when he crashed through the screen door and scrambled barefoot across the coarse ground, never feeling the goatheads jabbing at his toes. He yanked open Smokey's screen door and ran to the old man, bear-hugging him.

"Tell me you're not lyin'!" Dennis bellowed. "Because if you are, I'm gonna crush your stinkin' ribs."

Because there were no calendars or clocks, the boys had lost track of time. They weren't sure if camp had lasted six weeks or sixty days. Only Bryant and the coaches kept track of the dawns. It was hard for the players to imagine they'd labored only ten days in the broiling heat because so much had gone down and so many quitters were now miles up the highway. Teammates, roommates, and friends would never be seen or heard from again. Players who had come to A&M together from the same little towns—friends since childhood—were now separated and never again would share the misery and pain and the camaraderie and the ecstasy that only football could summon. The Aggie squad, 111 strong when the buses rolled out of College Station, looked more like a troop of Johnny Rebs limping home from a long war.

Just the mention of home, though, relit a fuse.

Many of the boys ran bare-assed for the river and dived in, splashing and playing and dunking one another in the cool South Llano. Boys again, there was energy in their voices and hope in their eyes.

Bryant leaned against a pecan tree, puffing on a Chesterfield and taking in the celebration. "If I'd known they had this much piss and vinegar, we'd have stayed a couple of more days," he told Phil Cutchin. "God knows I've got enough explaining to do when I get back."

Several times the boys had flirted with physical exhaustion. But they'd suffered more from mental duress in the final days. The gnawing feeling they wouldn't survive was a tall hill to climb with each dawn. Their biggest enemy in Junction had become the lingering component of fear.

There were times when the boys seemed to be speaking in tongues, times when the blind wobbles rattled their joints, a time when Dennis Goehring was haunted by a ghostly vulture. But the survivors had hung tough and somehow were bonded by a blind trust. In the end, a single thread bound them all. Each survivor knew he really had no better place to go.

· · ·

At nine o'clock, a single Greyhound bus sat humming on the edge of the unforgiving patch of land known as the practice field. As they climbed aboard, some of the boys felt giddy, others a sense of great relief. A few players were mindful of missing teammates and felt sad. Bebes Stallings said, "Look at it this way. We came out in here in two buses, and now we're goin' home in one."

That lone bus was half-empty as it rolled toward the front gate, raising yellow clouds that would float on the high wind for several days. Thanks to Bryant, there had been no welcoming committee. Now there was a farewell party of one—Elmer Parrot, the Adjunct grounds supervisor, who waved a straw hat at the big diesel as it pulled away.

Bryant yanked open a window and stuck his head out. "It wasn't heaven, but it wasn't hell, Elmer," Bryant said. "Tell the folks in town we'll not be back. Most of 'em will be happy about that."

"Bye, Coach!" Elmer yelled back. "Win 'em all this year."

Bryant had one last thought. "If Fred Broussard shows back up, tell him he still ain't playin' for me."

Elmer smiled knowingly.

Before the bus crossed Flatrock Bridge, leaving behind the gurgling blue water of the South Llano, every player was sound asleep. There would be no card playing or storytelling or dreaming of naked girls frolicking in the back creek. Dennis Goehring had forgotten about Laverne Johnston—at least for the moment. Boys who had played their transistor radios on their journey to Junction were no longer around. Now, they were far away, listening to Hank Williams and Bob Wills, probably wondering if Bryant had finally killed off the stragglers.

The outbound trip had been filled with energy and anticipation. Now the only sounds were of the eight tires singing against the asphalt and the wind whipping against the windows.

Coach Elmer took a slow walk down the aisle, counting heads. Though he had witnessed the steady parade of quitters, he was a bit unnerved by the vacuous feel of the bus. On the way out, boys had been crammed like sardines into the aisles and others had stretched out and slept in the overhead baggage compartment. Now, as he counted again and again, he shook his head in disbelief.

"How could this have happened?" he quietly asked himself.

Sauntering to the front, he knelt in the aisle next to Bryant and shifted his cap to the back of his head. He placed his right hand on the coach's left shoulder and began slowly. "Coach, we came out with a hundred and eleven. I know that for a fact because I counted them myself. But shit, son, you ain't gonna believe this. We're goin' home with only thirty-five boys. Thirty-five boys, that's all we got left."

Bryant gazed through the window at the gray and dusty hills. Tumbleweeds scuttled along the highway.

"I got a much bigger question," he drawled. "Just how many will be able to suit up for the season opener?"

Coach Elmer looked down and didn't speak.

"Come on. How many?"

"No more than twenty-four. I talked to Smokey and Billy before they took off in Billy's Ford, and they both agreed. We got boys recoverin' from heatstrokes. We got boys with casts on their hands. We got boys with casts on their arms. Even if we wanted to play 'em, the Southwest Conference wouldn't let 'em. We got boys so tired they can barely walk."

On the surface, the news from Elmer wasn't shocking. Bryant had known the players were leaving in droves. He knew that some of the boys were too battered, broken, and flat worn-out to play. But just the idea of having so few available for game duty was depressing. He never had faced this kind of predicament before, nor did he know of a successful coach who had.

The men rode in silence.

Bryant deeply trusted Coach Elmer, a wise old cuss who had coached college football all over the South. Coach Elmer's opinion was always valued, which was a far cry from the noise Bryant heard from some coaches. In Junction, Bryant and Elmer talked each day, and some of the theory sessions carried deep into the night. More than a philosophical guru, Coach Elmer was a resourceful and tenacious recruiter who had lured John Crow and Charlie Krueger to the Aggies. He understood every phase of college football—from targeting blue chippers in the deepest backwoods to motivating even the laziest boys.

One night, Coach Elmer had said, "Coach, you know, if we can just keep the dang wheels on this sucker for one season, we'll be choppin' high cotton pretty soon. We've got the best-lookin' freshman class I've ever seen. Krueger and Crow'll be All-Americans their sophomore years. Hell, Ken Hall gained 4,000 yards in one season. We got more stud blue chippers than Notre Dame and Oklahoma combined."

As the bus rolled through the ravaged Hill Country, past the town of Fredericksburg, Bryant's mind was clouded with many issues. How would he explain running off almost three-quarters of the team? How would he explain Billy Schroeder's brush with death? What would they do with all of the empty rooms in Walton Hall?

The phone would be ringing. He could just hear the alums crying in their beers at the Cibango Club.

Oddly, Bryant was having some self-doubts.

"Do you think this trip was a mistake?" he asked Elmer.

"I'm not saying it was or wasn't. I do know this. In three or four weeks, we'll have the toughest sumbitchin' team in the whole conference. But early on—shit, it's gonna be rough sleddin'."

Bryant lit a cigarette. "Tech'll have eighty players suited up, won't they?"

"A hundred. I've known their coach, DeWitt Weaver, for many a year. His boys'll have fresh legs. They'll be full of pep when they hit our stadium. Plus, there's another thing we gotta worry about. Tech's petitioned the conference for membership. Right now, they're gunnin' for respect. It'd sure be a feather in their cap to bust our butts."

Coach Elmer didn't mention that Texas Tech had finished the 1953 season 11-1 and ranked twelfth in the final A.P. poll.

Bryant hated to lose, but for the moment he wasn't overly concerned with what might happen against Texas Tech. More important was establishing the right tone and raising calluses and vanquishing the quitters.

Still, it would take weeks, months, and possibly the whole season to get his team on the fast track. In the meantime, he would be dogged by waves of wide-eyed alums.

At least the long bus ride back to College Station afforded much time for thinking and planning.

As the miles passed and the ashen country turned a pale green, Bryant felt himself starting to relax. By God, he'd been a problem solver all of his life. This crisis was no different than anything he'd faced since Arkansas. People had always been amazed at his ability to get chicken salad out of chickenshit.

Bryant suddenly realized that everyone else on the bus was asleep—except the driver, of course. Ten days in Junction had wasted them. But not him. He often drew peace of mind from his own physical and mental fortitude. There wasn't a man alive who could outwork him, much less outcoach him. Now he faced a challenge of a lifetime and, by God, it would be fun. Yeah, the critics would point the finger at him, and the sportswriters would take their shots and the A&M administration might call him on the carpet. But all they had to do was look at his record. He'd whipped the odds before.

Bryant reflected upon the sad face of John Crow as he waved goodbye to the varsity players back on campus. Then he had an uplifting thought. He would someday build a champion around Crow and all of the strong-willed boys who had survived Junction. It would happen, by God.

The next few weeks would be a royal pain in the ass. But there was much to be thankful for and plenty of reasons to drive on. Besides, his forty-first birthday was just two days away and that would give him something to celebrate.

As the bus turned off University Drive and entered Texas A&M, Bryant was struck by a pleasant sight—Crow standing on the same sidewalk where he'd bid the team farewell eleven days earlier. Then he chuckled to himself. Crow didn't know what had gone down. Before the varsity left, Bryant had canceled all of the newspapers coming to the athletic complexes.

"What must be going through that peckerhead's mind?" Bryant said, elbowing Coach Elmer and waking him.

"Thank the Lord that he's still here."

Now, as Crow watched the single bus crawling toward Walton Hall, his eyes widened. He stood in silence as a slim troop of sleepy boys trudged through the door. He then gazed back up the empty street, wondering if the second bus would ever appear.

"Hey, you guys," he blurted. "Where the hell did everybody go?"

14

Losers

The first thing a football coach needs when he's starting
out is a wife who's willing to put up with a whole lot of
neglect. The second thing is a five-year contract.

—PAUL "BEAR" BRYANT

SEPTEMBER 17, 1954

Bear Bryant's dark suit was soaked and matted to his skin, and a wet,
stringy curl sprawled across the edge of his brow.

For several minutes he restlessly paced the locker room, prowling and
thinking and balling his hands into fists. Resting on one knee, heads bowed,
each Aggie sucked air like a spent racehorse. Bryant rattled a metal locker
with his forearm and then turned his hot eyes on the players.

"After you get showered and get dressed, go on back to the dorm and
stay there tonight. Let the Texas Tech boys have the girls. You don't
deserve them."

The Aggies had been whipped 41–9. Both the margin and the manner
of defeat were unsettling to the quiet and restless crowd of 40,079 fans
and to the sportswriters now on deadline searching for words to describe
this hour of gloom. Most folks who had navigated the narrow asphalt into
College Station had expected a miracle from the man with prescient eyes.

He had practically walked on water in Kentucky. Now the writers knew Bryant hadn't been bluffing back in Junction when he had poor-mouthed his players and let almost eighty boys quit.

It quickly became evident that the leg-weary Aggies were defenseless against a rested Texas Tech squad that wore them down with waves of fresh reserves. Only twenty-five of Bryant's boys had suited up, compared to more than a hundred for the Red Raiders. All week, the A&M players had walked around campus like zombies. Bryant had blundered in lining up Jack Pardee at cornerback, where he was burned time and again by the faster Raider receivers. Pardee's natural position was linebacker, and everybody knew the thick-legged boy was better suited to stop the run. The Aggies were also hurt by Billy Schroeder's absence from the line.

Statistics told a large part of the story. Texas A&M had recorded no passing yards and had lost an unthinkable ten fumbles.

"If you've got a gut in your body," Bryant said, "you'll be on the practice field at three o'clock Monday afternoon. I also expect you injured boys to be out there." Then he turned and walked out of the locker room.

• • •

The call came Monday morning and found Bryant sipping coffee and plowing through a pile of newspapers from Houston to San Antonio to Dallas.

"Good morning, Paul," M. T. Harrington said. "I have something to discuss with you. I assume you wouldn't mind coming by my office before going to yours this morning."

Bryant felt like laughing. He'd already been to the office and had returned home to peruse the newspapers and drink Mary Harmon's coffee. He'd been watching and grading the Texas Tech film since four that morning.

"Don't know why I can't come by. Go ahead and get the coffee to percolating."

Bryant and his family had been living in a two-story brick home since June, when the school year ended in Kentucky, and Mary Harmon had moved the children and the family belongings to College Station. The house had two air conditioners, hardwood floors, and a large basement where the Bryants planned to entertain.

Mary Harmon had cried when she set eyes on the stark and empty countryside and the drab campus where the tallest structure was a silver water tower with the tall maroon inscription that read: WELCOME TO

149

AGGIELAND. At least she found Texas folks to be friendly. What depressed her, though, was readjusting to a new town and a fresh set of expectations. It seemed that her husband caused hopes to soar wherever he went and couldn't remember a place where fans had seemed more starved for winning than at Texas A&M.

"Papa," she said. "Everywhere I go, people are talking about you. I had no idea that football was that important down here."

A few minutes after nine that morning, Bryant studied Harrington's face. It was clear from his puffy eyes that the chancellor hadn't slept well. He nervously tapped a pencil on the desktop. After shaking hands with the coach, he paused for several seconds, his mind wishing for the magical words.

Bryant asked, "What's got you goin' there, Tom?"

"Paul, what's got me worried is what's going on here at Texas A&M," Harrington said in a soft voice.

"And the football team didn't help much Saturday night."

"Well, kind of. But I'm sure you'll bring them back. What worries me is the spirit around this place."

"How're you plannin' on fixing it?"

"Well, sir, college-aged kids just aren't accepting our gung-ho military rah-rah anymore. Our enrollment's slipped for six straight years. We're down by twenty-four hundred students since 1948."

"Maybe if you could get some girls in here, it'd help."

"The climate just isn't right to do that," Harrington said. "Oh, we've got some people and some politicians pushing for coeducation. But I don't think the time is right."

"You know," Bryant said, "I appreciate all the schoolboy soldiers cheering like hell and marching around campus. But maybe you could get a few civvies in here."

"We're making progress on that. This is the first semester in the history of this college that we're not requiring compulsory military training. I just don't know how long it's going to last. The ex-students like it the other way."

Harrington fixed his eyes on the coach and saw a rare smile taking shape at the edges of his mouth.

"Coach Bryant, I hate to put this on you. But I'm really depending on the football team to pick this place back up."

Bryant frowned but tried to remain calm.

"Oh, I know it's going to take some time. But I'm afraid, Paul, that if we don't turn the football team around pretty soon, potential Aggies will keep going somewhere else. God knows the enrollment is up at just about every other Southwest Conference school.''

Bryant peered through the window and tapped a cigarette on his fingernail. "Let me get this straight. You're telling me that the future of this college might just depend on wins and losses. Is that right?''

"That's right.''

"Hell, it seems you've got more problems than me. Besides, football was a losing proposition long before I got here.''

"I know we've got problems. But—''

"Then why don't you straighten out all the other BS?''

"Because we're handcuffed.''

"Dr. Harrington, I'm afraid you're asking a lot of me. I just got here.''

Bryant stood and walked to the back of the room, where he took several long pulls from his cigarette. His frustration with Texas A&M was growing by the second, and he'd been there only seven months. He could already see that recruiting stud players on a regular basis would be a constant battle. It quickly became evident that every school in the state was ganging up on the Aggies. Recruiters called it a cow college.

But Bryant was now married to this dung pile and he needed to make hay.

Turning toward Harrington, he said, "I'll take on some of the pressure. But I need some assurances. Are you ready?''

"Yes sir.''

"OK. I don't want my football players marching to meals anymore. I don't want my bottle babies like John Crow getting hazed by a bunch of buzz-cut upperclassmen. I keep hearin' that hazing gets pretty hairy around here. I don't want John Crow running off to LSU in the middle of the night because the military rats put him in a hole and pissed on him.''

"I can agree to that.''

"No, I want it in writing. No more hazing of the football team. Period. Hell, I do enough hazing as it is. Second, I want my football team eating alone—away from the soldiers. I need to put my own form of discipline on these boys night and day.''

"You have my assurances and I'll put it in writing.''

Bryant nodded and turned toward the door. He could feel hardwood beneath his feet, then marble, then the concrete sidewalk outside. Just what he needed, more pressure. He could never imagine expectations being so high so soon at a place where losing had become such a stubborn habit.

• • •

Bebes Stallings was the first player on the practice field fifteen minutes before three o'clock, and he spotted Bryant with hands clasped behind his waist, walking in tight circles around a football that had been placed at the fifty-yard line. Moving closer, he could hear the coach singing. Stallings made out the song but couldn't believe his ears.

"Jesus loves me, yes, I know, for the Bible tells me so . . ."

Bryant either was ignoring Stallings or didn't see him. But the singing continued for several minutes, until most of the team had gathered. Players wore dirty and wet game uniforms that had been lying in front of the lockers since Saturday night. The student managers had been ordered not to wash the pants and jerseys, which soon raised an acrid smell of sweat and ammonia. Bryant got a whiff of their sour outfits, and it pleased him.

His eyes suddenly were filled with fury. "We're gonna pretend the Texas Tech game never ended. There'll be no need for calisthenics. I want the offense on this side of the ball and the defense on that side. Boys, buckle up."

Smokey Harper and Billy Pickard assumed their normal positions behind the coaches.

"You guys get on over to the sideline," Bryant said, pointing. "We'll have no need for trainers today. If a boy's gonna bleed, a boy's gonna bleed."

Led by Elwood Kettler, the offense quickly gained control of the scrimmage. Halfbacks Joe Schero and Don Kachtik gained large chunks of yardage, and Kettler completed a few wobbly passes to Jack Pardee and Bennie Sinclair. The offense scored two quick touchdowns before Bryant devised an unusual strategy. He started adding players to the defense.

"I've seen Coach do some crazy things, but nothing like this," Kettler whispered to Stallings.

"Coach might be slippin' a little," Bebes said.

Bryant added more and more players to the defense. Kettler's lower back began to ache as tacklers piled on. Dizziness was setting in. Sliding out of bounds, he spotted a puddle created by an overnight rain shower. He dropped his face into the water and began slurping. After the defensive unit grew to twenty players, Kettler finally was stopped inches short on a fourth-and-one sweep.

"Goddamn, it's about time!" Bryant yelled.

He marched toward Lawrence Winkler and grabbed the tackle by the

152

face mask. Winkler had received consistently good grades for his blocking the previous two seasons. But Bryant was suspicious of every Aggie who'd played under Ray George, whose practices were short and sweet. The new coach had carefully reviewed the film of the final five losses of 1953, finding the opposing team more physical in each one.

Bryant grabbed guard Marvin Tate's helmet and pulled it over his ears and buckled the chin strap. Winkler barely had time to brace himself before Bryant was in a three-point stance, ready to charge. Winkler was neither as quick nor as strong as the forty-one-year-old man who rocked his sternum with a forearm thrust that sent the tackle toppling backward, the back of his helmet smacking the ground.

"Stand up, you sonofabitch."

Before he could steady himself, Winkler was down again.

Winkler wasn't the first Bryant pupil to discover he couldn't block, much less manhandle, the coach. At Maryland and Kentucky, Bryant had taken on players with bare hands and rarely bothered to buckle on a helmet. He worked with the ruthless abandon of a prizefighter. Bob Gain was considered the best lineman to ever wear a Kentucky uniform. But he couldn't avoid Bryant's wrath.

At six-foot-five and 240 pounds, Gain was considerably bigger and stronger than his coach, but a common sight was Bryant dropping into a stance and plowing through him. It had gotten to be humiliating. A few nights before Christmas in 1950, Gain was riding around Lexington with a carload of teammates when he insisted that Dude Hennessey stop the car at Bryant's house. Gain informed the boys that he intended to whip Bryant's butt. Bets were quickly placed, most in favor of the coach.

As the players crouched in the bushes, Gain garnered the courage to approach the house.

Bryant answered after a few knocks and stared icily at the visitor. "What the hell do you want?"

"Ah, nothing, Coach. I just wanted to wish you a Merry Christmas."

Player after player had become acquainted with Bryant's intimidating style and psychological maneuvering. He controlled the players through exhaustion and frustration. Now, after knocking Winkler down a third time, Bryant gathered the Aggies around him and then gazed into the distance at the clay brown buildings and the cadets marching across campus.

"When shit comes up to your neck, you need to suck your guts up. Needless to say, you played like shit the other night."

Long after darkness settled over the campus, the Aggies completed their four-hour scrimmage and some of the boys lay on the ground for thirty minutes before summoning the energy to limp back to the locker room. They drank from the shower nozzles until their stomachs could hold no more water. Then they puked into the drains.

. . .

The next Saturday night, Kettler was intercepted three times and the Aggies coughed up two fumbles in a 14–6 loss to Oklahoma A&M, a team that didn't bother to throw a single pass but gained 288 rushing yards.

Two days later, Bryant approached senior guards Marvin Tate and Sid Theriot in the lunchroom.

"I need to have a meeting with y'all boys in a few minutes."

"Yessir, Coach," Tate responded.

After Bryant walked away, Theriot grabbed Tate by the shoulder. "Oh, shit, Marvin, what does he want with us? What the hell did we do?"

Later, Bryant appeared deeply troubled as he sat down at the table across from the two players. "Boys, y'all are both seniors and you've been around here for a long time. I need to know what is wrong with this football team."

The players were instantly suspicious. Not once since his arrival had Bryant's tone been so abiding. This was not the same man who'd shouted and cussed and whipped them like mules.

Tate, however, sensed an opening. For months he'd listened to teammates complaining about the brutal ways of Bryant and his staff.

"Coach, with all due respect, players are getting tired of being cussed all the time."

Theriot looked at Tate as if he'd just burped in the coach's face.

Tate cleared his throat and continued. "I've never been called so many names in my life, Coach. Every time I turn around, one of the coaches is making fun of somebody's mother."

"I've been guilty myself of swearing."

"You gotta realize, Coach, we've got some boys here who've lived the straight and narrow. Coach, Bennie Sinclair wouldn't say 'hell' if his pants were on fire. He's more religious than John the Baptist."

A few months earlier, a carload of football players had been riding around campus, telling dirty jokes, when Bennie interrupted: "Does anyone in this car know any jokes that are funny?"

Bennie had been raised a devout Baptist in the piney woods town of Mineola. He was a straight-A student, an all-state end, and one of the most recruited high school seniors of 1951. He was months from graduating from A&M with a double major in petroleum and mechanical engineering and held a 4.0 grade average. Not many football players could say they'd been selected to the *Who's Who Among Students in American Universities and Colleges.*

Bennie also had the misfortune of being five minutes late to Bryant's first team meeting.

"You sonofabitch!" the coach had hollered. "Next time you're late, you'll be runnin' stadium steps till the Fourth of July."

Bennie tried to explain. "Coach, I had an important lab and I ran all the way across the campus." But Bryant continued to stare holes through him

Now as Bryant listened to Tate's suggestions, he tapped the table with his right index finger. Then his eyes widened.

"Boys, you're right about the cussing. Our mamas and our papas didn't raise us to talk like this."

He studied the ceiling and snapped his fingers. "Tell ya what we're gonna do. We're gonna start us a cuss bucket. Every time a player cusses, he'll throw in a quarter. An assistant coach, it'll cost him a dollar. Me, I'll throw in ten bucks."

"Yeah—"

"Then at the end of the season we'll have a party. Think of all of the stuff we could buy with that damn money. Bryant smiled and told the boys he'd see them at the afternoon practice.

The Aggies were thirty minutes into the workout when a rash of offensive mistakes inspired a volcanic eruption. Profanity rolled like thunder from Bryant's tongue.

The coach then spotted Bennie Sinclair a few feet away. "Shoot, Bennie, that's gonna cost me," he blurted. "I'll pay for every word of that."

Bryant's right hand dipped into a pants pocket and found two crinkled hundred-dollar bills. He tossed them both toward Billy Pickard.

"That oughta cover me for a while, Billy. When that's gone, run me a tab."

· · ·

Tom Tipps and Coach Elmer were waiting for Bryant when he arrived at his office an hour before daybreak. The coaches had been watching game films of the Georgia Bulldogs, and now they were itching to tell Bryant of an important discovery.

"You boys look like you've been up all night drinking coffee," Bryant said, noting the stains on Coach Elmer's T-shirt.

"God, Coach, you're not gonna believe it," Elmer said, his hands shaking. He flipped a button on the projector, and it whirred like a sewing machine. The sixteen-millimeter film was wound on a large metal spool that shimmied as it spun. Elmer had marked with a red crayon the spot where he would restart the film.

"Look at this," he said, flipping off the ceiling light.

Georgia quarterback Jim Harper was set under center, and he pivoted quickly to pitch the ball. The halfback gained four yards around the right end.

On the next play, Harper retreated five steps into the pocket and completed a soft pass to the tight end. Then he handed off to the fullback at left guard as Elmer shut down the projector.

"Notice anything?" he said to Bryant.

A cigarette butt glowed through the darkness.

"Rerun it."

They intently watched the three plays—the right end sweep, the pass to the tight end, and the fullback plunge.

"The quarterback's doin' something funny with his feet," Bryant said.

"That's right!" Elmer howled, slapping Tipps on the back. "Tom here noticed it first. And we've been peein' in our pants to show ya."

The Georgia quarterback had passed for 239 yards in the first two games of the season, and the Bulldogs had won both. But opposing defenses failed to notice that he was tipping the plays with his feet.

On passes and running plays to the right, Harper's habit was placing his right foot behind him as he set up behind center. This allowed him to pull away from center faster. On passing plays, he was able to retreat more quickly into the pocket.

If a running play was called to the left, Harper set up behind center like most quarterbacks—with both feet parallel to the line.

Shaking his head, Bryant muttered, "I can't believe the doggone Georgia coaches haven't noticed it. But I guess I won't be tellin' Wally Butts."

Bryant and Butts, the Georgia coach, had become close friends while competing against each other in the SEC. When Kentucky had played in Athens, Bryant dined on black-eyed peas and corn bread prepared by Winnie Butts and, conversely, Butts would join the Bryants for Friday-night supper when the Bulldogs played in Lexington.

For the third game of the 1954 season, the Aggies traveled with only twenty-five healthy players to Georgia. The afternoon game would be played in ninety-degree heat mixed with high humidity. Student manager Billy Pickard filled a trough with ice on the sideline for Billy Schroeder, who would lie in it during breaks from the game. Doctors were still trying to convince Billy to give up football.

The Aggies were twenty-point underdogs, and Bryant knew why. Georgia had more talent than Texas Tech and Oklahoma A&M combined. After arriving in Athens, Bryant was approached by Atlanta newspapermen Harry Mehre and Ed Danforth.

"Coach, where's the rest of your team?" Mehre asked.

"This *is* the rest of my team."

"Well, uh, why didn't you bring more guys?"

"Because these are the only ones who want to play."

The reporters walked away shaking their heads.

Bryant couldn't wait for kickoff. His little secret would be a powerful weapon.

Linebacker Don Kachtik had been informed on Thursday of the coaches' discovery. He viewed the Georgia game film and was shown how the Georgia quarterback tipped the plays. Kachtik's job on defense would be relaying signals to his teammates. If Harper lined up with his right foot back, Kachtik would place his left hand on his left hip. The defensive backfield would rotate to the left, expecting either a run in that direction or a pass. If Harper had his feet parallel to the line, the defense would rotate to the right, anticipating a run that way.

The plan worked to near-perfection. Kachtik intercepted two passes and Harper was held to sixteen passing yards. Three minutes before halftime, Kachtik's second interception was returned eighteen yards to the Georgia thirty-yard line. After a ten-yard completion to Pardee, Kettler lofted a high, wobbly pass to Stallings, who took the ball away from two defensive backs at the nine-yard line and stumbled into the end zone.

A&M won 6–0.

Bryant and Smokey danced an Irish jig in the locker room, and cigars were passed all around. Bryant handed over wads of cash to several players.

"Boys, when we get back to Texas, the girls are yours tonight!" he yelled. "Don't let anybody take 'em away from you."

As the boys boarded the chartered flight, they were handed beer, cig-arettes, and cigars. They celebrated that night as if they'd won a national championship.

Monday morning, Bryant called his old friend in Athens to tell him about the problem with his quarterback's feet.

"You silly sonofabitch!" Butts hollered into the phone. "You're just braggin'." Then he slammed down the receiver.

"Bragging?"

It had been a long time since anyone had accused him of that.

15

Aggies

When you make a mistake, admit it; learn from it and
don't repeat it.

—PAUL "BEAR" BRYANT

OCTOBER 10, 1954

When the boys weren't playing or practicing football or running stadium steps, they were searching for ways to have fun. This was a challenging task since the A&M student body lacked women. In years past,
males had danced with males at school functions. But Bryant's boys were
far too macho for that form of public humiliation.

As the pickup turned the corner and crept along the alley beside the
stadium, the boys slumped in the seat and pulled their caps low. Jack
Pardee flipped off the headlights.

"You sure you wanna do this?" Pardee whispered.

"I'm sure," Weasel Watson said.

A warm and sticky breeze drifted through the windows and reminded
them of summer nights down at Matagorda Bay, an inlet from the Gulf of
Mexico about two hundred miles south. The moist air raised lines of per-

spiration on their foreheads, but the boys were sweating for other reasons, too.

Several late-model cars were parked below Kyle Field, and most had full gas tanks. The coaches were working their usual late hours inside stadium offices.

The boys targeted a shiny dark four-door sedan that seemed a football field long. Pardee eased the dusty Ford into a parking space, and Weasel reached for the gas can and a green garden hose that had been shortened to four feet by one whack of a hunting knife. A single eighty-watt bulb dangled from the ridged concrete ceiling, sputtering and casting long shadows across the basement lot and making it difficult to determine the make and model of each car. Many were white four-door Chevys with black-wall tires that were the property of the state but, thanks to creative paperwork, had fallen into the hands of Aggie coaches. As they crept through the quiet lot, Jack and Weasel prayed they wouldn't disturb any automobile being driven by Coach Bryant.

At the moment, each boy had a few quarters jingling in his jean pockets, enough money for about four rounds at Fort Shiloh, a local honky-tonk where the country-and-western music was loud, the Lone Star beer cold, and the women slightly loose. What they lacked was enough money to push the needle on the Ford's fuel gauge above E. Hitchhiking three miles to Fort Shiloh was a boring chore, and besides, a gassed-up vehicle was necessary to pick up girls. If they got lucky, they'd drive the girls to a secluded parking spot by the air base where they could drink a few more beers and neck.

"This is crazy," Pardee said hoarsely as Watson plunged the green tubing down the esophagus of the gas tank.

Watson took a deep breath, arced his neck, and then sucked on the hose. After pulling it from his lips and exhaling, he jammed the tubing into the empty can. The gasoline streamed like warm piss from a grazing cow. The first time Weasel had tried to siphon gas years ago, he'd wound up with a mouthful.

"God, hurry," Pardee said, his eyes scanning the basement. The thought of being caught red-handed by Bryant almost made him pee in his pants. Watson finally removed the hose when the last drop had been drained.

"Let's get out of here," Pardee said. To his dismay, though, Watson slid beneath the car and began prying a plug from its underbelly. A mechanic would uncap the fuel tank if he wanted to clean out the dirt. But Weasel had other ideas. He wanted everything but the fumes.

"We're suckin' her dry," he whispered.

"Dammit, Weasel, get your butt outta there!" Pardee almost shouted, his voice echoing against the basement walls.

Grease and dirt smudged Watson's face as he reemerged with a can filled to the brim. He smiled broadly. "Shoot, we got enough for two trucks," he said. "We'll be runnin' up and down this highway for a long time."

The pickup's back tires spun gravel as Pardee tromped the accelerator and watched the dark stadium disappear through the rearview mirror. The boys figured it to be a clean getaway, given that nobody chased them. Pulling onto a deserted dirt road about five minutes later, they poured gasoline into the truck's thirsty tank, slapped each other on the back, and headed off to Fort Shiloh. Nothing could stop them now.

An hour later, Bear Bryant slid behind the wheel of the dark blue Cadillac and inserted the key into the ignition. He was the last to leave the stadium, the assistant coaches having been excused a half hour earlier. He heard the starter grinding and the engine coughing, and as he eyed the fuel gauge he could see the needle stuck below empty. The silence was broken with loud curses.

"Who the hell used all the gas? I filled this damn car up yesterday."

◆ ◆ ◆

Dennis Goehring loved to raise hell on the football field. That didn't mean, however, that he was ready to rest when he got back to the dorm room.

A footlocker was situated at the head of the bunk beds, and Dennis had been hiding some things there unbeknownst to just about everyone. He cracked the lid and peered at the loose collection of belongings—old shoes, two footballs, a bottle of Wild Turkey, three *Playboys,* and a box of Trojan rubbers. He began to dig.

Behind him and looking over his shoulder was Lloyd Hale, the small but scrappy Aggie center who wore a fresh flattop.

"You're a liar," Hale said. "A dad-gum liar. I'm never gonna believe a thing you say."

Before Hale could utter another word, Goehring turned and casually handed him a long stick of the most potent dynamite to be found in that part of Texas.

"If I'm lyin' you're dyin'," Goehring said, erupting into a spooky laugh.

Hale's hands began to shake. "Where'd you get this? This ain't funny."

"We were diggin' wells last summer," Dennis said nonchalantly. "Naturally, we needed dynamite to fracture the rock. So one day, I just stole a batch."

"Then put it up," Hale said, handing him the stick. "You're crazier than a henhouse rat."

Bobby Jack Lockett and Bobby Drake Keith walked quietly into the room. They had just returned from practice. "Is that what I think it is?" Lockett said. "God damn, Dennis, you mean I've been sleepin' two feet from that shit all semester!"

Keith had been Dennis's roommate the previous year and had slept with his head only a few feet from the same locker for two semesters. Now he felt the hair rising on the back of his neck.

Dennis's mischief-loving nature was widely known. The squatty guard with beefsteaks for forearms had virtually set a campus record a year earlier by doing more push-ups, running more laps, and marching more hours in the bullring than any other Aggie freshman. Upperclassmen had, in fact, grown tired of disciplining Dennis.

Cradling a handful of silver blasting caps, Dennis turned to the boys.

"Oh, shit," Hale said. "Put it away."

Bobby Drake and Bobby Keith made a quick exit. But Hale stayed, knowing he was the last line of defense between his crazy friend and the building's foundation.

Pranks were a way of life at Texas A&M and had been for decade upon decade. The absence of women seemed to stir up the boys' testosterone. Though football allowed the players to vent some of their frustration, some of them were still wound up at the end of the day. Dennis loved being the ringleader.

Like all of the dorms at Texas A&M, Walton Hall had no air-conditioning. So windows were raised most of the time and the screens had been peeled off. Residents had to be on guard for water balloons that sailed out of nowhere at all hours.

Waters fights were minor, though. A favorite pasttime was plucking a cadaver's arm from the biology vat and toting the formaldehyde-soaked limb back to the dorm. An unsuspecting Aggie would awaken to the grisly appendage being waved in his face, often with a lit cigarette stuck between the fingers.

After the boys hit the bars and drank a few beers, Dennis liked to culminate the night by returning to Walton Hall and belching into Redbird Granberry's face.

Redbird would snap awake and blurt, "Your breath stinks."

"Just good beer."

Most of the creative capers originated in Dennis's room, where nude photos of Marilyn Monroe adorned every wall. Hugh Hefner had launched the controversial *Playboy* magazine in 1954, paying the grand sum of $500 for the rights to all of Marilyn's nude photographs. Soon it seemed every red-blooded boy in America wanted a glimpse of the luminescent Marilyn. Dennis's favorite was Marilyn arching coyly on a red velvet drape, her body angled to hide her pubic area but her breasts fully exposed. Many of the Aggies fell asleep at night and awoke in the morning, thinking of Marilyn. Thanks to America's new sex bomb, *Playboy's* circulation soared to 100,000 subscribers by the end of 1954. Hefner could thank the Aggies for doing their share at fifty cents a pop.

Dennis carefully broke the dynamite stick in half and began attaching the blasting caps. Hale leaned over his right shoulder and noticed his friend was shaking. Sweat oozed from behind his ears.

"Why the hell you so dad-gum nervous?"

"Because I've never done this."

"Great."

Dennis held the dynamite in one hand and wiped away a sweat droplet from his nose. He slowly crimped the long fuse into the blasting cap and held the stick to the light, wires dangling like water moccasins from a willow tree.

"Good," Dennis said confidently. "Looks good. Time for a test."

The boys found Lockett and Keith pacing nervously and talking quietly on the front sidewalk.

"Come on, boys," Dennis said, gesturing like a cavalry leader. "We've got some shit we need to blow up."

Lockett and Keith reluctantly joined them but walked several paces to the rear. Beside Walton Hall was a dusty half-filled parking lot. With nothing stirring, and no one in sight, Dennis propped the dynamite next to a sidewalk more than thirty feet from the nearest car. His hands shook and he cussed the matches that kept blowing out. The others were already running toward the dorm when fire finally licked the fuse.

"Yee-haw!" Dennis yelled as he took off chasing the others. They dashed through the front door and down the hallway to his room. Slamming the door, Lockett flipped off the lights. They gathered at the open window, breathing hard.

"How long?" Hale asked.

"About another minute," said Dennis.

Then they spotted two cadets strolling down the sidewalk. Moments earlier, they had departed the Sbisa Hall Center en route to one of the corps dorms. Now, they were moving directly into the path of destruction.

"Thirty seconds," Dennis whispered.

"What are you gonna do?" Hale asked, panic in his voice.

Dennis stuck his head through the window and yelled. "Run, you son-ofabitches!"

Suspecting another water fight, the cadets smiled and waved at the young footballers.

A white light split the darkness and the cannonlike thunder rolled across the campus. The initial shock wave knocked Dennis off-kilter. He was amazed at the raw power of the blast. The cadets were now sprinting the other way, past Sbisa Hall and across the parade grounds and far into the night. They wouldn't stop running until they ran out of breath, and by then the lights of campus were dull specks.

"Goddamn!" someone yelled from the next room.

Within seconds, the rest of the residents were spilling onto the sidewalk, their eyes combing the grounds for the perpetrators. They searched for clues and wondered where the rascals had run. In the parking lot, they found shards of two shattered windshields. Several dorm windows were smashed along the first floor.

They gathered around a hole that was blown deep and wide in the dry earth.

"What in God's name?"

"It's gotta be dynamite."

Several months would pass before word leaked as to the identity of the dynamiters. Those with intimate knowledge of the blast were now hiding in a darkened room, paralyzed into silence. Even the garrulous Goehring was speechless. They sprawled on the floor, never moving, until the crowd went home.

• • •

Women were finally allowed on campus on weekends, but even then, they were banned from the dormitories. Any deviation could result in an automatic expulsion.

"The problem around here," Weasel Watson once said, "is that most of my fellow students are forced to use their bodies like amusement parks."

So the cadets routinely burned up Highway 6 between College Station and Waco, where the Baylor girls were charming and classically southern—just what you'd expect from a small, rich private school in Texas. Baylor girls were generally attracted to A&M boys since they seemed more rugged and manly than the Baylor boys. The problem was that Baylor girls were a bit goody-goody and, even when they agreed to park and neck, had to be home by nine. Males were never allowed in the girls' dorms, except through a fire escape that could be reached from a stout tree limb. Unlike the Baylor boys, the Aggies didn't mind the climb.

A round-the-clock option for carnal knowledge was seventy miles down the two-lane asphalt strip in La Grange, where the Chicken Ranch offered young and voluptuous women for three bucks an hour. Or the boys could stop halfway to La Grange at another whorehouse in Brenham that sometimes offered free beer. Many of the Aggies, however, preferred the Chicken Ranch because a good number of the working girls were University of Texas coeds. UT girls were the prettiest and most fragrant on earth. But they were snobbish to Aggies and wouldn't give them the time of day on the sidewalks of Austin. An Aggie's money, however, was always welcome in La Grange, where the UT girls were pleased to see them.

When the boys were out of money, they had another option closer to home and her name was Nadine.

She was twenty-something and worked at a dime store in nearby Navasota. She was so popular with the Aggies that she spent enough time on campus to earn two degrees.

Nadine became rooted in Aggie folklore one night when a cadet, fed up with being horny, stuffed her into a laundry bag and hauled her up two flights of dormitory stairs. He was halted in midsmuggle when an upperclass officer, also known as a bull, hollered, "Hey, piss head, Ten hut!"

Shifting the booty onto his left shoulder, the cadet snapped to attention and saluted the officer without dropping Nadine. The shapely laundry bag never wiggled, and the cadet managed to smuggle her into his room without the bulls catching him.

One night after football practice, Weasel Watson had a surreptitious meeting with Nadine and convinced her to come over to the athletic dorm. A hour later, they met at the back door, where Weasel had been patiently waiting, bag in hand.

"Darlin'," he said. "The boys are waitin' upstairs. I hope you realize it's been a while for some of these fellers."

She giggled as Weasel cloaked her in the long cotton bag and hoisted her over his shoulder. The little running back proved to be strong for his size. Hauling his prize up three flights of stairs, he never broke stride, never seemed short of breath, and whistled the "Aggie War Hymn" most of the way.

Topping the stairway and emerging into the hall, Weasel removed the sack from Nadine as a line began to form. The boys shuffled their feet and seemed nervous about this famous guest now in their midst.

"You boys have fun," Weasel said. "I'm asking y'all one favor. Don't let Bobby Ray get to her early. His pecker's too big and he'll wear the poor girl out."

Trysts with Nadine soon became the talk of Aggieland. The campus newspaper ran a picture of what the editors believed to be the back of Nadine's head. The *Battalion* caption read: "Nadine gives S&H green stamps."

. . .

While the players found creative ways to spend their limited time away from football, the work never seemed finished for Billy Pickard, the student assistant trainer whose job description should have read: "Fix everything in sight, including broken bodies." He'd recently been handed the unofficial title of equipment manager.

Some days, Billy had to tape all of the ankles, wash all of the uniforms, and shoo the boys onto the practice field five minutes before Bryant arrived. Billy also had to mend some broken hearts.

A week after beating Georgia, the Aggies had Houston on the ropes and victory was a quarterback sneak away. Trailing the Cougars 10–7, Kettler plunged from the five-yard line to the six-inch line with eleven seconds left to play. Then the football mysteriously disappeared from the pile.

Aggie players pointed their fingers and accused the Houston nose tackle

166

of flinging the ball into the end zone stands. The officials seemed befuddled and forgot to stop the clock.

"Hey, Ref, we can't run a play without the ball!" Kettler hollered.

The Aggies offense was lined up and ready to go when the final gun sounded. Bryant ran onto the field waving his arms. He confronted the referee and shouted, "How can you end the game when you don't know where the goddamn ball is?"

"Coach, the game is over."

"Where's the ball?"

"I don't know."

One by one, Bryant grabbed the Aggie players and began shoving them toward the dressing room.

"Get off the field," he growled. "I'm tired of lookin' at these cheaters."

The Aggies were heavy underdogs against TCU the following Saturday at Kyle Field, and the 14–0 halftime deficit was proof of the imbalance. But in the third quarter, Kettler led the offense on a six-play ninety-yard touchdown drive. Thanks to one-platoon rules of that era, teams were not allowed to substitute a kicker for extra points. So Kettler, the best kicker on the field at the time, was left with the chore. He hooked the kick past the upright, and the Aggies trailed 14–6.

Minutes later, the Aggies drove to the TCU fourteen but couldn't convert on fourth down. Then TCU sophomore Jim Swink dashed seventy-nine yards for a touchdown and the game seemed hopelessly out of reach at 21–6.

In 1954, Bryant's team lacked some important qualities like size, speed, depth, talent, and experience, just to name a few. But A&M did possess one important intangible called resiliency. After Herb Wolf recovered a fumble at the TCU thirty-three, Don Kachtik scored five players later. Kettler's kick was good this time, and TCU's lead was now eight points.

After a TCU punt, Kettler marched the offense down the field again with Kachtik and Joe Schero eating up yards between the tackles. Eight plays into the drive, Kettler sneaked over from the one. Rules of the time didn't allow for a two-point conversion, so Kettler's kick made it 21–20.

The game ended on that score. Texas A&M, a twenty-one-point underdog, had lost to one of the nation's top teams because a PAT kick had sailed right. Week after week, the Aggies were playing teams right down to the final gun only to have the football gods laugh in their faces.

Wearing face masks was a mistake from the start. Instead of choosing the single iron bar that had been invented three years earlier by Cleveland Browns coach Paul Brown, the Aggies ordered the awkward-looking two-inch Plexiglas shield that would soon be junkpiled. Even worse, somebody installed them upside down.

After six games, the Plexiglas was starting to work loose at the screws. The Friday night before the Baylor game, Pickard had worked later than usual. Somehow he'd arrived at the notion of soldering the Plexiglas tighter to the helmets. He toiled well past midnight, wielding the soldering iron as the smell of the metallic cement permeated the locker room and made his head spin a little.

Billy would be making the trip to Waco without Smokey. He'd been knocked out of commission during a practice by whiz-bang freshman halfback Ken Hall, who had flattened him from behind. The old trainer was standing on the sideline, smoking a cigar and cussing midnight last calls, when he got trampled. He was placed on the shelf with Johnnie Walker and Jim Beam.

Saturday morning, Billy and Dr. R. H. Harrison, the team physician, had no trouble finding seats on the bus that carried only twenty-five able-bodied boys to Waco. Watching the flat countyside pass by, Billy thought about his handiwork with the face masks and felt confident. But an hour before kickoff he felt like puking. His heart paused as he saw the face masks jiggling like Jell-O.

"God," Billy groaned to himself. He instantly knew the problem. The hot solder had melted parts of the Plexiglas.

Baylor fans were quick to insult. "You boys oughta peel off them sissy face guards!" a fan yelled. Baylor boys didn't wear face masks, and the prevailing opinion in 1954 was that real men didn't need them.

A half hour before kickoff, Bryant sauntered toward Billy, a half-grin forming, and Billy couldn't remember the last time he had seen Coach smile.

"The news is worse than you think," Bryant said, starting to chuckle. "Billy, you also went off and left the dad-gum mouthpieces back in College Station. Hell's bells, boy, you're more forgetful than Grandma."

The NCAA had recently handed down strict rules about the use of mouth protectors. So the Aggies were left with but one choice; they'd have to borrow discarded, chewed-up mouthpieces from the Baylor team.

In spite of the injuries, the losing, and the chronic pain, many players forged ahead. Senior guard Marvin Tate had suffered torn ligaments in his right ankle when he was blindsided by a blocker a week earlier in the Houston loss. His other ankle was so badly sprained that he could barely walk to practice, much less suit up. But he was sitting on the trainers' table before kickoff with ankles so swollen he couldn't tie his shoelaces.

"What do you propose?" Billy said.

"Just tape my shoes on," Tate said. "Then I'll think of somethin'."

Billy could feel loose fluids floating beneath Tate's skin. It took several rolls of tape to secure his high-top shoes over the bloated joints.

Billy Schroeder was feeling weaker by the game but tried not to show it. He still suffered from the effects of the near-fatal heatstroke. His weight had plummeted and even the starchy meals in Sbisa Hall couldn't put the pounds back on. Schroeder was no longer the lumberjack who had man-handled opposing players the previous season. But he never stopped trying.

Fullback Bob Easley had come to terms with the pain in his knees years earlier. On game days, his ally was the needle. Sitting stiffly on the training table, he studied the ceiling as Dr. Harrison pulled the six-inch needle from his bag and began to probe the mushy right joint. Easley felt the needle scrape the bottom of his kneecap, then the rush of hot liquid. Within seconds, he felt warm from head to toe.

Breathing deeply, Easley said, "Doc, that sure feels fine." He seemed to be floating in space.

Dr. Harrison then inserted the needle into the left knee and slowly worked the area beneath the patella. Fifteen minutes later, Easley would be warming up on the sideline, preparing for the game, feeling numb from his hips to his feet.

Elwood was another player who carried on in spite of the pain and four broken bones in his lower back. The Aggie quarterback still managed to lead the conference in total yardage and was second behind Rice All-America Dicky Maegle in scoring.

Charles Hall was trying to forget that he'd dislocated his right shoulder badly during a midweek practice. The joint had been taped for support, and Hall could barely raise his arm above his head. Wednesday, with his arm dangling to his side, he'd been driven to the hospital, where a young doctor had popped the shoulder back into place.

"Watch this," the doctor said to an emergency room intern. He wrenched Hall's arm, pulling the joint back out of socket. Hall, wringing wet with sweat, let out a scream that could be heard for four blocks. Then the doctor quickly reset it.

"I just wanted to show you how I did it," the doctor said, winking.

"I ain't no guinea pig!" Hall yelled. "You crazy sonofabitch."

Redbird Granberry's shoulder continued to pop in and out like a jack-in-the-box. When it dislocated on the first play of the game, Billy ran onto the field, stuck his foot beneath Redbird's armpit, and yanked on his arm. As usual, the shoulder popped back into place and Redbird didn't miss a down.

Minutes later, Don Kachtik rambled down the field like a cattle truck loose on a steep hill. As he piled into the Baylor kick returner, his nose spurted blood. Billy and Dr. Harrison ran toward the fallen player, who appeared at first to be unconscious. Dr. Harrison quickly snapped an ammonia capsule under the boy's nose, and he began to wiggle.

"Get that shit out of my face!" Kachtik howled. "I'm not asleep!"

No, but his nose had been shoved an inch to the left and his jersey was turning crimson. Billy and Dr. Harrison grunted in unison as they wrapped their arms around the fallen fullback's waist and walked him to the sideline. Kachtik's face mask had been shattered. The student manager who was sent to retrieve the helmet found it full of blood. As it was carried to the sideline, the crown leaked blood through the airholes, staining the grass.

"Why the hell'd you take Kachtik out of the game?" Bryant yelled.

"I think he's hurt, Coach," Billy replied.

Dr. Harrison inserted tongue compressors into both nostrils and maneuvered the lumpy patch of skin and cartilage back into the center of Kachtik's face. But his nose still didn't look right, and likely never would.

"It'll have to do for now."

As the doctor finished his work, the blood started to flow again. Billy stuffed gauze up the right nostril, and Dr. Harrison tried to dam the left one. It took five minutes to halt the flow.

"Can you play?" Billy yelled above the crowd. "Coach wants you back in there."

"I think I can. Hell, I'm all right, Smokey."

"I'm Billy."

"OK, Billy, whatever you say."

As Billy shuttled the news to Bryant, Kachtik's body slowly drooped to the right. His shoulder pads slid along the bench's metal back support until he was flat on his back, and as he looked up through the white haze he saw a blonde Baylor cheerleader standing over him. She wore a tight cream-colored cashmere sweater with a large felt green *B* sewn to the front.

Her hair was pulled into a ponytail, and she had sky blue eyes. High puffy clouds floated about her head, and Kachtik thought he was seeing an angel.

"You don't look all right to me," she said, leaning over the bench, eyeing the blood-soaked jersey. "Ew."

Seconds later, the big fullback's eyes rolled back into his head.

"What the hell am I going to tell Coach Bryant?" Billy muttered on finding Kachtik sound asleep. "This just won't do."

Minutes later, Billy rubbed his chin and plopped into a chair next to the training table. Kachtik, now awake but still groggy, had been carried on a stretcher into the locker room. Billy had heard a story about a Texas halfback who played against Rice with a broken nose. To protect the nose, the trainers had devised a mask that covered his face from forehead to chin. Of course, the Longhorns were light-years ahead of the Aggies in training and medical treatment and Frank Medina was the most competent trainer in the state, maybe the entire country.

At age twenty, Billy knew he was no Frank Medina. But thinking fast was something you just did with Bear Bryant on your back.

"I've gotta find a way to get this boy back in the game in the second half," Billy said.

"It'll take a miracle," the doctor replied. "He's lost a lot of blood."

Billy began to dig through a large green trunk. He found a clear plastic mask with two round holes for the eyes and a ridge for the nose.

"God, this thing's been rattlin' round in this trunk since Junction."

Ironically, Aggie fullback Bob Smith had broken his nose during a 1950 game against Baylor and the trainers doubted he would be able to play the following week against seventh-ranked SMU. But Smith was a rugged 215-pounder who had wide shoulders and a slim waist and ran like a freight train. A plastic mask was ordered from a medical supply company in Dallas. It was a clear, hard shell that could have passed for a NHL goalie's mask. Not only did Smith play against SMU; he rushed for a school record 297 yards and the Aggies won 25–20, leading sportswriters to dub him the Masked Marvel.

It was Smith's mask that Billy had found.

"Billy, you got Kachtik ready to play?" Bryant yelled as he paced.

"Yessir, Coach. We're gettin' close."

Bryant was confounded over the shrinking number of healthy bodies. Injuries had posed a weekly crisis, and the Aggies had yet to suit up more than twenty-six players. Bryant had kept former student manager Troy

Summerlin in uniform for insurance but didn't plan to send the 145-pounder into action until an emergency arose.

"Hurry up, Billy!" Bryant yelled.

In the first half, Baylor's enormous front line had run over the Aggies' defense. Quarterback Billy Hooper was seven-for-seven passing. But the determined Aggies had scored a touchdown on a pass from Kettler to Billy Pete Huddleston, and the score was tied at seven.

"Fishin' line," Billy whispered. "I've gotta have some fishin' line in this box someplace."

Then, with the mask stuck to Kachtik's face, Billy poked two holes in the clear plastic, and he inserted and then looped the fishing wire. He tied the line to the leather chin strap and buckled Kachtik's head into the helmet.

"I think it's gonna work," Billy said, tugging at the mask to see if it was secure.

"How do you feel?"

"Like shit," Kachtik responded, his voice muffled by the mask.

"Can you play?"

"Looks like I'm going to."

Kachtik was the last Aggie through the tunnel, and as he wobbled across the field toward the A&M sideline a few of the forty-one thousand fans felt queasy. His jersey was still soaked with blood. Billy didn't have a clean uniform to issue. Baylor players were astounded to see Kachtik lining up at linebacker for the start of the third quarter. But Hooper showed no pity as he sent the tight end over the middle into his coverage area.

Kachtik could see the ball arcing against the backdrop of blue sky. He backpedaled quickly. His plan was to pluck it from the air and sprint down the right sideline. But his legs were too heavy and his head too light. The day now moved in slow motion.

He reached for the ball with his right hand, but it grazed his fingertips and fell into the waiting arms of the tight end, who ran toward a wall of popping lights and cacophonic sounds. Snakes now curled and hissed in the western sky. Kachtik turned in time to see Bryant slamming a fist into his palm and his head jerking wildly.

The air seemed light, and Kachtik began to float. He toppled backward, the back of his helmet striking the hard, dry ground. He never heard the crowd groan or felt the trainers lift him onto the stretcher again and carry him away.

Monday morning, Billy drove Kachtik to Dr. Harrison's offices in the adjacent town of Bryan. His face was black and swollen, and his nose had turned purple. He had vomited blood several times. The boys were confused at first because there were two entrances. Above the left door, the sign read: DR. R.H. HARRISON—VETERINARY MEDICINE. The other sign read: DR. R.H. HARRISON—HUMAN MEDICINE.

The diagnosis was swift.

"This bugger doesn't look too straight," the doctor said. From the drawer he pulled a ball peen hammer. He placed a white handkerchief over the boy's nose and plunked it once with the head of the hammer, rebreaking the bone. Oddly, there was little pain. Seizing the nose between the index and middle finger, the doctor pushed it back into place and set it.

"That looks good. Your movie career's probably over. But you can play football in a couple of weeks." Having been an Aggie dropkick specialist in 1918 and '19, Dr. Harrison at least understood the violent nature of college football and the chances for reinjury.

"Sir," Billy said sheepishly. "Coach Bryant wants him back and playin' this week."

"Coach Bryant will do what Coach Bryant will do. But I recommend at least three weeks out of pads, maybe more. That nose is broken a lot worse than I thought. And those eye bones, well, they need some time to heal."

Kachtik stayed in bed until noon on Thursday. But by three o'clock he was suited up and on the practice field. The mask partially obscured a discolored face and a nose that looked like a month-old banana. He stayed after practice so Bryant could brief him on some strategy changes.

Saturday night against the Arkansas Razorbacks, Kachtik didn't last long. As he was diving to recover a fumble, his right forearm was propped on the ball when an Arkansas player landed on his elbow, forcing it downward and out of the socket. The arm dangled at a grotesque angle as Kachtik grimaced and walked slowly to the sideline. There wasn't enough Novocain in Texas to hasten his return.

With the score tied at seven, Bryant was in a fit of rage when he marched into the locker room at the half. He ripped off his brown fedora and threw it down. Twice the Aggies offense had moved inside the Arkansas five-yard line, only to fumble the ball away. He pointed to the back of the room where a cluster of assistant coaches leaned on the wall, their eyes studying the floor.

"Out!" he bellowed. "I want you riffraff and you sonsabitches out of here."

The coaches looked quizzically at one another, not certain whom he was talking to.

Taking no chances, Bebes Stallings and Bobby Drake Keith almost knocked each other down bolting for the exit, their cleats sliding and scraping on the concrete floor.

"Not you, you silly farts," Bryant rumbled. "I want the shittin' coaches out of here."

Keith stopped. Stallings, being 80 percent deaf in one ear, looked like a frightened deer, its eyes frozen in the headlights. Again he turned and lunged for the door, but he was halted in midstride by Dennis Goehring, who pulled him back into the room by his jersey.

For the next twenty minutes Bryant railed and preached and paced. He did everything but pray.

The Aggies trailed 14–7 when Weasel Watson fielded a punt at the A&M sixteen with fifty-eight seconds to play. He began to dance and weave as both Schroeder and Huddleston leveled defenders with cross-body blocks. Watson broke into the clear at the Aggie forty, and the Hogs didn't have a prayer of catching the fastest player in the SWC. The eighty-four-yard punt return sent the Aggies' sideline into orbit. Student managers scrambled to find the kicking tee for the extra point. More than forty thousand fans stood and cheered and sang as the band blasted out "Spirit of Aggieland."

Then the celebration crashed in the blink of an eye. Lying back at the fifteen- and twenty-five-yard lines were yellow penalty flags. Schroeder and Huddleston had both been called for clipping. The touchdown was nullified. Heartache had become as familiar as reveille in the morning.

Bryant seemed flattened by the defeat. He barely had the energy to speak. Not once in his previous nine coaching seasons had he lost more than four games, and now the loss count stood at six. It didn't matter that Arkansas was the conference's best team. Bryant hated losing to the biggest school from his native state.

No, he just hated losing.

It was time to seek a higher power.

16

Faith

What matters . . . is not the size of the dog in the fight, but the size of the fight in the dog.

—PAUL "BEAR" BRYANT

NOVEMBER 2, 1954

At one o'clock that morning all hell broke loose.

The door pounding was resonant and unsettling, and the terrorists worked with precision and speed, as football coaches are wont to do.

"Get your asses up and be in the lobby in five minutes."

It reminded the boys of that first night in Junction when they were rustled from their beds in the midst of darkness. They tugged on jeans and T-shirts and stumbled shoeless into the hallway. Many were too sleepy to think.

Weasel Watson cracked an eyelid and said, "Do I at least get a last cigarette?"

"Shut up, Watson," Phil Cutchin rumbled.

Panic gripped Watson. "Is this about stealin' a little gas?" he whispered to himself.

On hearing the *boom-boom-boom* and loud voices, Dennis Goehring leaped from his bed, swung open the footlocker, and thought about diving in.

"Shut it, Dennis!" Bobby Jack Lockett yelled. "Hell, they're gonna think you're hidin' something in there."

"I am."

Dennis hustled down the hall. His eyes met with those of Lloyd Hale. "Everybody'd better keep their mouths shut," Dennis said. "Don't tell 'em nothin'."

Half-asleep and scared, they were thirty boys with thirty guilty consciences. Each shouldered a worry, real and imagined. Some had sinned. Others had just screwed up time and again on the playing field. Heavy on their minds was a common belief that they'd let the big man down.

Bebes Stallings leaned toward Bobby Drake Keith and whispered, "I'm not sure what we did. But I'm sure we got it coming."

Bobby Drake shrugged. "I guess."

Losing week after week can test a man's sanity, especially when that man is accustomed to winning in a big way and has an ego to feed. Bryant had seemed deeply troubled in recent days. His walking the campus late at night in his pajamas was not a healthy sign.

Two candles had been set on a table, and they cast a flickering light across the foyer. The boys quietly filed in. No one, not even the assistant coaches, knew Bryant's purpose for the gathering. A seance perhaps? The hour, the mood, and the lighting certainly fit.

Bryant walked slowly into the room. It was rare when he appeared rumpled. But this night, his hair was uncombed and his pajama tops protruded from his shirt collar and pants legs. His face was stonelike and shadowy, and some of the boys thought of Vincent Price.

But Billy Pete Huddleston had another vision. "He'd look just like Moses with a beard," Billy Pete whispered.

"God, he would," Redbird Granberry responded.

Bryant cleared his throat and set his eyes on Herb Wolf. "Didn't I see you eating a bowl of chili at the Twelfth Man at ten-thirty?"

"Yessir."

"You're dismissed."

No one breathed as Wolf walked quietly from the room.

Stallings and a few others had been playing pool across the street from the Twelfth Man about ten-thirty. Had Bryant spotted them?

The boys didn't know that Bryant had been combing the campus earlier that night, hoping to catch boys goofing off. At eleven o'clock, the coach had quietly slid through the back of Walton Hall and rapped on the door of running back Charles Hall.

"Didn't I see you at the coffee shop across the street an hour ago?"

"Yessir."

"Doing what?"

"Eatin' pie and drinking coffee. Coach, I'd been studying and my eyes were—"

"Never mind. This morning, there'll be a meeting of the players downstairs. You are not invited. Understand?"

Hall felt weak and almost sick to his stomach as he slowly closed the door. "For eatin' pie and drinking coffee?" he said.

Two hours later, Bryant stood silently before the boys, barely moving, his eyes fixed on something far away. The boys studied his face through the eerie light. He lifted a King James version of the Holy Bible from a small table and slowly opened it, turning to Matthew, seventeenth chapter, twentieth verse, and began to read: " 'He said to them, Because of your little faith. For truly, I say to you, if you have faith as a grain of mustard seed, you will say to this mountain, Move hence to yonder place, and it will move; and nothing will be impossible to you.' "

Bryant carefully laid the Bible on the table and studied the faces of the boys. A clock ticked in the hallway. Dry, windblown leaves scraped the front sidewalk.

The boys were not aware that Bryant had a spiritual side. He had taken them to church during the dog days of Junction and had seemed quite comfortable singing from the Baptist hymnal. But his language on the practice field and around the locker room didn't suggest a godliness. Now, though, he seemed in the midst of a religious experience.

He clasped his hands and spoke in a low voice that had lost its edge. "Now, I know this has been a rough time on you boys. We lost a lot of players, a lot of your buddies, in Junction. We've already lost a helluva lot of football games. But there's just something I know about y'all. I can see it in your eyes and feel it in your hearts. If y'all will just hang in there, you're gonna win a championship. Maybe not this year, maybe not next year, but you'll take that championship before you walk off from A&M for good. I believe that. Now is the time for you to start believin' that, too."

He lifted a box from another table and began walking among the players. To each one he handed a tiny clear capsule with a mustard seed enclosed.

"Keep these; hide these; put them away in a safe place. Every once in a while, I want you to take them out, look at them, and remember what happened here tonight. Remember that if you have the faith of the mustard seed, you can move a mountain."

The boys were almost afraid to look at one another, too stunned to move. They had just been roused from their beds. Now their hearts were up and racing.

"Gentlemen," Bryant continued, "life's battles don't always go to the stronger or faster man. But sooner or later, the man who wins is the one who thinks he can."

He paused and drew a deep breath.

"I wasn't so sure I was going to tell y'all this story tonight. But now I am. When I was young, kinda like y'all, I left my mama at home and rode in a rumble seat all the way from Arkansas to Alabama. After I was there a few weeks, I got so homesick that I could barely swallow. So I wrote a letter to my cousin, Collins Kilgore, and I told him that I was thinkin' about comin' home.

"Well, a few days later, ol' Collins fired a telegram back at me. It read in all capital letters: 'GO AHEAD AND QUIT JUST LIKE EVERYBODY PREDICTED YOU WOULD.' Well, if that didn't knock me back on my heels. I stuck that telegram in my trunk. Whenever I felt bad or homesick, I'd pull it out and read it. It was a jolt in the pants. After that, I knew I wasn't gonna quit and give everybody back in Arkansas the satisfaction. I was gonna prove something to them, maybe even prove something to myself.

"That's why I'm tellin' you this story. I'm sure a lot of you boys have thought about quittin'. God knows, we've had our share of quitters the last couple of months.

"Like you, I'm sick of being heartsick. I don't know if I'll ever get over the Houston loss—you know, Elwood diving to the one-inch line. Their nose tackle throwin' the ball up in the air and the damn referee not stopping the clock. One more play and we win the game. Then the TCU game comes down to an extra point. And by God, we had Arkansas beat.

"One thing you've gotta learn. You gotta keep believing, even when everybody else thinks you don't have a pig's ass chance in a slaughterhouse."

Bryant stood quietly and stared straight ahead. Then he turned and walked into the shadows.

For several minutes the boys seemed bolted to the floor as they thought about these words. They quietly digested the sermon. Then, without a word being spoken, they returned to their rooms.

There would be no pranks or water fights or dynamiting that night. But most of the Walton Hall lights stayed on until five o'clock, because the boys were too charged up to sleep. They talked about turning their season around and were confident it could happen. Breakfast hadn't been served, but they were ready to play SMU at that very moment in the dusty parking lot next door—ready to line up and kick some tail.

. . .

Coach Elmer Smith could see the light burning in Bryant's office when he arrived at Kyle Field a few minutes after five o'clock. The coaches' offices adjoined the locker room, and there was nothing special about the place. The floors were concrete and the walls bare and in the wintertime, it turned cold and drafty and damp.

Coach Elmer heard the film projector whirring in Bryant's office and decided to keep walking. That morning, too restless to sleep and still keyed up from the mustard seed sermon, Bryant had awakened at three-thirty and stumbled around the house for almost an hour getting dressed.

Now, hearing Smith puttering about, Bryant polished off his third cup of coffee and telephoned a friend who was a local veterinarian. Then he stuck his head into Coach Elmer's office and said, "Come on and take a ride with me."

Bryant would often drive the empty streets of College Station and Bryan in the early morning for the sheer purpose of relaxing. Sometimes he flipped on the car radio and listened to the lonesome wails of Hank Williams or the Texas Swing of Bob Wills. This morning, though, they rode in silence with just the sound of brisk wind pressing against the windows. Bryant didn't explain why he was pulling into an animal shelter parking lot.

Minutes later, he emerged with a small brown dog squirming in his arms. The dog had long, floppy ears and a cute face and was busy licking Bryant's cheek. Coach Elmer surmised that Paul Jr. was getting a surprise birthday present.

Again they rode for several minutes without talking while Bryant aimed the car down a pothole-laden street where cheap government-funded houses had been slapped together just after World War II. They were dubbed shotgun houses because you could fire a shotgun through the front door and the pellets would reemerge through the back door. Propped up on foot-high concrete blocks, the houses had no underpinning. The walls were of thin plywood painted white. In the first light of morning, the car stopped at the third house on the left.

Standing on the front steps were a mother and her son, a sandy-haired ten-year-old who wore a white T-shirt and faded jeans. While the boy cried, the mother held his hands and tried to console him. Bryant approached the boy and rubbed his head. He leaned forward, placing his hands on his knees, and spoke quietly. Then he returned to the car and fetched the dog.

·"I'll be right back," he said.

The boy smiled as the dog was placed in his arms. Bryant patted him on his head as the dog licked the boy's face. The big man then hugged the mother. Then he turned and walked back to the car.

As he steered the car back onto the street, streaks of auburn light angled through the windows. Bryant turned to his old friend. "Guess you were wonderin' what that was all about?"

"Yep."

"Well, I was drivin' to the office about three hours ago when I ran over and killed a little dog. I didn't want to go around wakin' up people that early. So I just went on to work. Now you know the whole story."

"Uh-huh."

They rode in silence back to the stadium, where Bryant poured another cup of coffee and plopped into his office chair. Soon the film projector whirred again. After that day, the men would never discuss the little boy and his new dog.

• • •

Friday morning, *Houston Post* beat man Mickey Herskowitz came around looking for a story.

Bryant hadn't struck up many friendships with sportswriters around Texas. He was convinced that most of the big-city writers preferred the big-city schools. It bothered him that A&M, thanks to being stuck in the boondocks, missed out on having a major metropolitan newspaper to defend it.

But over the last few months, Bryant had developed an affinity for the young Herskowitz, who wasn't afraid to ask tough questions. This day, though, Herskowitz appeared nervous when he arrived at Bryant's office door and it took Bryant about three seconds to recognize it.

"Little buddy," he said as Herskowitz sat down. "Somethin' pretty heavy's on your mind today."

"Yessir, Coach. My sports editor sent me up here to ask you some questions. Seems there are a lot of rumors about dissension on your football team."

"What?"

"Well, you know, you guys've lost six in a row. That tends to make curious people start talking—"

"Especially when it's A&M."

"I guess."

"Well, you can write this down and I hope you print it. I don't think there's any dissension on this football team. But if I see anybody out there who's not giving 150 percent, there's going to be some and I'm going to cause it."

Herskowitz scribbled the quote into his notebook, and when he finished Bryant had more.

"There's one thing that always happens when your football team is winning. The alumni are coming around glad-handin' you and tellin' you how great your team is doing. But when you're losing, they all want to know how lousy your team is doing. Write this down, Mickey. This is my team and I'm proud to have 'em."

It was the truth. Bryant was deeply proud of his ragtag bunch that had played TCU, Houston, Baylor, and Arkansas to the wire. The only blowout loss had been against Texas Tech when the Aggies were still pooped from the Junction debacle.

Looking Herskowitz square in the eye, Bryant said, "This is the hardest-nosed bunch of little boys I've ever had. Every week, we're outweighed twenty to thirty pounds a man. Tomorrow those big ol' Methodists from Dallas oughta swallow us. But they won't. I guarantee you that."

Bryant wanted to let him in on the mustard seed story but decided against it. He didn't want to tip his hand, to let SMU know just how fired-up his players would be the next day in Dallas.

The afternoon broke sunny and clear at the Cotton Bowl, one of the country's great football stadiums. It had become known as the "House That Doak Built" in 1948, when SMU running back Doak Walker won the Heisman Trophy. Of course, Texas A&M's ultimate goal was to play in the Cotton Bowl on New Year's Day as the champion of the SWC. But it had been twelve years since that occurred, and according to the talk of Texas, the sun would burn out before it happened again.

As a sophomore, Dennis Goehring had been in and out of the lineup for most of the season and had all but begged the coaches for more playing time. Bryant decided SMU would be his big chance. At 180 pounds, Goehring was better suited to play noseguard, where his quickness was a great benefit. But Bryant had cooked up something much larger for his feisty little guard.

Minutes before kickoff, Goehring was informed that he would open the game at left defensive tackle. That meant he would come face-to-face with All-American Forrest Gregg, possibly the best lineman in the country and a man who seemed destined for a great pro career. Dennis knew he was up to his neck in snakes against Gregg, but it didn't take long for him to concoct a plan.

On the first play, Dennis charged offsides and smacked Gregg in the face with a forearm shiver, knocking the 235-pounder into his own backfield, where he landed on his butt. Bryant sent a sub into the game, and as Dennis trotted to the sideline the big man grabbed him by the collar and shook him. "Why'd you do that?"

"Because, Coach, I thought it was the only way I could beat my man. Besides, I needed to get the big ole boy's attention."

Bryant's mouth fell open. Then he popped Dennis on top of the helmet and said, "I always did like a lineman who could think in an emergency. Get your butt back in there."

The Aggies displayed a spirit that belied their last-place status. Kettler quickly moved the team fifty-nine yards on the first series and then booted a twenty-four yard field goal. The Aggie defense repeatedly whipped the Mustangs at the line of scrimmage. Gregg did seem discombobulated as Goehring shot past the big tackle and registered several tackles. In the press box, *Dallas Morning News* football authority Tex Maule noted that the smaller Aggies were controlling the game.

SMU didn't make a first down until minutes before halftime, and then the Aggies mounted a goal-line stand, stopping the Mustangs on four tries from the five. Typically, though, the A&M offense fizzled and stalled three times inside the SMU twenty on fumbles.

In the third quarter Mustang quarterback Duane Nutt plunged over from the one, and that was all the points they would need. A&M had lost again, this time 6–3, because it couldn't muster an offense when it really mattered. Kettler was so fatigued at the end of the game that he lay on the field and couldn't move. Two teammates wrapped their arms around his waist and virtually dragged him into the locker room, his cleats scraping the concrete floor. Kettler had played every minute of the game, making several tackles as a special roving linebacker. He had passed for eighty-eight yards and rushed for sixteen more.

"Men, you didn't lose today," Bryant told the players. "Our day is coming." Four of their losses were by a total of eleven points.

Long after the final gun, Kettler sat on the bench in front of his locker, unable to move.

"What's wrong, buddy?" Billy Pickard finally asked.

Tears welled in Kettler's eyes. "Billy, I'm too tired to even take my shoes off." Thirty minutes later, with the help of Billy and a few teammates, Kettler was dressed and ready for the long bus ride back to College Station.

17

Changes

I'm known as a recruiter. Well, you've got to have chicken
to make chicken salad.

—PAUL "BEAR" BRYANT

DECEMBER 10, 1954

A cold blue norther was singing down from the Texas Panhandle with
nothing between Amarillo and College Station to slow it down. Sitting in
his office, listening to the howling wind, Bear Bryant cocked his right
eyebrow and peered at Billy Pickard.

"How could it be so hot in the summer and so damn cold in the
winter?"

"Because, Coach, the wind just roars down outta the Rocky Mountains.
A blue norther sprouts wings across the plains and the prairies, and it'll
kick in and keep goin' and goin' and goin' all the way across Texas until
it piles smack-dab into the Gulf of Mexico."

Bryant reached across the desk and handed Billy an envelope. From
the touch, he knew it was filled with cash.

"I need you to go down to Fort Shiloh, that honky-tonk on the edge

184

of town. Seems a couple of our boys knocked down a wall the other night. Give this to the owner. He knows it's coming.''

The football season was over, and some of the pain was beginning to subside. Bryant was already starting to plan for spring practice. Minutes after sending Billy on his mission, Bryant hustled through the back door of the locker room, when he ran chest-first into Billy Schroeder, the big tackle from Lockhart. He still looked pale from the heatstroke he'd suffered months earlier. Once a robust boy with full cheeks, he seemed skinny and a bit stooped. Doctors continued to insist that he quit football.

But Bryant had plans for Schroeder in 1955.

"Billy, son, I've been thinkin' a lot about you. I know you played tackle last season and you did all right. But I want to move you back to your natural position—end. You can take Bennie Sinclair's spot next season."

Schroeder studied the ground for several seconds as the wind wailed down the plains. Bryant knew something was wrong. The normally outgoing boy couldn't even make eye contact.

"Coach," Schroeder said, "the doctors tell me that I've got to slow down. I gotta skip spring practice. They say my system's all messed up. They say that if I get some rest I can still play football next fall. I really want to."

Bryant cleared his throat and gazed at the empty practice field that had turned the color of a corn tortilla. He felt uneasy talking to a boy who had almost died in his preseason camp.

"Son, if you're gonna play end for me next season, you've got to suit up in the spring."

"I don't think I can do it, Coach."

"Think it over."

"No. The doctors and my parents won't let me."

"Then I don't have much choice."

"Are you gonna cut me?"

The words stung Bryant. The boy had shown so much courage. Now Bryant was faced with the decision whether to let him go.

"Billy, spring practice isn't gonna be that bad. It won't be nothin' like last year. There'll be a lot less hitting."

"Coach, I barely even have the strength to walk to class."

"Billy, if I excuse you from spring drills, I'll have to let other boys out, too."

It seemed hopeless. Rules were rules with Bryant, and no player super-seded the team.

"I understand," Billy said.

"I'm sorry," Bryant said, turning to walk away.

Bundled in his full-length navy coat, the coach moved slowly across the practice field, his hair raked by the wind and his feet raising plumes of dust. The sky began spitting snow. Schroeder thought about the man who had ripped off his coat on the Grove stage just last February and then spoken so profoundly to the crowd about winning again at A&M. He remembered his own exhilaration.

Though his voice was weak, he yelled to Bryant, "I think you'll bring the Aggies back! Win a championship, Coach."

Bryant turned and briefly smiled. Then he was gone.

Schroeder fiddled with loose items in his pocket. He pulled out a dime, a penny, and a quarter. Then his fingers located the clear plastic capsule with the mustard seed inside.

"So long, Coach," he whispered.

Schroeder turned and leaned on the wall.

"Don't cry," he said. It didn't work.

• • •

One of Bryant's favorite pastimes was relaxing on a wooden bench on campus next to the statue of Lawrence Sullivan "Sul" Ross, a former A&M president, the governor of Texas from 1891 through 1898, and the great Indian fighter. Bryant was perusing Christmas ads in the *Bryan Eagle* when he spotted Mickey Herskowitz half-jogging across campus. The re-porter wore black shoes with thick heels, and his swept-back hair bounced as he ran.

Bryant waved to Mickey but didn't look happy to see him. "Sit down, son. There's something you wrote the other day that pissed me off."

"What is it, Coach?"

It seemed that every soul in Texas was talking about the Aggie fresh-man football class. Months earlier, Bryant had brought to A&M three of the top recruits in America—running backs John Crow and Ken Hall along with Charlie Krueger, a monstrous lineman who could lift a barn with one hand and a silo with the other. And there were several other great freshmen like Jim Stanley, Loyd Taylor, Bobby Joe Conrad, Billy Dedney, and quarterback Jimmy Wright, who already had sneaked more girls into his dorm room than most seniors.

The Aggies had broken NCAA rules by paying some of the top recruits. But Bryant had spun his own magic in luring many of the boys to College Station. Instead of making his sales pitch directly to the player himself, he spent much of the time wooing the parents. He would typically show up at a boy's house late in the afternoon and then work his way into the kitchen, where he would help the mother prepare supper. Afterward, he insisted on washing and drying the dishes. His down-home charm was often effective, and it drove enemy recruiters nuts.

Smokey Harper had dubbed the freshmen class of 1954 the Million Dollar Boys. But Bryant had grown weary of reading miles of newsprint about the greatest recruits since Doc Blanchard and Glenn Davis hit West Point. He was especially steamed about a story that had appeared in the *Houston Post* under Mickey's byline. He'd written that the talented freshman class would soon flush the sour taste of a 1–9 season. What really peeved Bryant, though, was the line that read: "The Texas Aggies will be greatly improved by graduation."

Bryant deeply admired many of the seniors from the 1954 team—especially guys like Elwood Kettler, Marvin Tate, Don Kachtik, and Bennie Sinclair. To close out the season, the Aggies had lost 29–19 to Rice and 22–13 to Texas on Thanksgiving Day. After the season finale, Kachtik sat in the visitors' locker room and cried. Bryant put his hand on the big fullback's shoulder and said, "By God, son, you're one player I'd like to have back."

Tate had played the final four games with ankles so black and swollen he could barely walk. And in spite of the offensive blunders, Kettler finished first in the SWC in total offense and second in scoring behind Rice's Dicky Maegle.

But a 1–9 season? Given the presence of Bryant, no football authority in America would have predicted it.

Like Herskowitz, many of the state's sportswriters had become infatuated with Crow, Hall, and Krueger. Bryant tried to deflect the attention to his other players, but it didn't work. The Million Dollar Boys were the talk of Texas.

One Saturday, Bryant was forced to miss his own television show due to a prior speaking engagement. He asked Smokey Harper to fill in. The moderator was A&M sports information director Jones Ramsey, and the sponsor was Lilly Ice Cream. Ramsey and Smokey spent a good portion of the show shoveling ice cream from a bucket.

Ramsey finally asked the question that was on everyone's mind: "Do you think all of these great freshmen will make us a better team next year?"

"Sure do," Smokey said. "If the damn coaches don't run 'em off."

Ramsey almost swallowed his spoon. "Guess we better get back to eatin' some more of this good ol' Lilly ice cream," he said.

* * *

The SWC had called a special meeting for the Rice Hotel in Houston, and every writer in Texas figured it would be a bloodletting. Rumors of probation had circulated for months, and it appeared that A&M's number was up.

Bryant accepted the fact that some of the Aggie blue chippers had been paid. He knew that prominent Aggie ex-students had been beating the bushes with cash in hand. He had firsthand knowledge of a slush fund. But he also was aware that several other conference schools—especially Rice and Texas—had been paying studs under the table for years.

He didn't worry about his own players who had accepted money to play at A&M. They were not likely to spill the beans on their school. It was the ones who turned down the cash and went elsewhere. They were the potential loose cannons.

Baylor athletic chairman Abner McCall was only a few steps inside the front door of the old and famous hotel when he was met head-on by Henry Diggs, a member of the UT athletic council.

"We've got to kick A&M out of the conference," Diggs demanded, his nose a few inches from McCall's. His breath was thick with Prince Albert.

"What? Surely you're kidding."

"No," Diggs said. "We've got the goods on this Bryant character. He's bad for business. Let's kick his ass out."

"Slow down. That's preposterous."

The room where the representatives would meet was charged with enough energy to light downtown Houston. McCall and the other athletic representatives who had come from all over the state and the University of Arkansas campus in Fayetteville were now prepared to determine A&M's fate.

Many had Bryant on their minds. Amazingly, after just one season, he had singed nerve endings from Laredo to Longview. Blood foes were lined up all over the state. Jess Neely, Rice's banty rooster of a coach, resented the publicity heaped upon Bryant for his hard-nosed approach. Neely fashioned himself to be the biggest hard-ass in Texas. What really pissed off Neely was that Bryant had recently marched like Patton onto Neely's fertile recruiting turf and won key battles.

No one could remember a group of coaches canvassing the state during the spring of '54 and accruing a mother lode of talent as efficiently as the Aggie staff. For decades, college football in Texas had been a close-knit fraternity as the big institutions regularly awarded their top jobs to dues-paying high school coaches with flattops. Everyone got along because, each year, the talent was spread fairly evenly across the conference. With the exception of Texas A&M and Baylor, teams took turns going to the Cotton Bowl.

Then Bryant took a jackhammer to the old-boy network. Perhaps the only compliment from an insider had come from TCU coach Abe Martin, who said, "Bryant's gonna make the rest of us put away our golf clubs and go to work."

Many of the Texas writers were also hot on Bryant's heels. Lorin McMullen of the *Fort Worth Star-Telegram* had written that it was "regrettable that a few A&M people cling to the belief that they are responsible for and honor bound to support this professional from the scandalized Kentucky campus who had distorted their aims, mocked their spirit, and severed their unity."

Bryant suspected that McMullen held a grudge that dated to his Kentucky days. He had once invited *Dallas Morning News* writer Bill Rives to dinner when Texas A&M was in Lexington to play his Wildcats. He'd also invited the governor. McMullen was left out and apparently felt shunned.

Other writers resented Bryant's oft-quoted remark that any one of them could be bought with a fifth of whiskey.

Pacing the lobby of the Rice Hotel, Bryant could feel the glare of enemies. He strolled into an adjoining drugstore and, after perusing a rack of paperbacks, made a purchase. He returned to his suite, sat on the edge of the bed, and pondered the inevitable.

Almost three hours later, as Bryant strolled back into the ornate lobby, Jack Gallagher of the *Houston Post* dashed toward him.

"Two years' probation," Gallagher gasped. "No bowls and all your boys are released from their scholarships. What's your reaction?"

Over Gallagher's shoulder, Bryant could see the meeting breaking up—gray-haired men in dark suits walking with purpose toward the front door.

"Hey, you sonsabitches!" he hollered. "When's the last time you put a one-and-nine team on probation? We won one shittin' game last year. You sonsabitches."

Henry Diggs heard the remarks loud and clear.

"Hey, Coach!" Diggs shouted across the room, his voice echoing across the rotunda. "What about Sid Banker? Why don't you tell the reporters about Sid Banker?"

Bryant was silent. But the eyes could have burned holes in marble. He wondered how the sawed-off egghead knew about Sid Banker, the mystery man with dark whiskers, a man Bryant had encountered only once. He needed a stiff drink. His mind was filled with questions: How did the committee find out about Sid Banker? How much information did they have? Who fingered the Aggies?

A gaggle of reporters was suddenly upon him.

"Boys. Come on up to my suite. Let's talk awhile."

Bryant spent more time asking questions than answering them. He opened two bottles of Johnnie Walker and two of Jim Beam and sent Coach Elmer out for ice. Reporters had been briefed by Howard Grubbs of the SWC office. The committee had arrived at its decision through testimony and signed affidavits. Evidence was provided that the Aggies had offered money to two players. Neither had signed with A&M.

Bryant's premonition was right.

They were Yoakum quarterback Bob Manning, who had signed with Texas, and Gonzales end Tom Sestak, who had gone to Baylor. Their respective coaches had helped them file affidavits with the SWC office stating they'd been offered $200 to sign by A&M and $50 a month over tuition.

Bryant couldn't believe his ears. That kind of cash was chicken feed. Up front, he'd told the Aggie alums to "meet the competition" when it came to bankrolling players. Money cited by the committee would be considered pocket change by his Aggie bagmen.

"The shitheads put us on probation for pissant stuff," Bryant said. "Hell, that's jaywalkin' material."

Bryant pulled one of the friendly writers aside. "Did anybody mention the name Sid Banker?"

"Never heard the name."

"Good."

"Why?"

"Good. That's all."

Sportswriter Dave Campbell walked across the room and noticed a paperback novel lying on Bryant's bed. The title: *Prisoner in His Room.* Campbell summoned Jones Ramsey, and the two had a long laugh.

"Coach planted it there hopin' somebody would see it," Ramsey whispered. "He's big on irony."

After several drinks, Bryant and Coach Elmer were ready for the ninety-minute drive back to College Station.

As they burst through the hotel's front door, they felt the raw wind in their faces.

"That north wind here in Texas just don't care whose ass it stings," Bryant said.

"Just like a sad song that don't care whose heart it breaks," Coach Elmer said.

"And these damn people in Houston. These athletic whatchamacallits. They didn't mind breakin' our hearts one bit."

"Aw, hell, Coach. Those silly sonofabitches probably put jelly beans in chili."

It was a good thing that Coach Elmer had decided to drive back to campus because Bryant felt a long cry coming on.

18

New Blood

When we have a good team, I know it's because we have
boys that come from good mamas and papas.

—PAUL "BEAR" BRYANT

MARCH 27, 1955

Bryant didn't sleep well for several weeks after learning the Aggies
had been flagged for cheating. With the scholarships being invalidated, the
Aggies were officially left without a team. The players had the option of
either staying at A&M or signing with another college where they would
be granted instant playing eligibility.

"This means that John Crow can go scot-free off to LSU," Bryant said
to Jim Owens the day after the SWC slapped A&M with two years' probation. "This means that Jack Pardee and Gene Stallings and that fast little
Watson boy can just vanish in the wind. Shoot, my bottle babies will be
scattered a hundred miles down the highway."

His eyes again filled with tears.

The players were away on Christmas break, and no one was sure what
their reaction would be. Next morning, though, the telegrams started rolling
in:

Count me in.—Don Watson

Can't wait to see you after Christmas.—Bobby Drake Keith

Not going anywhere.—Dennis Goehring.

The boys who didn't have money for wires wrote letters. Others called. Within three days, all had been accounted for, and all were coming back.

Bryant almost fainted when he heard the news. "I told you these boys were winners," he said to Smokey Harper. They decided to toast their good fortune with a long night of Tennessee aged whiskey.

With the '54 season behind him, Bryant could look forward to finally having players like John Crow, Charlie Krueger, and Ken Hall on the varsity roster.

Crow intrigued Bryant for several reasons. He had been born with a noose around his neck. It was his umbilical cord. Moments after delivery, the eighteen-inch strand had to be unraveled by a midwife who moved swiftly and saved the baby's life. But there would be complications. A doctor later explained to Harry and Velma Crow that the nerves on the left side of their boy's face had been severely damaged. The snarled rope had restricted blood flow to the head.

That first day he walked onto the A&M campus, folks quickly noted a droop in the left corner of his mouth. That side of his face seemed to sag, and the left eye was sleepy. But it didn't bother Bear Bryant one bit. He could have hugged the stud running back from the backwoods town of Springhill, Louisiana, the first time he set eyes on him.

That didn't, however, satisfy the curious.

Houston Chronicle writer Dick Freeman asked in a sympathetic tone, "Coach, what's wrong with Crow's face?"

Bryant explained the complications at birth.

"That's a shame," the writer said. "If not for that he'd be handsome."

Bryant's response was quick. "Oh, Dick, he's handsome to me right now."

Crow could not have seemed more beautiful to a man with a lifelong devotion to rugged, manly types and it would have been impossible to clone a more perfect fit. John Crow came from a town of callused hands and dirty fingernails—a paper mill town. He was raised by a strict and demanding father. Unlike many players seeking cash, Crow settled for a promise. "If you get hurt and never play a down," coach Elmer Smith told him, "I'll see to it that you don't lose your scholarship." No one in Crow's family had ever graduated from college.

He was neither swift nor particularly agile, but he possessed powerful shoulders that dipped and then overpowered tacklers. He was perfectly suited for one-platoon football. He possessed explosive energy at the point of contact. Bryant had never seen a player hit harder or tackle better.

If Crow was a fastball, then Ken Hall was a crackling curve. And compared to Crow's hard and uneven face, Hall was movie-star handsome. He was a high-stepping runner with pretty moves—two fakes and see-you-down-the-highway. His numbers were astounding. At tiny Sugar Land High School, about thirty miles from Houston, Hall had rushed for 11,232 yards and scored 127 touchdowns. In a game against Houston Lutheran, he averaged 47.3 yards per rush. He'd shattered every national high school rushing record.

Back in the spring of '54, months before coaching his first game at A&M, Bryant was scheduled to address a booster club meeting in Houston. But the first order of business was the introduction of Ken Hall. A chatty Aggie alum had commandeered the microphone and proudly announced that Hall had decided to sign with A&M. The thunderous applause lasted for several minutes. Then Bryant walked slowly to the front, stepped to the lectern, and just stood there, staring at his audience. He didn't smile. "I'm damn glad to hear Kenneth Hall is coming to A&M," he deadpanned. "I just hope he goes out for football."

Some folks began to worry that Hall might not satisfy Bryant's blood-and-thunder style of football. A few weeks after the freshman reported for fall drills, Smokey stopped Bryant on the practice field.

"Somethin's wrong with the Hall boy," he said.

"What is it?"

"Well, he'll be fine if you change the rules."

"What do you mean, Smokey?"

"Well, he's the best two-hand touch player I ever seen."

Bryant shook his head and walked away.

There was no questioning the masculinity of Charlie Krueger, who was raised a poor sharecropper's son. Krueger, at six-foot-six and 240 pounds, couldn't comprehend his own strength. The first sound Krueger heard most mornings at Walton Hall was: "Fish Krueger, get your butt down here."

It was the voice of Dennis Goehring, and it meant trouble. "Push-ups, Fish Krueger!" Goehring would shout. "Let's see how many you can do this morning."

A fish, also known as an A&M freshman, was a bottom feeder. He was on-call twenty-four hours a day for both mental and physical abuse from upperclassmen.

The fun-loving boys lived to haze Fish Krueger. Until the morning he fought back.

"Mr. Goehring!" the freshman shouted. "Fish Krueger is tired of being picked on. I'm sorry, Mr. Goehring."

Before he knew it, Goehring was eight feet in the air, having been hoisted there by Big Charlie. Weight lifters would call it a military press.

"Help!" Goehring wailed. "Get this animal off me!"

Jack Pardee came running from the other room and tackled the big freshman. Krueger, however, didn't budge. He simply tossed Dennis onto the bed, grabbed Pardee by an arm and a leg, and lifted the fullback above his head like a rag doll.

"I'm sorry, Mr. Pardee," he said. "But Fish Krueger lost his temper this morning."

"Put me down, you big ape!" Pardee yelled.

Day by day on the practice field, Bryant watched the transformation from boy to full-grown man. "That boy's meaner than a bucket of rattlesnakes," he would say. "And he's bigger than the Jolly Green Giant."

So it wasn't surprising that Bryant would feel an ulcer attack coming on one summer evening in 1955 when the call came from Goehring. Several Aggies had been working a summer job at the Houston shipyards when Krueger vanished.

"Coach, you better sit down," Goehring said. "Charlie's long gone."

"Where to?"

"Texas A&I."

"Those sonsfabitches."

"Gil Steinke came and stole him."

Steinke had been an assistant coach for several seasons at A&M before winning the head coaching position down in Kingsville. He had spent the better part of the last year stockpiling Bryant's throwaways, including quarterback Dave Smith, who had quit in Junction. The previous summer he'd almost convinced Pardee to transfer to Texas A&I.

"Get down there and bring him back!" Bryant thundered.

"How? I don't have my car."

"Hop a freight train if you have to. Just get your ass to Kingsville."

A freight train it was. From Houston to Corpus Christi, the Cotton Belt Line rumbled through El Campo and Victoria and Refugio and Sinton. Goehring then hitchhiked to Kingsville, which was located on the legendary King Ranch. It was thirty miles east of Pardre Island and an hour's drive from the Mexico border.

He arrived in Kingsville to find assistant coaches Jim Owens and Willie Zapalac already there.

"He ain't comin' back," Zapalac said.

"He will if I tell him," Dennis said. "Y'all go on back to campus. I'll be there soon."

The boys spent almost four days talking. "Dennis," Krueger would say. "When I was growing up in Caldwell, I heard the sermons on the importance of being God-fearing. But I never actually saw God in Caldwell. Bryant was right there in front of me and he was real. I wasn't sure that God would kill me, but I knew Bryant damn sure could. Actually, I fear him a lot more than I do God."

Dennis pondered the words and knew what Krueger was feeling. He'd witnessed the exodus of almost eighty teammates in Junction. Some were scared out of their wits.

"This is what you gotta do with Bryant," Dennis said. "You gotta show him you're not afraid. Sometimes you've got to bluff him a little."

"I don't know how."

"Charlie, I wouldn't be here today if I acted scared. I just kept fighting. Bryant loved it."

"Hell, Dennis, I can't go back. He doesn't take quitters back."

"Officially, you haven't quit yet."

Goehring knew better. In Bryant's mind, Krueger had quit. But Dennis also knew the Man desperately wanted Krueger back. He had heard the worry in Bryant's voice over the long-distance line.

"You can come back if we leave right now."

Krueger stared into the distance at the dusty land, and his heart ached. He stuffed hands the size of catcher's mitts into his jeans pockets. He looked straight down Route 77 and thought he could see forever. The two-lane highway split the flat country like an arrow. Heat lay in shimmering clouds just above the blacktop.

"Shoot, Dennis, I made a bet with Jim Stanley on who'd last longer with Bryant. We bet a whole fifth of whiskey. We weren't joking."

"Go back now and you don't have to pay up."

"Let's go."

Minutes later, Dennis was on the phone to Bryant.

"We're comin' back. I think we'll have to hop a train."

"No. There's a small airport on the west side of town. Go there and wait. If nothin' happens in three hours, call me."

Two hours later, a maroon-and-white jet with TEXAS A&M AGGIES inscribed on its tail descended from the high white clouds.

That evening, with Krueger standing behind him, Dennis knocked on Bryant's front door.

"Coach, I think we'll just hitchhike on back to the dorm."

"Oh, no, you won't." Bryant turned and shouted, "Mary Harmon, where are the keys to your car? Mother, these boys need to borrow it."

With Krueger riding shotgun, Goehring drove the Cadillac ninety miles to his old stomping grounds in San Marcos, where the beer was cold and the girls were glad to see them. They stayed a week, and Bryant never mentioned it.

. . .

All that Bryant could think about was the opening game of the 1955 season against UCLA. That's why he spent three weeks of spring practice preparing for nobody but the Bruins.

He cut the team in half, and the scrub players were assigned blue-and-gold uniforms—UCLA colors. Coach Elmer was assigned to coach the B team. It was a collection of second-rate misfits who Bryant figured wouldn't play a down with the varsity in the fall. He called them rinky-dinks.

For three hours every afternoon, the rinky-dinks worked on the UCLA offensive plays and defensive schemes. Bryant wanted the annual Maroon-and-White spring game to be a dress rehearsal for the season opener, and everything was on schedule. Then the unthinkable happened. On the opening kickoff, Redbird Granberry aimed his five-foot-seven, 155-pound frame down the field like a torpedo. He hit kick returner Ken Hall head-on, stole the ball, and ran the other way for a touchdown. Coach Elmer threw his cap into the air and did a high-stepping dance that lasted almost five minutes. The rout was on. The rinky-dinks beat the varsity by three touchdowns.

When the scrimmage ended, Bryant sent the rinky-dinks in early. Then he led the rest of the players to the end of the field for another scrimmage—this one on the goal line. Players grunted and bled. Bryant put sixteen players on defense and instructed quarterbacks Jimmy Wright and Donnie Grant to run the ball between the tackles. The noise that emanated from Kyle Field sounded like seven-car pileups.

Charlie Krueger had invited Bryant that night to address his high school booster club in Caldwell, which was thirty miles down the road. Bryant passed and ordered assistant coach Pat James to take his place. As nightfall approached, both James and Krueger were becoming nervous about getting to Caldwell on time. James finally approached Bryant with his predicament.

"Ah, hell, you and Charlie go on," Bryant said. "Get out of here."

James and Krueger were hustling across the field toward the locker room when they heard Bryant's voice bellowing, "When you get there, don't forget to tell 'em how *horseshit* you are!"

Three nights later, with the spring semester coming to a close, Bryant held a farewell party at his home for the seniors, using the proceeds from the cuss bucket. The boys found him in the backyard in an apron and chef's hat, grilling enough steaks to feed a brigade. He was sipping on Jack Daniel's and seemed as comfortable with spatula in hand as he did on the sideline. When Marvin Tate didn't ask permission before turning a well-done piece of meat, Bryant yelled, "Get your ass away from that! I'll have you runnin' stadium steps."

"Coach, I'm graduatin' Sunday."

"Son, I'll tell ya when I'm through with ya."

After dinner, Bryant and his wife, Mary Harmon, chose up sides for charades. The boys only *thought* they had seen the coach's competitive side.

The teams stood on opposite sides of the room. Girlfriends and wives were included. Bryant drew *Birth of a Nation*. Gesturing with his hand, he drew a wide arc around his stomach.

"Fat Mama."

"Belly of Laughs."

"Tub of Goo."

"No, Tate, you silly sonofabitch," Bryant said. Bryant fell on his back and, with a great expression of pain, moaned loudly.

"*The Agony and the Ecstasy.*"

"*As I Lay Dying.*"

"Pig Latin."

"Elwood, dammit, can't you see I'm pregnant?"

"That's cheating, Paul."

"Ah, Mary Harmon, these boys are so dumb they need some help."

Bryant pointed to a globe across the room, and someone yelled, "*As the World Turns.*"

Then he pretended to be waving a flag.

"Yankee Doodle Dandy."

With his ulcers burning, Bryant dropped to the floor again and pounded it.

"Paul, we're not playing for the national championship."

"Mary Harmon, given the collective IQ of the football players around here, I don't think we ever will."

19

Deliverance

Hell no! A tie is like kissing your sister.

—PAUL "BEAR" BRYANT

SEPTEMBER 18, 1955

The season opener against UCLA didn't go as Bryant had hoped, and the Aggies lost for the tenth time in the coach's first eleven games at Texas A&M.

Now they were packed into the smoke-filled room below the Los Angeles Coliseum and the press had Bear cornered. Showers hummed while players wrapped in towels stepped over wet uniforms, pads, and piles of twisted tape, moving in silence through the warm, steamy haze.

"You didn't really think you were gonna win, did ya?" said *Los Angeles Herald-Examiner* columnist Melvin Durslag, biting a thick cigar.

"Why, hell, yes," Bryant said. "Why else do you think we'd come out here, you silly sonofabitch?" He moved toward the sportswriter and was of a mind to pop him in the nose.

So much had been riding on the trip to the West Coast. Bryant had counted down the days, the hours, and then the minutes to the start of a new season—a new era?—against UCLA. What better time to flush the bile and the bitter taste from 1954?

It had been twenty years since he had played in the Rose Bowl in nearby Pasadena, and he had often longed to see the palm trees, the jagged coastline, the mountains, and the movie studios of Southern California again. Alabama had defeated Stanford before a crowd of 84,474—more fans than had seen the Crimson Tide play the entire regular season. That week, he met former Alabama All-American and Western movie star Johnny Mack Brown and had lunch with Ray Milland and Dorothy Lamour. He even sneaked away from a team function one afternoon to take a screen test at Paramount Studios, turning down an offer of sixty-five dollars a week to try his hand at acting.

Now Bryant felt like a college kid as the Aggies toured Universal Studios and gathered for dinner at the Brown Derby with actor William Bendix. With them wearing their new blue blazers purchased by the athletic department, Bryant no longer thought of them as roughnecks and ranch hands. When the players had gathered in the foyer at Walton Hall before leaving on the trip, he'd told them, "We're goin' first class from now on. We're gonna dress first class, fly first class, eat first class, meet first-class people, and win first class."

Two high school buses then rattled up to the curb outside the dorm, coughing black smoke. Both had worn tires and were badly in need of paint.

"Look at those yellow dogs out there," sophomore Jimmy Wright said for all of the players to hear. "Yeah, boys, we're really goin' first class." Bryant overheard the remark but decided to take it up with his quarterback at another time.

Thirty minutes later, as the buses approached Easterwood Airport, they encountered a hill that couldn't be climbed. Running backs, ends, quarterbacks, and Bryant rode in the lead bus.

"Dammit, bus driver, is this thing runnin' out of juice?"

"Sir, we're in trouble."

"This bus *will* make it over this hill."

"I'm not so sure, Coach."

"Will we make it over this hill if we all get off?"

"That might be the ticket."

They filed off, and moments later the yellow dog crawled over the crest of the hill. Then the second bus was unloaded.

"All I know," Bryant said, "is that airplane had better fly."

Fly it did. It was a four-engine TWA Convair 121 identical to the aircraft that ferried Pres. Dwight D. Eisenhower about the country. Flying to Los Angeles would be the experience of a lifetime for most of the boys, since a handful had ever traveled beyond state borders and only two had ever flown. They were like wide-eyed kids when the plane touched down at Los Angeles International. The fresh haircuts and new clothes still couldn't hide country boys in the big city.

As the chartered buses rolled past the tall, modern buildings of Westwood, Bryant hollered, "If you boys don't stop lookin' up, folks are gonna think you're from the sticks!"

Saturday night before eighty thousand fans, they fell to earth with a thud. The Aggies moved the ball on the ground but couldn't push it into the end zone. UCLA quarterback Rodney Knox threw three touchdown passes. Bryant's expectations had been skewed. Of course, he should have known that UCLA was a powerhouse since the Bruins had shared the national title the previous season with Ohio State.

The Aggies lost 21–0. Hell was explaining it again to the writers.

Not since Junction had Bear's life been so filled with angst. As the boys prepared for the return flight to College Station and the Convair 121 awaited takeoff, he spotted a large box of chocolates weaving its way from row to row through coach class. Players were chowing down on nut clusters and bonbons. He seized the box and marched toward an open exit.

"Who brought this shit on board?"

Chocolates flew and then skittered across the tarmac like ants under siege from a Raid can.

After UCLA, Bryant didn't know how much more losing he could stomach. Now his ego was squarely on the line with a game coming up against LSU, a team that had lost its season opener to Kentucky, his former team. Folks from Lexington to Little Rock would be laughing if the Aggies lost to LSU.

"If we lose," he told Smokey, "they're gonna say I don't have sense to pour piss from a boot."

Practices that week lasted well past dark. Right and left, players screwed up and lost their meal privileges as punishment. Several quit. Hardly a word was spoken during the four-hour bus ride to Dallas, where the game was scheduled for the Cotton Bowl on Saturday night.

Minutes before kickoff, Bryant stood before the players.

"As you leave this locker room, I want each and every one of you gentlemen to come by me and shake hands and look into that mirror right over there.'' The mirror was situated above a sink next to the door that led to the stadium tunnel.

As they left, Bryant said, ''When you come back in here tonight, take another look in that mirror. Then you'll know if you gave your best.''

Smiles reflected their relief. The Aggies pounded LSU 28–0 as John Crow rushed thirteen times for 130 yards. A seventy-seven-yard touchdown run seemed more thrilling than a ride on the Comet, the State Fair roller coaster that clacked and rumbled over steep, twisting hills behind the south end of the Cotton Bowl. Crow had encountered heavy traffic at the line of scrimmage thanks to a mix-up between the two guards. Both had pulled and run headlong into each other. But Crow managed to weave through the traffic jam, breaking several tackles along the cluttered route. Fabled radio man Kern Tips said in his lilting drawl, ''John Crow tonight announced his arrival on the Southwest Conference scene with the quiet modesty of an elephant stampede.''

After the game, Bryant stood before the press, buttons bursting. ''That was the single greatest run I've ever seen in my life. Boys, he must have broke fifteen tackles. That John Crow is the real thing.''

Crow was the answer to a desperation prayer. But Bryant still couldn't find a quarterback to match the grit of Elwood Kettler. He'd opened the season with Donnie Grant and the offense had been flatter than Amarillo. The switch to Jimmy Wright lit a fire against LSU, but Bryant fretted over the quarterback who had been dubbed Tab Hunter by his teammates. He was flashy and cool, with sandy blond hair and movie-star looks. He was also a distant cousin of Weasel Watson and walked with the same Rebel swagger. Watson and Wright had spent a lot of time together growing up, and some folks even confused them for brothers. Both were great athletes and neither was afraid to speak his mind.

Jimmy was a prankster and a rounder from the day he walked on campus. The previous night, he and guard Jim Stanley had taken the stage at a local honky-tonk called Uncle Jimmy's. They brought down the house by singing Hank Williams's number-one hit, ''Your Cheatin' Heart.'' Then they chugged two pitchers of Pearl.

Wright was feeling frisky during practice one afternoon when he pulled a joke on Bebes Stallings, who had trouble hearing the plays. Bebes played left end and stood in the left corner of the huddle. To hear the quarterback Bebes had to lean forward and crane his neck. He tried to position his right ear—the good one—as close to the quarterback's lips as he could.

Jimmy had quietly tipped his teammates on the little prank that he had planned. He would lip-synch the play so Bebes couldn't hear it. But the other players would know the play in advance. As the team broke the huddle and headed for the line of scrimmage, Stallings blurted, "What? I didn't hear it." He smacked left tackle Charlie Krueger on the shoulder pad and said, "Hey, Charlie, what's the play and the snap count?"

It was too late. Before he could drop into a three-point stance, Jimmy barked the signals and the ball was snapped. Coach Pat James made a beeline for Stallings.

"What the hell is wrong with you, son?"

"Coach, I didn't hear the play. Besides, I'm deaf in one ear."

"I didn't know that." James planted a shoe in Stallings's backside and pointed a finger at Jimmy. "Don't ever do that again, son." Jimmy giggled.

Jimmy, of course, gave the coaches plenty to worry about. But they couldn't quibble with his tight spirals that hit the receivers between the numbers like slugs from a .44.

"That boy chunks it better than Babe Parilli," Bryant told Smokey. "But I gotta watch him like a damn hawk."

After Wright fumbled on the first play against LSU, Bryant yanked off his hat and slammed it to the ground. Three plays later, though, Stallings intercepted a pass and Jack Pardee scored the Aggies' first touchdown of 1955 on a four-yard run. Pardee ran for two touchdowns and Crow added two others, and that's the way Bryant liked it. He could care less that college coaches across America were subscribing to the principles of Paul Brown, the NFL's resident offensive guru. Bryant was still plowing with a team of mules. He didn't care that Brown was rewriting the book on offensive football by flanking out two receivers and using a split backfield. He didn't care that some of his college peers believed in throwing the ball more than five times a game. He'd been a T-formation man since the day he walked into Texas, and nothing was about to change that.

In moments of free thinking, he would occasionally move a halfback all of about three yards to wingback. That was the closest A&M would come to having a wide receiver. Aggie ends were blockers 90 percent of the time. Bryant's most daring play was a bootleg. Rolling either left or right, the quarterback had the option of passing to a back in the flat. The ball would travel five or six yards at the most.

"Jimmy!" Bryant often hollered during practice. "If that's man not wide open, dammit, son, don't throw it. Run it."

Telling Wright not to pass was like setting a whiskey bottle in front of

Smokey and insisting he drink straight Coke. Jimmy came from a shoot-'em-up offense at tiny Edinburg High, where passing came as naturally as breathing. Edinburg ran both the pro-set and the shotgun offense well ahead of their day. Coach Bill Cooper could have taught Paul Brown a thing or two about spreading the field.

Edinburg is situated deep in the Rio Grande Valley about twenty miles from the Mexico border. Aggie coaches had spent weeks and weeks eating tamales and hot peppers and recruiting the boy with the cannon arm.

"We can throw the ball with the best of them," Bryant had told Wright on his recruiting trip to A&M. "You come on to A&M and we'll light up that goddamn scoreboard."

"Light up" apparently meant to turn it on. That first day, Wright was handed a playbook straight from the Knute Rockne era. The Aggies practiced the passing game about three minutes a day. The other three hours, they ran between the tackles.

Wright knew there was no use arguing with Bryant. But he did take up the matter with assistant coach Jerry Claiborne.

"This is the silliest shit I've ever seen."

"Jimmy, please don't tell Coach Bryant that."

The fifties were a troubling time for a control maven like Bryant. Coaches were allowed to neither shuttle plays into the games or signal from the sideline. This meant that quarterbacks were free to call their own plays. Referees kept close watch on the frustrated men who prowled the sideline. They were prohibited from even signaling for a punt on fourth down. If a coach wanted to attempt a field goal, he was allowed to heave the kicking tee onto the field. Some coaches got cute and would place a strip of tape on the bottom of the tee to signal a fake. But if they were caught talking to players on the field or flashing the smallest signal, they were flagged.

So having the strong-willed Wright boy at quarterback raised a few gray hairs on Bryant's head.

"I am in charge, dammit!" he would yell, pounding his fist into an open palm. Bryant held long chalk-talk sessions with the quarterbacks each day. A few hours before kickoff, he'd walk the field with the signal callers, explaining in detail the plays he wanted called for every situation. His demands were clear

Folks just didn't know just how badly Bryant wanted to prove himself in Texas. Anger had motivated him since the day he set foot in College Station. Texas A&M was regarded as a stepchild, and he considered it unfair. He wanted to wear the opposition down by running the ball and break them mentally, physically, and spiritually. He wanted Jess Neely and the other coaches to feel the sting of his whip.

"Boys," he often said to the players. "Folks around this state regard you as nothin' more than yard dogs. Nothin' more."

In the third game of the season, when the Aggies scored on a four-play drive against Houston, Wright pranced to the sidelines, his helmet cocked back on his head.

"Buckle your shittin' chin strap!" Bryant yelled.

"What?"

"Son," Bryant said, grabbing his jersey, "don't ever let my offense score that fast again."

"What?"

"You start spoilin' my offense, boy, and you'll never play quarterback for me again."

"I don't get it."

"Get this. *Run the damn ball!*"

In the third and fourth weeks of the season, the Aggies drubbed Houston 21–3 and Nebraska 27–0 at Lincoln. They were 3–1 with the biggest game of the Bryant era coming up.

Every team in the SWC feared TCU. The Horned Frogs had won a national title in 1938 and now boasted their greatest player since that championship season, when Davey O'Brien had won the Heisman Trophy. His name was Jim Swink and he could shake, rattle, and roll like Bill Haley himself.

Swink was considered the second-favorite in the Heisman balloting behind Ohio State's Howard "Hopalong" Cassady. After watching some film, John Crow had an idea on defensing Swink. But it took him two days to build up enough courage to approach Bryant.

"Coach, I think I know how to stop Swink."

"Why, John, so ya feel like coachin' now?"

"No, sir. I just have an idea." Crow's voice was breaking.

"Spit it out, son."

"Well, Coach, why don't you let me shadow Swink? I mean, let me kind of follow him around. If he lines up right, I go that way. And every time he gets the ball, I try to meet him in the hole."

Not in his twenty-three years of coaching had Bryant seen a tougher player than Crow, who lived for a good hit as much as he did for a long touchdown run. He always had the dirtiest uniform on the field. The scary part for opposing running backs was that Crow, who played safety, was bigger than most Aggie linemen.

"I tell ya what," Bryant said. "I might just give it some thought."

Bryant felt dizzy watching Swink scooting and spinning as he ran the TCU film back and forth late at night. Bryant studied teams all over the country and knew the unbeaten Horned Frogs were a national power.

"They're just about as good as Bud Wilkinson's bunch up at Oklahoma," he told Jerry Claiborne. Bryant knew a lot about Oklahoma football. His Kentucky team had broken the Sooners' thirty-one-game winning streak in the 1951 Sugar Bowl.

Bryant decided to try Crow's defensive strategy. Then, during his pregame walk with the quarterback, he decided to loosen the reins a tad on his quarterbacks, even though it troubled him. He expected a high-scoring game with Swink on the other side. So he added several passing plays to the game plan.

Early in the second quarter, his worry began to subside when Wright arced a perfect spiral into the left corner of the end zone. Watson had beaten the defensive back on a fade route and managed to snag it over his left shoulder while tapping both feet in bounds. The twenty-yard touchdown put the Aggies ahead 6–3.

Swink seemed to be wearing Crow like a cheap suit until Crow heard a loud pop in his left knee. Billy Pickard helped the limping boy to the visitors' locker room. The door was locked. They had to settle for the men's rest room beneath the east stands, where Pickard tried to secure the joint with tape. But the knee continued to wobble and Crow was unable to return to the game.

The A&M sideline had grown quiet and restless until Billy Dedney, another member of the Million Dollar Boys, shot through an opening at left tackle, slid to the outside, and dashed twenty-one yards to the end zone. Given the anxiety that accompanied the loss of Crow, the 12–3 halftime lead looked and smelled better than aged whiskey.

In the third quarter, the Aggies were dominating both sides of the ball until Donnie Grant replaced Wright and drilled a perfect strike between the numbers of TCU's Hugh Pitts. The big linebacker lumbered ten yards with the interception to the Aggie eleven. Bryant walked several steps onto the field and greeted his quarterback with words he would never forget.

"You stupid sonofabitch," Bryant growled. "We've got a 12–3 lead and you throw a stupid goddamn interception. Sit your ass down, boy, and don't get up till I say."

On the bench, a moping Grant muttered to Wright, "If he ever cusses me again, I'll quit."

"Hell, son, he cusses everybody but his mama."

TCU scored quickly on a touchdown pass from Chuck Curtis to Brian Ingram. Then, in the fourth quarter, Swink slipped into the end zone from the five. The A&M lead was gone, and hope had become a leaky balloon. The T-formation was designed for three yards and a cloud of dust—not quick comebacks.

It would have behooved the Horned Frogs to remember that the fastest man in the conference was lining up in the A&M backfield. They must have forgotten.

Kern Tips had the call on the Humble Oil Football Network:

"Trailing 16–12, the Aggies need a kicker here late in the fourth quarter. . . . The ball's at the Aggie forty-nine and the toss goes to that Lilliputian leather lugger from Franklin. . . . Don Watson does a Hoooola Hoop at the forty and slants back across the grain. . . . Look at the little rascal go over the clover. . . . Watson rides the rail down the right sideline at the twenty, the fifteen, the ten, and it's pay dirt for the Cadets. . . . Boy howdy, Bear Bryant's boys are for real. You can send a postcard home to Mama!"

The Aggies won 19–16. They were stepchildren no more.

* * *

Weasel and Jimmy knew the alley door would fly open with a hard yank. They had sneaked into the G. Rollie White Coliseum many times and had yet to be tossed out by the campus police.

On Tuesday night something really big was happening. The boys were determined not to miss it. From the practice field late that afternoon they had watched the caravan of cars pulling onto campus, and many were filled with teenage girls who poked their heads through the windows and waved and squealed.

"I hear there's some guy playing over there tonight who's better than Bo Diddley," Lloyd Hale said. "This cat really knows how to play guitar."

After wind sprints and quick showers, the boys were off and running across campus. The others were Jack Pardee, Dee Powell, Jim Langston, Loyd Taylor, and Hale. They were in a hurry because the main attraction was scheduled to be the first onstage as part of the seven-act Louisiana Hayride Jamboree. This kind of excitement was rare for Texas A&M, where the biggest event each year was the building and then the lighting of the massive

Wednesday-night bonfire that preceded the Texas game on Thanksgiving. Other than water fights, football games, and the smuggling of girls into the dorms, the campus didn't offer many chances for excitement.

Though times were rapidly changing across America, the clocks seemed frozen at Texas A&M, where 90 percent of the students were still members of the Corps and most resented the abolishment of compulsory membership. World War II had ended almost a decade earlier. But given the daily military maneuvers in Aggieland, you would have thought WW III was being hatched in a campus boardroom.

Administrators had attempted to polish the college's image by banning hazing. But the students aggressively fought back, and a secret organization called the True Texans, also known as the TTs, emerged for the purpose of challenging the administration's new ideas on campus life. Some of the cadets confused tradition with patriotism. Customs such as yell practice, muster, the bonfire, and observance of memorials took on the mantle of sacred rituals.

Whenever talk of admitting women surfaced at Texas A&M, ex-students across Texas wrote letters and fired off telegrams and telephoned school officials. One Aggie who went against the grain, often voicing his approval for coeducation, almost suffocated when an ammonia bomb was tossed into the open window of his dorm room.

It seemed the cadets never stopped complaining about the scarcity of females. But most didn't want to share classrooms with them. The only women admitted into lectures were the daughters of professors. According to a poll of the student body, the Aggies were overwhelmingly against coeducation, even though many longed for female companionship. For the "Senior Sweetheart" section of the 1955 yearbook many A&M students submitted a picture of their mother.

Across America, the era had provided a chicken for every pot. There were air conditioners, dishwashers, and all forms of electrical gadgets. The new age produced drive-ins, supermarkets, FM radio, high fidelity, and a black-and-white television set for many homes. But it failed to propagate any meaningful changes at a place called Old Army.

So it wasn't surprising that the new sound had yet to arrive at A&M, where students listened to swing music from another age—the big bands of Harry James and Guy Lombardo.

This night, in spite of a clear sky, a storm had rumbled onto the prairie and the air seemed electric. For hours, students had been lining up at the box office and swapping stories about the young singer who had hit town.

While the cadets and their dates and a flock of teenage girls streamed through the front door, the football players sneaked along a darkened alley on the back side of G. Rollie White next to Kyle Field. They weren't about to pay for tickets.

"Lloyd," Watson whispered. "You go ahead and yank open the door. The rest of you boys follow me. And don't do no loud talking."

The stocky center with powerful hands cracked open the door in seconds, and the boys rushed into the cool darkness. They could see a bright yellow light flashing in the space between the bottom of the curtains and the floor. They were now behind the stage. Without uttering a sound, they descended the stairs into the auditorium and quickly located seats in the corner by the wall.

As the thick maroon curtains slowly parted, a low, booming voice rose from the amplifiers situated at both ends of the stage.

"Ladies and gentlemen, please welcome . . . Elllvis Presley!"

He was dressed in a pink dinner jacket, black open-collar shirt, pink pants, pink socks, and red shoes. He just stood there with his chin thrust forward, sneering. A wave of long black hair cascaded over his brow. Like a sledgehammer, his right hand rose and then crashed across the guitar strings, splintering two.

He sneered and glared at the crowd.

"Golly," Jack Pardee said. "I don't think I've ever seen a guy dressed in pink before."

In the summer of 1954, Elvis had broken onto the Memphis music scene on radio station WHBQ. Lately he'd been storming the southern states, gyrating as he had seen the gospel singers gyrate. To some, the music and pelvic thrusts were new and fresh. Others accused him of stealing from Bo Diddley, the great black rocker. Asked if he was upset about this, Diddley said, "If he copied me, I don't care—more power to him. I'm not starving."

Elvis was a white man with a black beat, and naturally there was some confusion in 1955 as to who he really was. His career began to ascend when he picked up on a piece by bluesman Arthur "Big Boy" Crudup called "That's All Right (Mama)."

Elvis gained national attention when he joined the Louisiana Hayride, which was broadcast on the 150 stations of the CBS Radio Network. Stations across Texas began playing songs like "Blue Moon of Kentucky" and "Baby, Let's Play House." It had become a Saturday-night ritual in small towns for the teenagers to gather in empty grocery store parking lots.

They would crank their car radios full blast to the Louisiana Hayride and, in the light of the Texas moon, dance unabashedly and undisturbed.

Elvis's reputation as the "Hillbilly Cat" was starting to fade, even though some of his songs were still ranked on the country-and-western charts and "I Forgot to Remember to Forget" had climbed to number one. But most of Elvis's music was still undefined. It was a combination of C and W and blues, which became the roots of rock-and-roll, and it sounded like nothing before it. It proved to be a combustible mix in the spring of '55, when he appeared before fourteen thousand screaming fans at the Gator Bowl in Jacksonville, Florida. Thousands of girls stormed the stage and tore at his clothes. They climbed through the window of his dressing room, and he barely escaped in one piece to a waiting Lincoln Continental. It was the first full-scale riot ever reported at a rock-and-roll concert. Little did anyone know that the Memphis kid was just getting warmed up.

When Elvis's motorcade rolled onto campus that evening of October 2, "Baby, Let's Play House" was climbing the pop charts. Though most of the low-watt stations around central Texas were behind the times, Elvis's records got lots of airplay.

The Aggie footballers couldn't believe their eyes, much less their ears, as hundreds of squealing girls straddled the theater seats and wiggled and cavorted like Elvis himself. Most were dressed in poodle skirts, scarves, bobby socks, and saddle oxfords. Their hair was pulled back in ponytails. Their dates, who had come in military fatigues, were growing restless and frustrated at the lack of attention. The girls had gone gaga over the man onstage. Some pulled their skirts to midthigh, seeking an approving glance from Elvis. Others pulled off their panties and threw them onto the stage.

"Boys," Jimmy wailed, watching the girls dance, "I think I'm in love, but I know I'm in heat."

Elvis needed to look no farther than the front row to know this wasn't your normal college crowd. Military Corps officers wearing sabers on their hips stood shoulder-to-shoulder facing the raucous fans. They were, at the moment, busy rebuffing a blitz of worked-up girls who wanted to be on-stage and ran screaming through the aisles as if their hair were on fire. No one had ever seen anything like it at A&M. But, for the most part, the kids seemed to be having fun. Until Elvis did the unthinkable.

He spit his gum onto the stage floor.

In the blink of an eye, the crowd had rushed to the edge of the stage. Corps members moved in waves, shoving their dates aside. They shook their fists and cursed the swivel-hipped rocker. They didn't care that it was all just part of his act.

"You desecrated our stage!"

"Nobody does that to our building."

"Somebody knock that sonofabitch off of there."

Swords were suddenly drawn. Cadets were scaling the stage when a company commander grabbed the microphone and began barking orders: "Men, get back to your seats! This boy didn't mean any harm. We've already picked up his gum. Everybody get back. Now, goddammit."

Amazingly, the place grew quiet. The cadets retreated. Elvis held his arms above his head and apologetically smiled.

"Here, Elvis," the commander said, returning the microphone, "get on back to work. We're enjoyin' the show, son."

Elvis was suddenly transformed from a sullen hood to a polite, smiling teenager. "Sirs and ladies," he said. "I'd like to say I didn't mean anything by it. I'll try to do better."

With two strings still dangling from his guitar, Elvis broke into a song made famous by Bill Haley and the Comets—"Shake, Rattle and Roll." Even the cadets started moving to the music. By the time he broke into "Good Rockin' Tonight," the audience was his once more. He played for more than an hour and had never heard a louder ovation. He returned to the stage for three encores, including "Maybellene," a song made famous by Chuck Berry.

It was a night like no other in the eighty years of Texas A&M. Rock-and-roll had arrived. Women had frolicked unabashedly and even the hard-line cadets had demonstrated a forgiving side. The campus no longer seemed like a penitentiary. Aggie footballers couldn't wait to get acquainted with some of the young girls worked into a tizzy over Elvis. The other six acts on the Louisiana Hayride Jamboree performed to a lot of empty seats.

. . .

As the two buses rolled through the Ozarks and finally onto the street adjacent to Razorback Stadium, a drunk man with a round red face shoved the door of the first bus open and was suddenly standing within inches of Bryant.

"I'm your cousin," he slurred, his breath stinking of Old Crow and unbrushed teeth.

"Yeah."

"Yeah. I wanted to tell ya I'm proud of ya. But today I'll be pullin' for the Razorbacks."

Bryant planted his right palm firmly in the man's sternum and shoved him backward down the three steps. His hat and pennant flying, the drunk smacked the asphalt with his backside. He belched.

"He ain't my cousin," Bryant said. "My relatives don't drink whiskey that stinks that bad."

Early that morning, before the sun peeked over the Arkansas mountains, Bryant had welded on his game face. Not since leaving his native state and rumbling off to Alabama at age seventeen had he ever played in a game or coached one in Arkansas. God knows he had tried to come home.

Now Bryant had much to prove. The boys could read the determination on his face when they gathered for the early-morning buffet of eggs, smoked ham, bacon, sausage, waffles, pancakes, grits, biscuits, and gravy. They walked around the Man as if he were a poisonous snake. No one wanted to sit close to him during breakfast.

The team had bunked the previous night in Fort Smith, forty-five miles from Fayetteville, and it had been a long and tedious ride as the twin diesels rolled through the winding mountain roads. The lead bus had been library quiet until John Crow became amused with a sign nailed to a roadside store that read: GET YOUR SMOKED BACON HEAR. After he pointed it out, laughter rippled across the back rows and Bryant was quickly down the aisle.

"All right. Nobody's interested in playing Arkansas today. So let's all get out, sit under a big shade tree, and have a picnic. I'll send the driver into town for hot dogs, Cokes, and marshmallows. Then we'll call the game and spend the day tellin' stories."

The boys looked straight ahead, and some held their breath. The lead bus pulled over onto the gravel shoulder, and the second one followed. They had been parked for almost five minutes when Bryant spoke up again. "OK, bussie. I think the boys are ready. Let's go on to Fayetteville."

More than a homecoming for Bryant, the game represented a symbolic leap for the Aggies, who were 5-1 overall and undefeated in conference play. In spite of a 3-3 record, the Razorbacks were still defending SWC champions. An Aggie win in Fayetteville would make heads turn.

Neither team scored in the first half. The scrappy Arkansas defense had shut down Crow, and Bryant had tried all three quarterbacks with little success. At halftime, a scowling Bryant went from locker to locker.

"Goehring, you sonofabitch, you block somebody.

"Stallings, some days I like you. Some days I don't. Get your head out of your ass.

"John Crow, dammit, you're spendin' too much time readin' your own press clippings.

"Krueger, I can't believe a boy your size is gettin' pushed around by those little-bitty boys."

Then he stood over Henry Clark, who sat on his stool with his head bowed. Bryant grabbed the chunky tackle by the shoulder pads and lifted and shook him like a sack of potatoes. "Henry, you let that man shoot the gap on you one more time and you'll walk all the way back to Texas."

Henry gazed at Bryant with dark, sad eyes. "Coach," he said in a high-pitched voice. "I haven't even been in the game."

Like the Aggies, Arkansas was a conservative team. The teams traded punts for three quarters until the Aggies moved to the Arkansas ten early in the fourth. Bryant seemed to become more comfortable with the pass the closer his team moved to the end zone. Wright rolled right behind blocks by Crow and Pardee. Expecting a run, the Arkansas linebackers and defensive backs ignored Loyd Taylor, who slipped behind them into the flat and was wide open at the goal. Wright's arcing pass fell into his arms, and moments later Taylor added the PAT kick.

The Aggies played tenacious defense, and it appeared the 7–0 lead might stand up. Then Arkansas quarterback George Walker rolled right from the Aggie thirty-one-yard line and flipped a pass to All-American halfback Preston Carpenter at the twenty-four. He weaved past four Aggies along the sideline and was finally knocked out of bounds at the two by Pardee and Crow.

Walker sneaked behind center into the end zone, and the extra point gave rise to a historic quote.

"A tie," Bryant told the press after the game, "is like kissing your sister."

The writers scribbled it into their notepads and made certain the quote appeared high in their Sunday-morning game stories.

In spite of the tie, Texas A&M still held a half-game lead over TCU. Most folks expected Bryant to stick to the conservative path in the final weeks of the season. That's why the players were rendered almost speechless two weeks later when he announced that the starting quarterback against Rice would be Don Watson. All three quarterbacks had performed poorly against Arkansas, and after a punchless 13–2 win over SMU a week later Bryant decided to shake things up.

Jimmy Wright looked at his little cousin and shook his head. "Nadine'd have a better chance playin' quarterback than you. Son, they'll kick your ass all the way back to Franklin."

Not once had Weasel played quarterback in peewee leagues, junior high, high school, or college. But Bryant was fed up with Wright, Grant, and Bobby Joe Conrad, another one of the Million Dollar Boys. Conrad was one of the best athletes on the team, but Bryant still didn't know what to do with him.

Bryant could have chosen a softer spot in the schedule to tamper with the offense. The Aggies were hardly facing the Little Sisters of the Poor. Two years earlier, Rice had been ranked sixth in the final A.P. poll. The Owls had beaten the Aggies ten straight times, and the game was scheduled for Houston, where seventy thousand fans would pack Rice Stadium.

"Bryant's crazy," Jimmy told Weasel. "He's just showin' off. He wants to show Jess Neely that he can beat him with an All-Nobody playin' quarterback."

"Thanks for your vote of confidence."

"No problem."

For three quarters, though, Bryant had Rice right where he wanted them—in a scoreless tie. The Aggies played their best defense of the season, allowing one drive to the ten-yard line before shutting the Owls down. Predictably, Rice stacked nine men at the line of scrimmage to stop Crow and Pardee. It was clear that Watson couldn't pass.

Finally, in the fourth quarter, the dam broke. Rice halfback Paul Zipperlin followed a wall of blockers off left guard and plowed five yards into the end zone for a 6–0 lead. Minutes later, on a power sweep, Zipperlin rumbled around left end and scored on a six-yard run. Dee Powell blocked what seemed to be a meaningless extra point, and fans from both sides started heading for the exits.

Trailing 12–0 with 4:31 to play, Bryant pulled Watson and inserted Wright, his designated passer. But it was a running play that got the Aggies started from their thirty-nine-yard line.

"Option left, fullback lead," Jimmy called in the huddle. Then he said to Taylor, "Loyd, son, get wide. The end's been takin' the quarterback all day. Look for the pitch."

Jimmy was right. Running left, he was quickly confronted by the Rice end. Jimmy pitched with his left hand to Taylor, who for the first time all day got loose in the secondary. Twenty yards downfield, Pardee steamrolled an Owl defensive back, and Taylor dashed fifty-nine yards before being knocked out of bounds at the two.

Taylor then broke two tackles on the end sweep and rolled into the end zone. He also added the extra point, and the Aggies trailed 12–7.

Everyone in the stadium knew the onsides kick was coming. The Owls had nine men on the front line. Neely even called a time-out and summoned the receiving team to the sideline to make sure each player understood the gravity of the situation.

Aggie kicker Jack Powell had been instructed to punch the ball along the ground with hopes a teammate could recover it ten yards down the field but his right toe missed the ball and he caught it with his instep. The spinning action caused the ball to make a slow left turn, like a hanging curveball. It was ambling toward the left sideline and would have gone out of bounds if Stallings hadn't smothered it at the Rice forty-three.

In the days leading to the game, Bryant had admitted to himself that the Watson experiment might be a mistake. He knew his team might face a come-from-behind situation. So he'd pulled Wright aside before kickoff. "If we get behind, you're goin' in," he said. "I want you to throw it deep. Keep an eye on number 15. He's a sucker for the long pass. He likes to play about three yards off the line of scrimmage."

Number 15 happened to be Zipperlin.

Jimmy stepped into the huddle and said, "Full T. Seventy series. Loyd, go deep. And haul ass."

"Hold on," Taylor said. "I ain't worked on it."

"Hell, son, all you gotta do is run past number 15. I'll throw it to the flag. You just make sure you get there. OK?"

"I'll try."

With Weasel and Pardee flaring right and Taylor sprinting downfield, Jimmy decided no fake was necessary. He dropped seven steps into the pocket, locked his eyes on the speedy right halfback, and let it fly. Just as Bryant had envisioned, Taylor was five yards behind Zipperlin when he caught the ball at the goal. The pass couldn't have been more perfectly thrown, the play more perfectly planned or executed.

Taylor again kicked the extra point, and in a span of forty-six seconds all fourteen points were his.

Now Rice was on the short end, 14–12, with a little more than two minutes to play. Inexplicably, the Rice quarterback misfired and threw straight into the arms of Pardee, who was wearing the dirtiest uniform on the field. Pardee rumbled down the right sideline from the forty-eight to the eight-yard line. After the Owls were penalized five yards to the three,

Don Watson followed Pardee's block into the end zone and the shocking comeback was complete.

The Aggies had scored three touchdowns in two minutes and sixteen seconds, the fastest comeback in college football history. Only four snaps from center were required. Folded into the sequence were two kickoffs and three extra point attempts.

Perhaps the most surprising fact in the 20–12 comeback was that John Crow spent the final six minutes on the bench. He had been inexplicably pulled from the game and replaced at halfback by Watson. Thanks to the substitution rules of one-platoon football, Crow was rendered "dead" and therefore ineligible to return.

Though Bryant had watched the miracle comeback from the sideline, he still seemed bewildered.

Mickey Herskowitz ran toward him and shouted, "Coach, I got caught on the press elevator. I missed most of it. What happened?"

"Damned if I know," he said. "I was too busy praying."

Ten stories above the field, Herskowitz and a handful of writers had boarded a slow-moving elevator at the press box level. The car made several stops, and each time the doors opened they could hear wild cheering from the stadium. But they didn't know until they reached the ground floor and sprinted across the concourse and into the stands that the Aggies had taken a 14–12 lead.

As the players hugged one another and hollered, Bryant seemed in denial. They had won the game. But football in his world wasn't played like this. It was played according to scouting reports and game plans and sound fundamentals. The Aggies had beaten Rice with a dash down the sideline, an onsides recovery, a flick of the wrist, an interception, and a sprinkling of pixie dust. Jimmy Wright, a boy Bryant still couldn't control, had led the comeback, thrown the winning touchdown pass, and coronated the hero. For God's sakes, his teammates were now dousing Jimmy with Cokes.

"Who the hell pulled John Crow out of the game?" Bryant asked Smokey.

"You did."

"Why didn't somebody kick me in the butt?"

"We still won."

"I still can't believe we did."

Things were happening fast. One year removed from a 1-9 record, the Aggies had crept into the A.P. top twenty for the first time since 1941. They hadn't lost since the season opener against UCLA and had a 7-1-1 record.

Going into the tenth week of the season, almost everyone in Aggieland expected a victory over Texas, even though A&M had defeated the Longhorns only once since 1939. Even more remarkable was that A&M still had a shot at the SWC crown. If they defeated Texas on Thursday, they were conference champs, even if TCU beat SMU two days later.

Thanks to probation, they were banned from representing the SWC in the Cotton Bowl. But Bryant had promised the boys an exhibition game in Hawaii if they could beat Texas. He had already arranged a date with the Hawaii coach, and they'd decided to call it the Probation Bowl. The NCAA couldn't block the game since there were no rules on the books against it. Bryant was the master at asking for forgiveness, not permission.

After sparring with Texas in the first quarter, the Aggies came out throwing in the second. Jimmy Wright completed a seventeen-yard pass to a leaping John Crow. From the Texas thirty-five he sent Crow into the secondary and then looped an arcing pass over his left shoulder. Tipps described it: "This one goes airmail special delivery to John Crow, and Crow lays this one right on the lip of the cup." Jimmy sneaked the final six inches into the end zone. The sold-out crowd at Kyle Field unleashed a thunderous wave of sound that hit Bryant in the gut.

But the Aggies' 6–0 lead melted like April snow in Texas. The Longhorns returned the kickoff to midfield, and quarterback Joe Clements quickly completed a twenty-yard pass to Phil Hawkins. On the next play, he passed twenty yards to John Tatum in the right corner of the end zone.

In the third quarter, running back Walter Fondren increased the lead with a seven-yard touchdown run. After an Aggie fumble, Hawkins broke four tackles down the left side for a twenty-yard gain and then scored the final touchdown from three yards out. Texas had prevailed again, 21–6.

On Saturday, TCU clinched the conference title by beating SMU. The tie with Arkansas had cost A&M the championship. The Aggies finished with a 7-2-1 record and were ranked seventeenth in the final A.P. poll.

Bryant never again mentioned the trip to Hawaii, and the players were too afraid to ask about it.

Sadly, the season had ended on a thud. The Aggies had come farther faster than anyone had ever expected. But Aggie alums and fans all over the state had tasted a conference championship after wins over TCU and Rice and wanted to drink from the golden chalice.

Bryant had accomplished the unimaginable. He had raised a very heavy bar at Texas A&M. But it still wasn't enough.

20

Transition

One man doesn't make a team. It takes eleven.

—PAUL "BEAR" BRYANT

APRIL 1, 1956

Smokey was standing near the back of the training room in the first light of morning and didn't realize that someone was behind him. Bryant was already in one of his moods.

"Hey, Smokey. You seen my butts?"

The old trainer didn't respond. He had the *Houston Post* sports page spread across the training table and was puffing on a Cuban cigar. Something in the newspaper tickled him, and he threw back his head and brayed like a mule. Bryant marched across the room and tapped Smokey on the shoulder and, as the trainer turned, seized the volume control on his hearing aid and cranked it to full blast.

"Now, goddammit, have you seen my cigarettes?"

Smokey flinched and put his hands over his ears. "No. And if you don't stop jackin' with my hearin' aid, you'll be lookin' for a new trainer, too."

"What do you mean?"

"I mean I wanna go back to Kentucky. This place is flatter'n a skillet and hot enough most days to fry eggs on the sidewalk."

"What's got your goat?"

Smokey grabbed Bryant by the arm and led him toward an open window where a light breeze invaded the room. "Look out there at them trees. They're the only things worf a shit around here. And they're gonna cut 'em down, I hear."

Many aspects of life at Texas A&M had made Smokey unhappy, and Bryant had similar feelings. In spite of the Aggies' first top-twenty ranking in fourteen years, the alums were still prowling the campus in their Bermuda shorts and black socks and meddling in football business. It seemed that each new dawn brought more problems. Probation had caused many of the blue chippers to sign with other SWC schools, and the Aggies' spring recruiting class was a flop. A day earlier, Bryant had learned that he'd lost the best high school quarterback in America to SMU.

Bryant had flown in the A&M plane to Mount Vernon in East Texas to make one last sales pitch and the boy's eyes filled with tears as he walked into the small farmhouse.

"Coach," Don Meredith said. "If you were anywhere in the world except A&M—anywhere in the world."

Bryant asked himself each day if the Aggies really had the right stuff. Their stockpile of talent had inspired tall newspaper headlines all over Texas. But something was missing.

Kenneth Hall, the overhyped back from Sugar Land, had become disenchanted with his lack of playing time and quit the team. Hall thought he'd been promised his first starting assignment against Baylor during the '55 season. That week during practice, he'd sent three boys to the infirmary, two with broken noses and one with a separated shoulder. Assistant coach Willie Zapalac pulled Hall aside afterward and said, "You're the starter against Baylor. You play this hard the rest of the time, and you'll never sit the bench again."

Hall listened intently as Bryant read off the starting lineup just minutes before kickoff. When he didn't hear his name, tears of anger welled in his eyes. Bryant waited until the second quarter to put Hall in the game, and on his first carry he gained twenty-seven yards. Then, just as he was getting warmed up, Bryant yanked him out. Hall had been passive about his lack of playing time. But now he was seeing red. "Why don't you just let me run the damn ball?" he said to Bryant.

Hall was finally back on the field in the third quarter, and he gained twenty-one yards the next time he touched the ball. Then he turned to see Jack Pardee trotting toward the huddle to replace him. After the game, Hall walked up to Bryant. "Coach, I'm packing my stuff. This'll be my last game."

Bryant rolled his eyes. "You'll change your mind."

"No, I won't."

Hall drove home to Sugar Land and two weeks later married his high school sweetheart. Months would pass before he talked to Bryant again. But a few days before the start of spring practice, Hall had knocked on Bryant's door and asked to rejoin the team. To everyone's surprise, Bryant let him.

Now, with the 1956 spring practice getting started, Bryant had far bigger worries than Ken Hall. He still didn't have a quarterback he could trust. Donnie Grant had quit the team over the cussing he'd received in the TCU game. Spirits were low because of the NCAA probation and Bryant had yet to figure a way to break the hex of the Texas Longhorns. It had been thirty-three years since A&M had beaten the teasips in Austin.

Granted, the Aggies had stud hosses like Pardee, Goehring, Crow, and Krueger. But some of the other boys seemed dumber than dirt. Smokey had recently discovered Ty Hunterford soaking his head in the whirlpool. Now Smokey considered the whirlpool his cure-all. But he never recommended it for a head injury. He was so shaken to find the boy upside down, his head soaking in the swirling water, that he grabbed Ty by the hair and yanked his head out. The boy came up spitting and snorting.

"You crazy fool, what're you doin'?"

"Well, Smokey, you said five minutes in the whirlpool cures anything. I'd been in there two minutes. I guess I wasn't gonna make five. Thanks for savin' me."

Billy Ray Bowman was considered one of the best linemen in Texas and might have been headed for the Kodak All-American team if he hadn't outsmarted himself in the classroom. As he prepared for a final exam in an English course, he asked his tutor to prepare six papers. The professor had announced in advance the six possible topics he would ask the class to write about. Billy Ray placed all of the papers in his sock and walked to class. Throughout the three-hour exam, he scribbled in his notebook and appeared to be in deep thought. At the end, he pulled out his six papers and handed in the three correct ones. A few days later, he got a call from the professor.

"You flunked. In fact, I'm recommending that you be expelled."

"Why? I answered all of the questions."

"Yes. And all of the answers were typed."

Some of the Aggie footballers liked to get snot-slinging drunk and start fights all over town. Bryant had recently dispatched Billy Pickard again to Fort Shiloh with an envelope filled with cash to pay bills for broken windows and torpedoed walls. Bryant tried to look the other way, especially when the fast-living player happened to have talent. For instance, Bryant greatly admired Jim Stanley, one of the Million Dollar Boys, and since the graduation of Don Kachtik, Bryant considered Jim the second-toughest player on the team behind Jack Pardee. Jim led the Aggies in fifteen-yard penalties for late hits and poking opponents in the eyeballs, but Bryant rarely complained.

"It always seems that boy gets his fifteen yards' worth," he said.

Several players were throwing back Lone Star pitchers one night at Fort Shiloh when Stanley asked a young woman to dance. She happened to be the date of an A&M cadet, but Stanley didn't care and danced with her anyway. When confronted by the cadet, Stanley invited him into the parking lot to fight. Several other cadets followed. From across the bar, a group of Aggie players watched Stanley lead the contingent through the door. Dennis Goehring, Weasel Watson, Jack Pardee, and Lloyd Hale thought nothing of it.

Finally, Pardee sauntered outside to check on his teammate and returned a few minutes later.

"I got there too late," he told the others. "Jim's already whipped all five of 'em."

Bryant had dipped into the athletic budget to buy furniture, a television, and a radio for the lounge in the athletic department. It was one of the few TVs on campus. Some of the boys who'd grown up on ranches or in small towns had never seen the quiz shows or Milton Berle because, at the time, America had only a million TV sets and most were in New York.

One day, the boys found the TV set smashed along with the radio and most of the furniture. Dennis Goehring pointed the blame at 225-pound guard Gene Baker from West Virginia. Baker liked to chugalug his beer and stir up trouble. He had a bad temper, and many of the football players were afraid of him. That evening, Dennis spotted Baker wearing new slacks and a new shirt and standing on the front sidewalk. It was obvious from his dress that Baker had a date. So Dennis sneaked quietly through the front door and dumped a bucket of water over his head. The fight was on and Dennis managed to land a roundhouse right to the larger boy's mouth, causing blood to spurt. Baker hit the floor and didn't get up for several minutes. After seventeen stitches closed the gash, Baker spent the night in the hospital.

The next afternoon, Baker walked into the dormitory, sipping a milk shake. Without saying a word, Baker walked toward Dennis and landed a haymaker to his jaw, sending him reeling across the foyer. Baker tackled Dennis and held him to the floor, pounding him with both fists. But Dennis managed to stick his hand into the boy's mouth, and began tearing at the stitches as blood gushed onto the floor. Baker howled in pain. Then he jumped up and ran away. Dennis figured the fight was over until he heard something shatter in the next room. Baker returned with a broken Coke bottle in his right hand. He walked toward Dennis and brandished the glass shards. At that moment, assistant coach Jerry Claiborne ran through a side door and into the foyer.

"Stop!" he hollered. "That's enough."

But Dennis was in no mood to stop. He grabbed a wooden Coke case and broke it in half. Now he had a wooden club.

"Stay out of this, Coach Claiborne," Dennis said. "I got this sonofabitch."

Blood streamed onto Baker's shirt, and the pain was evident on his face. He threw down the broken Coke bottle, stared at Dennis, and then turned and walked through the door and onto the sidewalk. He walked past the Sbisa Hall and out of sight.

Two days passed and no one heard from Baker. Dennis was having lunch at Sbisa Hall when he felt a tap on the shoulder. He turned to see Baker standing behind him, his mouth bandaged.

"That's it. I'm leaving."

"Let me help you pack."

"OK. Let's go."

An hour later, Dennis stood on the sidewalk and watched Baker drive away in a gray Ford. Lloyd Hale was returning from class and approached his friend.

"What happened?"

"I just weeded out one of the turds."

"Oh."

No one was sure where Murry Trimble stood on the badass pecking order, but it was somewhere in the top ten. He had come from the West

Virginia coal mines, like Baker, and at age thirteen had been playing with firecrackers when there was an enormous explosion. The firecrackers turned out to be dynamite blasting caps. He felt his left forearm blow off near the elbow and watched it land about ten feet away. The boy didn't cry or whimper.

Coach Elmer had found Trimble at a high school all-star game and convinced Bryant that he was the toughest customer playing football in the state of Alabama. That turned out to be an understatement. Trimble exacted his revenge on the world by ramming his left stub into the stomach of unsuspecting opponents. Folded over and out of breath, Trimble's victims looked funny as they limped toward the sideline. Opposing coaches complained about Trimble's stub, calling it a lethal weapon, but they didn't get much sympathy from the officials.

"Coach," the referee would say, "I can't very well kick a boy out of the game who's got only one arm."

Murry also had a creative sense of mischief. He and two other students concocted a prank that had the town talking for years. Murry was standing in the line at the Palace Theater, along with a hundred or so other movie-goers, on a Saturday night when a black Packard roared through the streets and came to a screech at curbside. A man in a black suit jumped out and yelled, "Murry, you sonofabitch, I told you to stop messin' with my girl-friend!" He then aimed a high-caliber rifle at Trimble and fired two rounds of blanks. The big football player writhed and kicked on the sidewalk and managed to puncture a concealed package of ketchup, and a red substance suddenly covered his stomach and chest.

The moviegoers were so shocked that they ran off into the night and didn't look back. The police were called and soon arrived to investigate. They found no gun, no car, and no corpse. They did find a befuddled theater manager who sold no tickets and had no customers for the 7:30 movie.

Bryant had plenty of reasons to worry about his players when they left the practice field. Big Jack Powell liked to walk around campus yanking parking meters out of the ground. He then banged the meters on the ground until they coughed up some change.

Don Watson was one of the best all-around players in the conference and always seemed to be in the right place at the right time. His last-minute heroics had helped the Aggies beat TCU and Rice. The speedy halfback rarely had a scrape or a bruise on his body. So Bryant was a little surprised one Monday afternoon when he noticed that Weasel was limping. He approached the boy and said, "What the hell's wrong with your ankle?"

"Ah, Coach, I was snoopin' around one of the professor's offices and he walked in on me."

"What'd you do?"

"I jumped three stories."

"Don. Why don't you try studyin' a little bit harder."

Jimmy Wright and several of the boys had recently made a trip to Galveston for Splash Day, which was the Texas equivalent of spring break in Fort Lauderdale. They spent a lot of time on the beach, drinking beer and chasing girls. On the way back, Jimmy, Bobby Marks, and Loyd Taylor decided to stop at the Chicken Ranch in La Grange. They drank several Lone Star beers and promised the girls they would return the following November after beating Texas in the annual Thanksgiving game.

A few days later, Bryant got wind of the trip. He sauntered up to Jimmy and said, "Son, I hear there's nothin' you like more than women and beer."

"Nah, Coach, that ain't totally true. I like pizza, too."

$\bullet \quad \bullet \quad \bullet$

Bryant was starting to call him John David Crow and it pleased him. His mother had called him John David since birth, and his wife, Carolyn, thought it added a ring of character to his name.

During his first ten years as a coach, Bryant steadfastly believed that players should neither be overly praised nor criticized in print. But John David had become the exception to most rules.

"John David gives so much of himself without regard for his well-being," Bryant told the press, "that he's got a chance to be the greatest player I've ever coached."

Someone should have read that quote back to John David in the second quarter back in 1955 against SMU. Though he was one of the best kickoff returners in the conference, he ran himself into an embarrassing corner when he started retreating to avoid a wave of tacklers. He gave up twenty yards to the ten. On the next play, he lost another five yards as he tried to loop around a defensive back on an end sweep. He then saw his substitute, Billy Dedney, trotting onto the field. John David tried to avoid eye contact with Bryant as he ambled to the sideline and took a seat on the end of the bench. As he studied the ground, John David soon saw the tops of Bryant's shoes in front of him. The coach knelt, put one hand on the boy's knee, and said, "John, our goal is *thataway*."

Now, on the second day of spring drills, John David had jumped the gun on two snap counts and Bryant halted practice.

"John David. Does your mama back in Louisiana have a scrapbook of your press clippings?"

"Yessir."

"Well, you oughta tell her to burn it."

It still bugged Bryant that fans and ex-students gathered around the practice field to watch John David and the boys scrimmage, run wind sprints, and hit blocking dummies. But he couldn't do anything about it. There was no fence around the field, which was situated next to the stadium. Besides, he'd already stirred up enough trouble by publicly telling the alums to keep their noses out of his business.

On a warm and humid afternoon, Bryant worked the boys for three hours without water breaks. They ran twenty gassers, and many of the boys suffered from the blind wobbles as they chugged from one end of the field to the other. As the workout ended, Bryant smiled and waved at the all-male audience. Under his breath he said, "Good-bye and good riddance."

John David was so tired that he dragged a chair into the shower room and sat there for several minutes while the water poured over his body. Some of the boys lay on the concrete floor, letting the water soothe their aching bones. Then a student manager walked to the entrance of the shower room and announced, "Coach Bryant wants everybody back on the field in five minutes. Put 'em back on."

"You're crazy!" John David snapped. "There's no way."

Several of the other players protested.

"Look," the student manager said. "I'm just the messenger. The man said to put 'em back on."

They tugged on the wet, stinking uniforms and trudged back onto the field where Bryant stood at the fifty-yard line, smiling. The sidelines were now free of witnesses.

"Everybody get down on one knee," he said. "I've got a few things I need to tell ya."

All of the players knelt except John David. "Coach, I think I'd rather stand, if you don't mind," he said.

Bryant could see the boy's face was pale and that he was breathing

225

unevenly. He cleared his throat and said, ''Boys, we were tied last year by Arkansas and we lost to Texas because we ran out of gas in the second half. We ain't losin' no more games in the fourth quarter. Period. Got it? That's why we've gotta work harder than we ever have. So buckle 'em back on. We're gonna have a little scrimmage before it gets dark.''

Bryant heard a thud. Then he turned to see John David flat on his back.

''Billy!'' Bryant hollered. ''Get your butt over here. Seems that John David doesn't want to practice no more.''

Billy Pickard ran toward Crow and quickly recognized the symptoms of heatstroke. His mind flashed back to Junction, to the day when Billy Schroeder had toppled forward into the cactus and thick dust and they had rushed him to the infirmary. Unlike Schroeder, though, John David wasn't turning purple and blue and his heart rate was only slightly above normal. Student managers placed the unconscious player on a stretcher and carried him into the locker room, where Billy followed a procedure learned from Dr. Wiedeman back in Junction. He packed John David in ice before transporting him to the A&M infirmary.

For more than an hour, as John David lay unconscious in the emergency room, Bryant paced the hallway, chain-smoking Chesterfields, distress evident on his face. While his favorite player was having saline and glucose injected into his veins, Bryant was experiencing second thoughts about the slave-driving practices. He wondered if God was trying to give him a warning, letting him know he was lucky that the Schroeder boy hadn't died in Junction.

Charlie Krueger and Carolyn Crow watched Bryant walk the floor. All three were standing beside John David's bed thirty minutes later when he opened his eyes. Carolyn was holding her husband's hand. From the foot of the bed, Bryant peered at the groggy boy. ''Hell, John David, if you were tired, why didn't you just tell me?''

The Man was starting to change.

21

Thunder

If anything goes bad, I did it. If anything goes semigood, we did it. If anything goes real good, you did it. That's all it takes to get people to win football games.

—PAUL "BEAR" BRYANT

SEPTEMBER 16, 1956

Jimmy Wright had the Villanova Wildcats in the palm of his hand on a cloudy and windswept Saturday afternoon at Kyle Field. But he didn't know the dice he was rolling had turned stone cold.

Jimmy was challenging a Bryant edict that football games are won on the ground. He hit a streaking Loyd Taylor with a perfect spiral at the Villanova fifteen-yard line, a completion reminiscent of his winning touchdown pass in the improbable Rice comeback. Taylor caught it over his right shoulder and dashed untouched to the end zone, and the Aggies led 7–0 in the opening game of the 1956 season.

It was the hit of confidence Jimmy could have lived without. In the second quarter, the Aggies faced a fourth-and-inches situation at midfield. Jimmy sneaked a glance to the sideline and saw Bryant's secret signal for a punt. Under NCAA rules, coaches were not allowed to communicate in any way with players on the field. But Bryant knew the officials wouldn't flag him for casually placing his right foot in front of his left.

"Coach wants you to punt," center Lloyd Hale said.

"Piss on Bryant," Jimmy said. "Let's go with halfback lead, fullback counter."

"You're out of your mind, Jimmy."

"Shut up."

"Your ass is gonna be grass."

"Shut up."

This was the play: Jimmy would fake the handoff at right tackle to Crow and then spin 180 degrees and hand the ball to Pardee, who would dive between the center and guard. Hale and Goehring opened a hole that should have sprung Pardee for a long gain. But as Jimmy pivoted his right leg tripped the big fullback. Pardee sprawled a yard short of the line of scrimmage. A hush fell over the stadium.

Bryant marched onto the field and grabbed the quarterback by the face mask and wrenched the boy's head almost ninety degrees.

"You will never play another down of football for me, you bucket-headed sonofabitch," Bryant growled. He shoved Jimmy toward the locker room and yelled, "Get your ass in there and take off your suit! You'll never wear this suit again."

Jimmy knew he was in trouble, but he wasn't about to endure the embarrassment of walking to the locker room in front of a capacity crowd. "I ain't taking off my suit."

Bryant pulled off his hat and threw it down. "Then stand down there at the end of the bench with the centers, the guards, and the turds."

Bryant had prepared for the day when Jimmy would prove him right. That's why he had moved Roddy Osborne from fullback to quarterback. Like Elwood Kettler, Roddy was a tough hombre who possessed far more grit than flash. He had a weak throwing arm, and that pleased Bryant. If Elwood looked like he was slinging shit, then Osborne was flinging something far more odorous.

The Aggies didn't throw another pass against Villanova. After Murry Trimble recovered a Villanova fumble, the offense moved like a team of mules, needing eleven plays to cover fifty-eight yards with Crow scoring on a sweep from the seven. Taylor missed the extra point. Then it was run, run, run again in the fourth as Pardee, Crow, Watson, and Osborne ate up yards and the clock and Osborne scored on a quarterback sneak. The Aggies came away with a punishing 19–0 victory. Bryant loved it.

Monday morning, Jimmy discovered that his locker had been cleaned out. He slumped into a chair in the training room and was on the verge of tears when Smokey said, "Don't worry, boy; I've got somethin' for you to wear to practice. Shit, son, there'll be better days."

Smokey wasn't in the habit of consoling players, especially mavericks like Jimmy. But he admired the cocky quarterback who had never missed a practice and didn't even know how to turn on the whirlpool. He was usually the first to practice and the last to leave and never complained about aches and pains. He had never missed a meeting or a workout and could have been the best quarterback in the country in another offense. Smokey knew this. But until Jimmy relented to Bryant's thinking, the rest of the country would know little or nothing about him.

"Some folks think they can change Coach Bryant's mind," Smokey told the boy, biting into a cigar. "They're the dumb ones. Coach Bryant don't change." Smokey reached into a drawer and pulled out sweatpants, a T-shirt, and a jockstrap and handed them to Jimmy.

"Thanks, you old cuss."

Jimmy checked the bulletin board. As expected, he didn't find his name on the practice list, but that didn't stop him from being the first player on the field, and it didn't stop Bryant from ignoring him like a meddling alum. Assistant coach Jerry Claiborne walked toward Jimmy and said, "Buster, I thought you'd just give up and go home."

"Which is harder, Coach? Quittin' or goin' to work as a roughneck?"

"Roughneckin', I suppose."

"See?"

Though the Aggies had won eight of their last eleven games, practices were getting no easier. Pat James was demonstrating blocking techniques when he turned his cap backward and dropped into a three-point stance in front of Jim Langston. James was a burly man with a beer-barrel chest and thick arms. Before becoming a coach, he'd played guard for Bryant at Kentucky, and during the 1951 Sugar Bowl he had been photographed as he flew through the air, his eyes larger than saucers.

Langston was often picked on by the coaches because he stood five-seven and weighed almost 220 pounds. They called him Round Man. James charged from his stance and was about to rattle Langston's jaw with a forearm shiver when he felt himself being plowed under. Round Man ran straight over him, leaving the coach facedown in the dust. As James stood and brushed himself off, Round Man dropped into his stance, ready for more.

"That'll be enough," James said. "I think you get my drift. Just keep doin' it that way, goddammit, and you'll be fine."

Round Man might have won that battle, but Bryant cut him no slack at the end of practice when overweight players were ordered to run extra laps. Twenty minutes later, Bryant sat on his stool and was pulling off his shoes when Round Man burst into the coaches' dressing room, his face caked with yellow dust.

"They call me Round Man," he blurted, waving a soaked practice jersey. "And they'll call me Round Man when I'm fifty. But I can tell you one goddamn thing." Round Man pointed at Bryant. "You'll never run me off this football team."

Bryant leaned back as a smile creased his lips. "I guess you've been hangin' around Dennis Goehring."

Round Man huffed and puffed and suddenly realized he'd said enough. He turned away, his shoulder pads rattling as he waddled through the door leading back to the locker room.

"He's a peculiar boy, isn't he?" Bryant said to Jerry Claiborne.

"Yeah, Coach."

Bryant studied Claiborne's face and could see there was something on his mind.

"There's somethin' I've been thinkin' about, Coach," Claiborne said nervously. "You ready to hear it?"

"Spit it out."

"Coach, you're not gonna like this. But as you're makin' travel plans for LSU, you'd better put Jimmy Wright on your list."

"Why's that?"

"Because LSU's a lot better team than you think. We beat 'em pretty good last year. But they've got a big fullback, boy named Jimmy Taylor. He's got jackhammers for legs. Coach, some folks are pickin' LSU to win their conference. Paul Dietzel is a heckuva coach. I'm just worried that we'll get behind and we won't be able to catch up. That's why I think we'd better take Jimmy Wright along for insurance."

Friday morning, Jimmy found his name at the bottom of the travel squad, listed with the student managers. When the team arrived in Baton Rouge that afternoon, he was assigned a hotel room but not a roommate. The next evening, Bryant didn't acknowledge him during the pregame quarterback walk and Jimmy chose to tag along at the back. Bryant now focused all of his attention on Osborne, and the instructions were to pound the ball between the tackles.

To everyone's surprise, though, Wright opened the second quarter behind center in what amounted to a strategic ploy by Bryant. The plan was to reinsert Osborne after the first offensive series and then have Wright available late in the quarter if the Aggies needed a quick score. One-platoon rules allowed for a player to return in a particular quarter if he'd been on the field when it started.

It didn't go according to hoyle. Jimmy quickly pumped life into the offense, even though Pardee and Crow were on the sideline, suffering from the flu. Without a strong running game, Jimmy was left in the precarious position of improvising. Jimmy knew that he should check the sideline to see if Bryant had more instructions. But it didn't matter since sixty-one thousand drunk and rowdy fans were yelling at the top of their lungs.

With backup quarterback Bobby Joe Conrad lining up at Crow's half-back position, Jimmy had an idea. Conrad had played several positions and might have been the best punter and placekicker on the team and Bryant had once toyed with the idea of making him the first-team quarterback. Jimmy pitched the ball to Conrad, who rolled right and passed to a wide open Carlos Esquival in the corner of the end zone. Again Jimmy had lit a fire, and the Aggies grabbed a 7–0 lead.

The Aggie defense was being rocked by the bullish Taylor, but LSU still couldn't move the ball with any consistency. Tackle Bobby Jack Lockett turned to Lloyd Hale and said, "I don't know if number 31 cares more about gaining yards or just runnin' over you."

Hale sighed and said, "I think you're right."

In the third quarter, Dee Powell blocked an LSU punt through the back of the end zone and the Aggies had a 9–0 lead. But the Tiger offense took on a new dimension when they started passing. They moved the ball eighty-four yards to the end zone, cutting the lead to 9–7 with 1:35 to play. Then LSU executed the onsides kick just as the Aggies had done against Rice the previous year.

With less than a minute to play, LSU had the ball at the Aggie twenty-five yard line. On fourth down, a Tiger pass was completed at the three, and the receiver appeared to be in bounds. Bryant ripped off his hat and marched toward the closest official, pointing and hollering, "If you've got a gut in your body, you'll call it incomplete!" The official waved off the pass, and the Aggies held on for one of the biggest wins in Bryant's tenure.

Against Texas Tech the next week, Jimmy started the game and threw a ten-yard touchdown pass to Weasel Watson at the back of the end zone. Pardee and Crow each had two rushing touchdowns. The game was a testament to the different roads the teams had taken since the start of the '54 season, when the Red Raiders had clobbered the Aggies. A&M won 40–7, improving their record to 3–0. Coming up was the toughest stretch of the season, a stretch that would determine if the Aggies had truly arrived.

. . .

The captains for the 1956 season were seniors Bebes Stallings, Lloyd Hale, and Jack Pardee—all Junction survivors. Only eight Junction Boys were still around when the team had gathered for preseason drills. Their freshman class three years earlier had numbered *115*.

The others who'd perservered in Junction were Don Watson, Bobby Drake Keith, Bobby Jack Lockett, Dee Powell, and Dennis Goehring. Bryant told the press several times that if the Aggies were to win their first conference championship since 1941, the Junction Boys would the driving force, and it went without saying that John David Crow and Charlie Krueger would also play leading roles.

Not since 1939, when coach Homer Norton led the Aggies to a national championship, had there been such talent or football fever in College Station. Players were gods again on campus, and Corps members didn't dare to haze any footballer. The process of building the Aggies into a championship-caliber team had taken less than three seasons. Bryant had run off the heartless quitters and then molded the keepers into a winning squad. One of his favorites was Bebes Stallings, who played each down as if it would be his last. Stallings and Goehring had been named to the all-conference team in 1955.

Already Bryant was privately sharing his coaching philosophy with Stallings, who knew as much about *X*s and *O*s as some of the assistant coaches. As the players were preparing to leave campus during the summer break a few months earlier, Stallings had knocked on Bryant's door and the coach was happy to see him, as usual.

"Coach, I've got somethin' I need to tell you."

"Shoot."

"Well, Ruth Ann Jack and I are planning to get married this summer."

"That's not a good idea."

"I don't understand, Coach."

"It's not a good idea. My captains live in the athletic dorm. If you're married, you won't be livin' there."

"I see."

Bebes and Ruth Ann quickly postponed their marriage plans. Though the couple had been sweethearts since schools days in Paris, Bebes knew there was no use arguing with a man who walked around with his mind made up.

Bryant tried not to show favoritism toward Stallings, although the other players could see it. Stallings was neither big nor fast nor particularly athletic, and when he ran his legs seemed heavy. But he had a penchant for making big plays, like the onsides kick recovery against Rice in '55 that triggered the miracle comeback. Stallings had scored the only touchdown in the Aggies' lone win in '54.

Bryant appreciated Stallings's work ethic and the way he studied the game. But the coach also admired his grit and toughness. During spring drills two years earlier, Stallings had caught his finger in a helmet and almost ripped it off. The finger was dangling from his hand by the skin, but after several stitches, the boy was back at practice the next day.

An influx of talented players was making it more and more difficult for Stallings to hold onto his starting job. As the season progressed, he found himself being replaced by junior Bobby Marks, who was proving to be a more skilled receiver.

"Bobby Marks is just better than me," Bebes told Bobby Drake.

"Nah."

"Yeah he is. And if it makes the team better, so be it."

"You're crazy, Bebes."

The ultimate Bryant player might have been Hale, the tough-as-nails center who was a roughneck and a street fighter. But you wouldn't have known it by looking at him since he weighed 180 pounds and had choirboy cheeks.

Hale was from the West Texas boomtown of Iraan, a tiny place that also produced a guard named Bud McFadin who made All-American at Texas in 1949 and '50. McFadin helped lead the Longhorns to a number-two ranking in the final A.P. poll in 1950. McFadin, however, had worried the bejeebers out of the coaching staff when he went AWOL during pre-season drills. Coach Blair Cherry quickly dispatched one of his assistants to retrieve the boy from Iraan.

The coach found him working on the family ranch. "Bud," the coach said. "Did we do somethin' to make you mad?"

"No."

"Did you leave because you didn't like Coach Cherry?"

"No."

"Did you leave because you didn't like our food?"

"No."

"Then why did you leave?"

"I missed my horse."

The coach arranged for the bay colt to be trailered to Austin, where it would be stabled close to campus. Bud never left the team again.

Though college players across the country were getting bigger, Bryant still preferred small but bullish linemen who had quick feet. A scramble blocker like Hale attacked opponents at the knees and swept them out of the hole. Teams always put a noseguard over Hale, because if they didn't, he would wipe out their linebackers.

One afternoon, Bryant paid a surprise visit to the athletic dorm to make sure all of the players had landed summer jobs. After knocking on Hale's door, he heard someone inside say, "Just spit on the floor and slide under."

"What?"

"You dumb sonofabitch. Just spit on the floor and slide under. Or slide a dollar underneath and we'll let you in."

Bryant thought the words sounded slurred, and his ears didn't fail him. Hale and his roommate, Billy Pete Huddleston, had been concocting what they called Tahitian drinks, mixing strawberry Kool-Aid with rum. They were getting smashed.

Bryant knocked again.

"If you're lookin' for the maid, come on around back."

Then Bryant pounded the door. Hale looked stunned as he swung open the door and saw the Man.

"Coach," he said. "How's about a drink? Of 7Up, of course."

The smell of booze quickly filled Bryant's nostrils. He glared at Hale and then shook his head and then slowly walked away, mumbling to himself, and he didn't look back. Another player would have been running stadium steps until the next dawn.

Texas A&M received some unexpected bulletin board material from the *Houston Post* as they prepared to play the Houston Cougars in the fourth week of the season. Asked to assess A&M's unbeaten season, Cougar guard Bob White said, "All they got is one big ol' crippled boy and another boy with polio." He was referring to Murry Trimble, who had half an arm, and John David Crow, whose drooping face was often confused with a polio disfigurement.

In spite of the verbal challenge, Bryant noticed that his team was listless during practice leading to the Houston game. He couldn't figure out why.

He didn't know the players barely respected Houston, a team they'd whipped 21–3 the previous season. He didn't know the Aggies already had TCU on their minds. They were scheduled to play the Horned Frogs a week after the Houston game and everybody in Texas was already talking about it. Both A&M and TCU were ranked in the top ten. So the Houston game had become a fading priority.

The Aggies seemed to be sleepwalking in the first half. Roddy Osborne fumbled on the first play of the game, and the Cougars grabbed a quick 7–0 lead. Then the A&M offense moved seventy-four yards to the six before Ken Hall fumbled. John Tracey, a hard-hitting end from Philadelphia, blocked a punt and recovered for a touchdown. Otherwise the Aggies would have had no points at halftime. As it was, Bryant had enough to rant and rave about in the locker room.

A gruesome injury to Bobby Drake Keith had sickened some of the boys. Bobby Drake had tried to cross body-block cornerback Billy Bob Sweet, and the Houston player had kneed him in the chin. Keith's jaw snapped in three places. Part of the fractured jawbone severed a large vessel, and blood spurted from his mouth. It didn't deter Bobby Drake from walking back to the huddle and saying, "Call another play, dammit. I'll get even with that sonofabitch." Several of the players had seen Sweet purposely ram his knee into Bobby Drake's chin and heard the bones snap.

Roddy looked at his injured teammate. "No, bud, you're gettin' outta here. Hell, you're bleeding all over the place." Blood poured from his nose, and his face looked as if it'd been squeezed in a vise.

As Bobby Drake weaved and stumbled almost blindly toward the sideline, Bryant felt his stomach jump. A pall fell over the sideline, and many of the fans in the lower rows had to turn their heads. An ambulance roared down the tunnel and across the playing field and the game was halted as Bobby Drake was loaded in the back of the ambulance and rushed to a local hospital.

It was the third quarter before the Aggies felt like concentrating on football again. Crow and Pardee battered the Cougar line, and Osborne operated the option with a masterful touch. The Houston defense was near exhaustion when Osborne ran three yards for the tying touchdown around right end.

It seemed the Aggies were on the verge of seizing control of the game in their normal grinding fashion. But it wasn't long before they started fumbling again.

The past two seasons had been nothing but hell and frustration for Ken

Hall. He rarely even got into the games, as John David Crow, Loyd Taylor, and Weasel Watson had the halfback positions nailed down. Bobby Marks often made fun of Hall by wearing a sign around his neck that read: KEN HALL FAN CLUB.

Bryant really wanted Hall to play fullback but knew it wouldn't work. The fullback in the Aggie system also had to play linebacker, and Hall wasn't hardwired with a head-hunting mentality. He was a fast and fluid halfback who at six-one and 205 pounds could run the 100-yard dash in 9.7 seconds. Unlike Pardee, Hall was neither a power-driving back nor a good tackler. Aggie players were defensive players first in the Bryant system. Hall would have been better off at a place like Oklahoma, where Bud Wilkinson cashed checks and won national championships with graceful ballcarriers.

There was something that Bryant didn't like about the boy. Hall had the gall to approach the coach one day and say, "You know, that practice we had yesterday was pretty hard on the team. I was dog tired when it was over."

"I got tired, too," Bryant snapped. "And I bet your daddy was pretty tired when he got off work yesterday, too."

Bryant had cussed and embarrassed and tormented Hall in front of the other players. There had been times when he even dreaded suiting up for practice. It seemed that someone was challenging him for his second-string jersey almost every day. Bryant would walk through the locker room and holler, "Billy Bob Jones from the fifth string is challenging Hall for his jersey today!" Then he'd line up four or five players to take Hall on. He was normally worn out before practice even started.

Now Bryant was trying to rethink his position on the boy and had promised him more playing time against Houston. His teammates, however, weren't surprised that he fumbled the third time he carried the ball to kill a drive inside the Houston ten. He fumbled again when the Aggies reached the Cougar six in the third quarter.

"Get that sonofabitch out of the game!" Jimmy Wright yelled. "Hell, we're a lot better off with Watson or Loyd Hale in there." Bryant apparently agreed. Hall was quickly back on the bench, where he would stay for the rest of the game.

Houston had its chances in the third quarter, moving all the way to the Aggie one-yard line, where the Cougars had a first down. But Jack Pardee made four straight tackles for no gain.

Osborne kick-started the Aggie offense late in the third quarter as Pardee and Crow took charge by running the ball down Houston's throat. Osborne completed a seventy-yard drive with a two-yard run around left end, and the Aggies had a 14–7 lead. The Aggies expected the Cougars to coast in the fourth quarter, just as they had done the previous season. Instead, they were hell-bent on tying the game and did so five minutes later.

The Aggies knew they had to cover ninety-five yards for the winning points in just three minutes. Bryant almost called for Jimmy Wright but stuck with Osborne at quarterback. Crow and Pardee pounded the line and, with the clock winding down, it still appeared the Aggies had time to push the ball into the end zone.

From the three Crow plunged over right guard, and the Aggie sideline erupted into a celebration. It was premature. The official marked the ball inches from the goal with seven seconds to play and Bryant used the final time-out, summoning a student manager to tote the kicking tee onto the field. The Aggies simply needed a chip-shot field goal to win the game. Their most consistent kicker, Loyd Taylor, was already on the field. Osborne walked to the sideline, where Bryant was in a heated discussion with two assistant coaches.

"Goddammit," Bryant growled. "If we can't push it over from there, we don't deserve to win. Field goals are for sissies." He wheeled toward Osborne and cupped his hand over his mouth. "Throw back the kickin' tee and run 'option right.' Give it to Pardee."

Osborne didn't give it to Pardee, who could have walked into the end zone. He decided to run it himself around right end and was pinned between the tackle and the linebacker. The officials didn't signal touchdown and, instead, the ball was marked inches short of the goal as time expired. Bryant walked across the field, through a gate, and onto the team bus. He had nothing to say worth quoting about this tie.

• • •

The Aggies were heartsick after the long bus ride home from Houston, and Fort Shiloh was nothing more than an empty saloon. But the newspaper hype for the TCU game began the next day and it seemed everyone was talking about the SWC showdown of the decade—Texas A&M versus TCU at Kyle Field.

TCU was loaded with headliners. Jim Swink had finished second in the 1955 Heisman balloting behind Howard "Hopalong" Cassady of Ohio State. Froggie quarterback Chuck Curtis was considered the best passer in the conference. Abe Martin was arguably one of the best five college coaches in America, and after opening the season with wins over Alabama, Arkansas, and Kansas, the Horned Frogs were the fourth-ranked team in the country, with aspirations of being number one.

Two tropical storms in the last three weeks had churned up the Gulf of Mexico. Though College Station was two hundred miles from the coast, it felt like the Congo that Saturday afternoon when temperatures settled into the midnineties and the relative humidity hovered around 80 percent. The teams started warming up at one o'clock as the sun beat down mercilessly from a cloudless sky.

Each Aggie was propped on one knee in the locker room and drenched in sweat as Bryant paced, pulled on a Chesterfield, and prepared to deliver his pregame speech.

"The team that wins today is gonna be the one that concentrates every minute. I don't care if it's a hurricane, a tornado, or a typhoon that's comin' our way. By God, you'd better brace yourselves."

The boys traded quizzical looks. The weather forecast hadn't mentioned a hurricane or tornado and most weren't sure what a typhoon was. Was their coach speaking metaphorically? Or did he know something that even the weathermen hadn't predicted? It worried some of the players that Bryant seemed to possess powers of wizardry.

The crowd of forty-two thousand looked resplendent in a vast array of colors. Many of the women had donned floral hats that were more suitable to spring. Knit dresses were especially popular. The ALL SOLD OUT signs had been hanging in the Kyle Field ticket windows for more than a week. But thanks to a last-minute surge of walk-ups, athletic officials decided to sell about three thousand more standing-room-only tickets. As the players walked down the tunnel toward the playing field, they could see rows and rows of fans ringing the sideline. They were bunched tightly, and some stood only two or three feet from the sideline. Not since the Los Angeles Coliseum had the boys seen a larger crowd.

Beneath a bright sun, TCU began to drive the ball midway in the first quarter as Swink got loose in the secondary for runs of sixteen and twenty-two yards. But the Frogs were halted on fourth-and-inches at the Aggie twenty-eight when Pardee rammed through an opening at center and nailed Swink. The Aggies were not as fortunate on TCU's next possession, as Swink scored on a five-yard end run. But just as the A&M fans spotted a penalty flag, thunder rang down from the sky. A wall of black clouds and a smattering of dry lightning appeared from the south. The referee walked off a five-yard penalty against TCU for illegal motion. Then sheets of rain swept across the stadium and the scene turned almost biblical. Fury and darkness followed.

In spite of the dramatic weather shift, TCU still had no call to change its strategy. Swink carried to the four-yard line and, in the blinding rain, was tackled again by Pardee. Frog coach Abe Martin wasn't aware that Pardee was playing with a separated shoulder. But it wouldn't have mattered. Pardee never allowed pain to stand in his way, and besides, the shoulder had been numbed with a heavy dose of Novocain minutes before kickoff when Dr. Harrison worked the six-inch needle deep into the AC joint. Pardee had barely grimaced.

On second down, Pardee stopped Swink for a one-yard gain. On the next play, the TCU halfback drove within inches of the goal, where he was pummeled by Pardee. Water was starting to gather in small rivers, and the playing field was barely visible from the press box. Lloyd Hale moved from linebacker to noseguard. The Aggie linemen had their noses on the ground and their butts in the air. Their strategy was to halt the surge of the TCU line to give Pardee a clean shot at the ballcarrier.

Both sides dug in and Swink took the pitch from Curtis. He could feel the powerful wind pushing him from behind. Pardee again drove his injured shoulder into the running back, but Swink was certain that he'd broken the plane of the goal. The side judge disagreed and signaled that TCU had been turned away inches from the goal. The ball changed hands on downs.

"You shithead!" Swink hollered at the official. Pardee rarely opened his mouth during games, but he turned to Swink and in a high, girlish voice said, "Sorry, Jimmy."

Many of the fans were familiar with violent weather. Some had witnessed the raw force of a hurricane as it piled into the Texas coastal towns of Galveston or Corpus Christi. This storm felt no different. It struck with straight-line winds that roared at close to ninety miles per hour. Hats flew out of the stands, and the tall light standards swayed back and forth on poles turned rubberlike by the gale. Some seemed ready to snap. It was so dark and the horizontal rain so thick that the Aggies couldn't see the Horned Frogs on the other sideline, and vice versa. Teams were no longer worried so much about moving the ball as they were about hanging onto it.

Players with the wind in their faces had to pump their arms and lean forward just to reach the line of scrimmage for the next play. The stadium lights were turned on, but they flickered and spit sparks.

Lloyd Taylor tried advancing the ball around the right end and somehow reached the sideline before he was gang-tackled. He slid twenty feet with four players riding him like a pleasure boat. They landed in a swale where a deep pool of rainwater had gathered. Taylor's head became submerged. He couldn't breathe for several seconds and feared he might drown. Garnering superhuman strength, he shoved the Horned Frogs off his chest and gasped for breath.

Taylor was still breathing hard when he returned to the huddle. He grabbed John David by the jersey and shouted through the rain, "Don't let them sumbucks push you into that pool yonder! You'll drown."

Taylor watched as John David swept end on the next play and stepped nimbly out of bounds before he could be tackled. Two Frogs lost their balance and slid headfirst into the gathering lake. Waves rippled across the surface as powerful winds continued to punish the stadium. Lightning danced and thunder crackled. Two miles from Kyle Field, a tornado plowed into Easterwood Airport and damaged more than 150 planes. Ten aircraft were destroyed. The Bryan Air Base reported several other twisters touching down in the area, but the game was never stopped. It could be said that the fair-weather fans either ran for cover or went home. But almost thirty-thousand folks braved a storm that might be best described as a land-bound minihurricane.

Fans who stuck around were soon apprised by the public-address announcer that paper raincoats were for sale in the stadium concourses. The supply went fast but didn't last long. The wind swept away the raincoats along with thousands of hats. As Taylor drew a bead on Swink, he was suddenly blinded by a flying object that had sailed out of the stands. Taylor pulled the tangled raincoat out of his face mask with one hand and tackled Swink with the other.

Officials spent a good part of the first half chasing down footballs that were blown all over the field. Between plays, the referee kept his foot on the ball so it wouldn't roll away. The Aggies broke the huddle, and center Lloyd Hale prepared to squat over the ball when he realized it had disappeared. A fast-forming river had swept it down the field, all the way to the end zone. From that point on, the referee held the ball between plays and handed it to the center.

The Aggies spent most of the second quarter with the wind in their faces and their backs to the goal. They were barely able to move the ball more than five or six yards before either fumbling it away or punting. Neither team had scored. Four times TCU had the ball inside the ten-yard line as Pardee put the hammer down on Swink. Fans thought Swink was injured as he staggered to the TCU sideline. A shaken Abe Martin ran toward his star halfback and shouted, "What's wrong?"

"I can't breathe."

The howling wind had grown so intense that players were forced to turn their faces away from it to catch their breath.

Late in the second quarter, the Aggies were forced to punt again from their own twenty-yard line. Hale's snap to Osborne was quite accurate considering the conditions, and Roddy punted it away. Players for both teams searched the sky for the ball as it vanished into the low black clouds. They waited. Then they heard a thud. The ball had traveled about twenty yards before smacking into the jet stream and making a U-turn. Then it down-spiraled straight into the punter's helmet. Roddy, whose ears were now ringing, had punted for a negative ten yards.

The Aggies managed to hold TCU out of the end zone once more before halftime, and the teams scurried like drowned rats toward shelter. Aggie student managers had laid out fresh jerseys for the first-team players, but the numbers didn't match up. John David Crow, who wore the number 44, slipped into number 84. Weasel Watson traded 24 for 26.

Bryant lit a cigarette and his eyes scanned the locker room. "Where the hell is Coach Elmer?"

The room was silent. Everyone knew that Coach Elmer was Bryant's right-hand man on game day. He watched the action from the press box and then relayed pertinent information on the opponent's formations to Bryant. But when the storm moved in, the press box phones had gone out. So Coach Elmer had run down the stadium steps to the sideline to inform Bryant that he was going to seek out a perch above the end zone.

No one would have predicted that Coach Elmer, a man in his early fifties, could scale the tall and shaky wooden ladder that led to the scoreboard. But he did. He squatted on a ledge, where he removed his shoes and socks. He scribbled TCU's formations on a sheet of paper, stuffed it into a sock, and dropped it twenty feet to a student manager, who would dash to the Aggie sideline and hand the sock to Bryant. When Coach Elmer's socks became soaked, he started stuffing the charts into his shoes.

The job turned perilous in the second quarter as the hurricane-force winds intensified. Coach Elmer's hat blew off. He steadied himself by wrapping his left arm around a pole. The rain was almost blinding, but he kept scribbling.

Bryant was still searching for Coach Elmer when he heard a voice from the back of the locker room.

"Coach," student trainer Jerry Rhea said. "I hear that Coach Elmer might be stuck up on the scoreboard."

"Well, goddammit, son, go get him."

Three student managers dashed through the locker room door and up the stadium steps. They quickly discovered that the ladder leading to the scoreboard had blown down.

"Help!" Coach Elmer yelled, holding on for his life. "Help, you son-sabitches."

The boys propped the ladder back up, and Coach Elmer wasted no time climbing down. He fished a wet cigarette from his shirt pocket and stuck it in his mouth.

Minutes later, Coach Elmer looked like a soaked alley cat as he walked into the locker room.

"Where're your shoes?" Smokey Harper said.

Coach Elmer looked down at his bare feet. "I suppose Coach Bryant's got 'em somewhere."

The heart of the storm had blown through College Station before the players returned to the field. But the playing surface was a sponge and the wind still gusted at around thirty miles per hour. Not since the storm blew in had the boys been able to see the stadium crowd. They were shocked to discover that most of the fans had stuck around. Fans who had rung the field for the opening kickoff had returned after seeking shelter beneath the stands.

One of the toughest jobs belonged to Kern Tips, who could barely see the field through the blowing rain and gathering darkness. There were times when he couldn't see the ball. Several players had vanished into gloom, and others were sticklike figures.

"Folks," he told the radio audience, "all I can tell ya is that the Aggies are backed to their goal, but the Froggies have yet to ram it home."

The scene in the third quarter became even more confusing. Several Aggies had changed jerseys and now wore numbers that weren't listed in the game program. Tips sought emergency help from Jones Ramsey, but even the sports information director couldn't identify the players. Ramsey quickly sought out Bobby Drake Keith, who was sitting out the game with a broken jaw. He had taken a seat in the press box. Bobby Drake had seen the boys almost every day and could identify them by the shape of their bodies and by the way they ran. But with his jaw wired shut, he couldn't talk. So Bobby Drake scribbled down the name of the Aggie ballcarrier and tackler and handed it to Tips.

"Is there anyone out there in radioland you'd like to say hello to?" Tips said.

Bobby Drake scribbled: "Folks in Junction."

"Oh, yes, Bobby Drake Keith sends along his regards to all of the fine folks in Junction. Hope you people are gettin' some of this rain out there. We know you need it."

Almost three hundred miles to the west, Junction was still bone-dry and had been suffering for six years from the worst drought in Texas history. Hardly a drop of rain had fallen since the Aggies left town more than two years earlier.

Playing on a faster track, TCU finally ended its dry spell with a long touchdown drive. From the Aggie six Chuck Curtis side-armed a wet and heavy ball toward the back line of the end zone and the high, wobbly pass seemed far out of the reach of the receiver. But O'Day Williams, who had Crow riding his back, leaped and made a one-handed stab, dropping both feet inside the line and just inches from the left goalpost. Weasel Watson blocked the extra point, and the Frogs led 6–0 midway in the third quarter.

For the eighth time in the game, TCU moved inside the Aggie twenty-yard line early in the fourth quarter. They failed to score for the seventh time when Watson leaped over Frog halfback Jim Shofner in the end zone and intercepted Curtis's pass.

With the wind in the Aggies' faces and the end zone eighty yards away, Bryant realized it might be their last chance. But he continued to forsake the pass. Goehring and Hale drove the center of the TCU line backward as Crow gained twenty-one yards around the right end. Fans cheered but still wondered who the new boy was wearing 84. It was equally as confusing when Watson, wearing number 26, followed blocks by Stallings and Krueger for twenty-seven yards.

From the nineteen Crow gained eleven yards around the right end. Everyone in the stadium was expecting a running play. A sweep seemed to be developing when Osborne pitched to Watson heading around the left end. But Weasel stopped, planted his foot, and threw to Crow, who was behind the secondary in the end zone. It was the Aggies' only pass that day and it covered eight yards.

Watson, the hero of the day, was the holder on Taylor's extra point kick, and the 7–6 upset of TCU triggered a celebration like none other in College Station. Rules against women in the dorms were unofficially lifted because, after all, the ladies needed to change out of their wet clothes. They would look quite fashionable wearing battle fatigues.

On a crisp and sunny Sunday morning, more than five-thousand women's hats would be retrieved from beneath the grandstand. And for many years to come, female undergarments would be found in almost every room of every dormitory at the Agriculture and Mechanical College of Texas.

22

Prophecy

Every time a player goes out there, at least twenty people have some amount of influence on him. His mother has more influence than anyone. I know because I played, and I loved my mama.

—PAUL "BEAR" BRYANT

OCTOBER 22, 1956

Peggy Sue admired her perfectly shaped breasts in the vanity mirror as she brushed her shoulder-length auburn hair. She was a senior at the University of Texas and paying her own way through school.

"Do you think y'all are gonna beat us this year?" she asked, catching the boy's eye in the mirror's reflection. "You know, it's been a long time."

The Aggie footballer tapped the end of a Camel on the table and noticed something moving outside in the darkness. He strode quickly across the room and raised a window that groaned stubbornly against the freshly painted sill. Dennis poked his head out and said, "Damn you, Bobby Jack. You're grinnin' like a bug-eatin' possum. How long you been sittin' there?"

The big Aggie tackle was perched on a thick tree limb about five feet from the second-floor window, exposing almost every tooth in his mouth.

245

"Get your butt in here, you cheap sonofabitch," Dennis groused. "It only costs three dollars."

Bobby Jack Lockett and Hustlin' Billy Rose had ridden with Dennis Goehring to the Chicken Ranch, where they'd downed a few Lone Star beers in the first-floor saloon. Dennis paid the tab and dropped some nickels into the jukebox. Billy and Dennis had struck up a conversation with a well-endowed barmaid wearing red lingerie. That's when Bobby Jack vanished.

About thirty minutes later, Dennis closed the window and turned and smiled at Peggy Sue. "That Bobby Jack is the cheapest sucker I know. He won't come in because he won't pay three dollars. Heck, he won't even buy his own toothpaste. He borrows mine every morning." Dennis scratched his head. "I wonder if he was watching."

He sat down and lit an unfiltered cigarette as Peggy Sue continued running the brush through her hair.

"I didn't know you smoked," she said.

"I don't."

Dennis carefully set the cigarette in an ashtray with the glowing butt touching the tip of the fuse. He stood and said, "I gotta go. Maybe I'll come back next month when we beat the shit out of you teasips." His hand was on the doorknob when the cherry bomb exploded. The sound tore through the old house and Bobby Jack almost fell out of the tree. Peggy Sue tumbled from her stool and frantically crawled under the bed. Screams could be heard from the adjoining bedrooms.

"Adios, senoritas!" Dennis hollered as he dashed down the hall and ran chest-first into Hustlin' Billy, who had burst through one of the bedroom doors.

"Who's doin' the shooting?" Billy asked.

"Nobody yet."

The boys scrambled down the stairwell and were almost through the front door when Miss Mona raised the .44 above her head and fired a slug into the ceiling. Plaster rained down on her hair like snowflakes. "You Aggies get your asses out of my house!" she yelled. Miss Mona was wearing a large white housecoat and a scowl that suggested she could whip an army. "You boys never come back, ya hear? I hope them Horns whip your asses."

Bobby Jack stood trembling next to the big Chevy as Dennis and Billy sprinted down the gravel driveway. Dennis jumped behind the wheel and they sped off into the night toward the main highway. As the tires screeched onto the asphalt, Dennis hit the horn and hollered, "Yee-haw! The Aggies score again!"

Some bad news greeted Dennis the next afternoon as the players suited up for the afternoon practice. He learned that tackle Jack Powell had left school. According to the practice roster, Dennis was moving from nose-guard to tackle. Dennis grumbled incessantly during practice about the position change and swore he would take it up with Bryant. His teammates warned him to approach the coach's office with caution. He didn't.

"Now, I've got one thing to say," Dennis said, pointing across the desk at Bryant. "I'm the best damn noseguard in this conference. But I might be the worst tackle. If you want to beat Baylor, you'd better move me back to noseguard."

So much about the relationship between Dennis and Bryant had changed. Dennis had been a seventh-team guard when Bryant arrived. Now Jones Ramsey was pushing him for All-American and Bryant thought he deserved it.

Dennis was useful for many reasons. Dennis helped keep a lot of play-ers in line even though he stirred up a lot of trouble himself. When Bryant needed for one of his players to handle a team matter, he often called on Dennis.

For instance, when Krueger showed up without a coat and tie for the spring team party, Bryant pulled the Cadillac keys from his pocket and said, "Dennis, I want you to drive Charlie here over to my house and get him one of my sports coats." They drove into a neighborhood of plush lawns and two-story prairie-style homes, and Dennis pulled into one of the familiar driveways. A middle-aged woman answered the door.

"Evenin', ma'am," Dennis said. "Coach said we should get a sports jacket for Charlie here. Seems Charlie forgot to wear his to the party."

The woman smiled and said, "Well, of course; come in." She led them to a large walk-in closet where they found more than a hundred expensive jackets and suits. Krueger and Bryant were about the same size, and the boys figured they could find a quick fit. Instead, the sleeves on each jacket were several inches short. Confused to no end, they finally gave up and drove back to campus.

A month later, Krueger was attending another campus function when a familiar-looking middle-aged woman approached him. "You're the big fella who came to my house to try on my husband's jackets." Charlie's mouth fell open. Dennis had taken him to the wrong house—the one next door to the Bryant's.

Now Bryant peered across the desk and snuffed the spent Chesterfield into a tin ashtray. "Son, this is gonna be the toughest game of your life. I'm gonna move you back to noseguard. But I expect you to play your butt off for sixty goddamn minutes."

Baylor and A&M were unbeaten. The Aggies had jumped from fourteenth to ninth in the A.P. poll after the upset of TCU, while Baylor weighed in at number fifteen. Baylor had three All-Americans—linebacker Bill Glass, tackle Bobby Jack Oliver, and halfback Del Shofner. Given the distance of ninety miles between the schools, it was a natural rivalry. Players from both teams had played one another in high school and they'd dated the same girls.

Situated on the lazy Brazos River, Baylor was a quiet, pastoral college that was deeply rooted in the ultraconservative Southern Baptist faith. Church attendance was mandatory and dormitory curfews were strict. But there were no choirboys on the football team. The Bears, in fact, were considered the dirtiest bunch of ballplayers outside the NFL, which, at the time, was stocked with goons. They were known for kicking and eye gouging and grabbing testicles in the bottom of a pile and for roughing up an opposing player or two who strayed into their bench area. Baylor fans went straight home after the Saturday-night games because they had church to attend early Sunday morning. Maybe the Bible Belters begged forgiveness for their own sins.

Twenty minutes before kickoff at Baylor Stadium, the Aggies trotted from the field to the dressing room for final instructions. They had to dodge flying Coke bottles. A&M players were accustomed to whiskey bottles whizzing out of the stands in Arkansas. But these folks were Baptists!

"Goddammit, if that bottle throwin' don't fire you up, nothin' will!" Bryant bellowed as the team gathered in the locker room. Shards of glass had flown everywhere when the bottle throwing started. Several of the players were still picking razor-sharp particles from their jerseys. A layer of glass was forming on the locker-room floor.

The Aggies didn't wait for Baylor to land the first punch. Murry Trimble sent linebacker Bill Glass to the sideline by stubbing him in the *cojones*. On the next play, Goehring grabbed tackle Bobby Jack Oliver, slung him to the ground, and kicked him.

On defense, Goehring was grabbing and holding two players at a time so the Aggie linebackers could make the tackle. But the Aggie defense lacked its normal punch without Jack Pardee, who was on the sideline. Pardee had taken another Novocain shot for his separated shoulder, but

Bryant had decided not start him. Ken Hall was getting one more chance at proving himself. Early in the game, he had broken a long run before fumbling again. He was now standing by himself at the end of the bench.

Pardee was almost beside himself after spending the first quarter on the sideline. Not once in junior high, high school, or college had he missed a start for any reason. But Bryant had a rule that players who didn't practice wouldn't play on Saturday, even if their name was Jack Pardee. As Bryant paced the sideline, Pardee walked right behind him. At times, Pardee was so close that Bryant could smell the pregame meal on the boy's breath. Finally, he turned and said, "Jack, dammit, will you stop looking at me that way?"

Pardee didn't say a word but kept tracking Bryant's every move.

In the second quarter, Osborne intercepted a pass and returned it six yards to the Baylor twenty-two. But for the second straight week, as A&M closed in on the end zone, Osborne called for someone else to throw the touchdown pass. He pitched to Crow, who tossed a four-yarder to tight end John Tracey for the score. Baylor tied it at six late in the second quarter when fullback Larry Hickman plunged over from the two-yard line.

Bryant relented, and Pardee charged into the game to start the second half. With Goehring grabbing and holding the center and guards, Pardee was able to shut down the Baylor rushing attack after the Bears had driven to the Aggie five. When Baylor turned the ball over on downs, the Aggies' running game finally cranked up. Near midfield, Crow was knocked out of bounds at the Baylor sideline and was lying on his back when several Bear players started kicking him in the head and ribs. His teammates rushed into the melee and pulled their star halfback out of danger, but he suffered several bruises and a bloody nose. Two Baylor players were ejected from the game, and flags littered the field.

Crow was in pain but decided to stay in the game. Otherwise, he'd be stuck on the bench until the fourth quarter. On the next play, Osborne completed his first pass in almost two games, a thirty-two-yarder to Weasel Watson down the right sideline. Pardee then broke through the grasps of three Bears, spun, and rumbled backward into the end zone. Though Bobby Joe Conrad consistently kicked forty-yard field goals in practice and pre-game warm-ups, Bryant stuck with Loyd Taylor, who missed his second PAT kick of the night. Texas A&M led 12–6.

When Baylor's Bobby Peters scored on a four-yard run and Junior Beall added the extra point kick, the Aggies found themselves in the familiar role of trailing in the fourth quarter, this time 13–12.

"I want you boys to take a look at this," Crow said, lifting his jersey to reveal bruises in shades of black, blue, and purple. He looked like he'd been kicked by a horse. Dr. Harrison feared he might have a broken rib or two. The Aggie guards, Goehring and Trimble, were enraged, and when the Aggies took over the ball at their own thirty-seven the A&M offensive line started carving huge holes in the Baylor front. "Let's kick these sonofabitches in the balls," Goehring growled.

With a top-ten ranking and an undefeated season on the line, the Aggies started plowing up the field. Crow gained twenty-three yards at right tackle, and Osborne added five more on the option. But Pardee fumbled at the Baylor twenty-six, and the game-saving drive seemed dead. Then an official ruled that Pardee was down before the fumble. Osborne got loose on his best run of the season, slipping through six tackles and spinning to the Baylor four. But the Aggie offense bogged down on the next three plays and they could barely hear themselves think as the voices of fifty-thousand Bible Belters rained down. Tension was thicker than a Baptist hymnal.

On fourth down from the two, Osborne glanced to the sideline to see if Bryant had thrown the kicking tee on the field. Turning impatient, Crow said, "Give me the cockeyed ball and I'll put it in there." Osborne did, and Crow burst through a hole cleared by Goehring, Hale, and Trimble. The PAT kick made it 19–13. The Aggies had come from behind in the fourth quarter for the second straight week. They were destined to climb even higher in the national polls.

Nothing had seemed sweeter than the victory in the "Hurricane Bowl" against fourth-ranked TCU. But the Aggies had survived a field of land mines and practically walked on glass to beat Baylor. Most of the boys were happy just to walk off the field with their bones and joints intact. The A&M band jammed the concourse just outside the team's dressing room and blared the "Aggie War Hymn." The press could barely hear Bryant as he began to dissect the game. They circled the coach and turned their ears toward his voice.

"I gotta take my hat off to Pardee," he rasped. "I thought he was gonna whip me if I didn't put him in the game."

Crow had gained eighty-four yards, passed for a touchdown, rushed for a touchdown and made fifteen tackles. He was now laid out on the training table as Dr. Harrison inspected his bruises. Bryant, who had shed his coat and tie, drew on a cigarette and said, "I thought John David was magnificent." Then his eyes widened. "God, I've never used that adjective. Boys, you'd better scratch that out and make it 'good.'"

Players poured Cokes over one another's heads as Goehring and Trimble danced arm in stub. In the corner of the locker room, one player dressed in silence. Ken Hall packed his bag and silently made separate plans for the trip back to College Station because he couldn't stomach the thought of riding a jubilant team bus for ninety miles.

The next afternoon, Bryant wasn't surprised when Hall didn't answer roll call. He'd promised the boy more playing time against Baylor, but Richard Gay had lined up for most of the snaps at fullback in the first half before Pardee virtually clawed his way onto the field. Bryant had run out of ideas on what to do with Hall. Changing the lineup wouldn't make any sense now that the Aggies had a 5-0-1 record.

As he steered the long car into the driveway late that afternoon, Bryant thought he saw someone sitting on the steps of the front sidewalk. An orange light angled across the row of lawns that sat crinkled and brown. The boy stood as Bryant got out of the car.

"Ken, what can I do for you?" Bryant said, walking toward him.

"Coach, I'm sorry I missed practice today. I had some things to do today. I really meant to be there." Tears welled in his eyes and Bryant could see that he was confused.

Bryant leveled his eyes on him. "Just be there tomorrow. No more misses. OK?"

Hall was absent again on Tuesday but showed up at Bryant's house again that evening to ask for forgiveness.

"If you don't come back tomorrow, that's it. I'm gonna have to discipline you before practice anyway. So come ready to run some stadium steps."

Bryant had hoped to see Hall on Wednesday. When he didn't show for the afternoon practice, the coach called a team meeting to announce that the boy was finished at A&M. There was muffled laughter and then silence. Some of the boys respected Hall's talent, but others could care less.

John David raised his hand. "Coach, can I go get him? I know where he is. I think he'll come back if I talk to him."

"He's had enough chances."

Later that afternoon, Crow stood outside Bryant's office, trying to summon the courage to knock.

Willie Zapalac walked by. "Go on in, John David. He won't eat ya."

Crow finally knocked and nervously took a seat across the desk from Bryant.

"Coach, he's the best running back I've ever seen. I still remember the first time I saw him. He looked like Adonis."

"I know. But we gotta let him go. I just don't know what else to do."

Newspaper headlines blared the news across Texas the next day. Bryant's team had lost only two games in two seasons. But columnists wrote extensively about lingering troubles at A&M and questioned how a stud blue chipper like Hall could slip away. They speculated that he'd been beaten down both physically and mentally. It wasn't the first time that ugly rumors had flown about brutality in Bryant's program. He had often been asked about a "bloody pit," where players supposedly fought with bare knuckles for starting positions. Bryant knew that A&M recruiting had been hurt by stories of the so-called pit because parents had called to ask about it. Bryant adamantly denied its existence, and none of the Aggies players ever came forth to say such a bloodletting took place.

As the Aggies prepared for their game against Arkansas at Kyle Field, Ken Hall and his young bride, Gloria, were packing up their belongings. By the time the Aggies kicked off against the Hogs that Saturday afternoon, Hall would be pumping gas back in Sugar Land.

Bryant was both surprised and a little worried at the emotion that he felt for Hall. He'd awakened around one o'clock the night before the Arkansas game with the boy on his mind. He could see the thick muscles in his arms and the sinewy ropes in his calves. Hall just looked like a football player, even if he wasn't tough enough to be one. In the end, there was no place to play him. Bryant had racked his brain and even tried to imagine a lineup with John David at fullback and Hall playing halfback. He probably would have moved Hall into the starting lineup the next season with Pardee graduating. But Bryant couldn't justify begging a player to come back after quitting twice. Not once in his coaching career had he allowed anyone to come back after walking away the first time.

• • •

About the only bump in the road in the 27–0 victory against Arkansas was a broken nose suffered by Richard Gay in the fourth quarter. Gay was dizzy and blood poured from his nostrils as Smokey helped him to his feet. "You'll be all right, boy," Smokey said. "I'll get ya fixed up. You don't have to play no more today."

As the two walked toward the sideline, Pat James yelled, "Smokey, he's gotta stay in the game! Pardee is dead."

Pardee had been standing on the sideline with a shoelace draped around his neck, signifying that he was "dead," or officially finished for the game. He had retired to the bench early in the fourth quarter to rest his aching shoulder. With Hall gone, the Aggies were out of fullbacks.

Smokey turned to Gay, whose jersey and face were smeared with blood. "You'll be all right, boy. Go on and get back in there. I'll have an aspirin ready for ya later." Both the Aggies and the Razorbacks were shocked to see the bloody fullback wobbling back onto the field.

As the Aggies prepared for the next game against SMU, Bryant knew he would be hearing from the man who wore boots and blue jeans and a big rodeo belt buckle. He came every Thursday and Bryant stopped whatever he was doing when the tall cowboy showed up. His name was Bum Phillips, and high school coaches across Texas knew him as the best of their lot.

"Hello, Bun," Bryant said, grasping his thick hand.

"Coach, you can call me Bum. My mama does."

"OK, then I've got a question. Why do ya always take off your hat when you walk in here?"

Bum pulled a toothpick from his mouth. "Because my mama says you never wear your hat in the house."

Bum drove three hours from Nederland once a week in his weathered pickup to watch the master at work. Nederland was located in southeast Texas in an area known as the Golden Triangle. He gave his football team the day off on Thursday. "Go on down to the drugstore and be with your friends," he would say. "But be ready to play Friday night." Nederland High rarely lost a game.

When they were together, Bum and Bear seemed like soul mates as they sat on bar stools at Bixby's Barbecue, their elbows propped on the counter, talking football. They ate ribs and chopped beef and beans and cole slaw and pickled tomatoes. They ran plays on the countertop using salt shakers as blockers and pepper shakers as defensive linemen. On this day, the Tabasco sauce was playing quarterback and the ketchup was at safety.

"Let me show you a new blockin' scheme we been gettin' mileage out of," Bum said. Rearranging the shakers, he said, "It's simple. The guard blocks the man to his right, the tackle the man to his right, and the end the man to his right. The center takes the linebacker." Years later, the scheme would be called zone blocking.

Bryant slapped his knee. "By God, I can see how it works. It just makes too much sense."

The two wiped their mouths, paid their bill, and walked back across the campus for the start of the afternoon practice.

Bryant quickly gathered the players and the coaches around him.

"Bun Phillips here is the best dern high school coach in Texas. Most of y'all have met him. We're gettin' ready to add a new blocking scheme that he invented and I'm sure that you boys are gonna like it."

It wasn't unusual for Bryant to experiment with a new offense or defense during practice, because it kept the days fresh and the players awake. But now he was installing a blocking scheme that he planned to use in forty-eight hours at the Cotton Bowl against the highly respected SMU Mustangs.

After the practice, assistant coach Willie Zapalac pulled Phillips aside. "Coach, we appreciate you bringin' us your ideas. But next time, could you do it before Thursday?"

In spite of the rush to install Bum's blocking schemes, the Aggies had it all down by kickoff as John David Crow scored on touchdown runs of fifteen and thirteen yards, and Weasel Watson added a twenty-three-yard touchdown run in the first half. The Aggies led 33–0 before the Mustangs posted a touchdown late in the game. Bryant told the press that Phillips had contributed greatly to the convincing victory.

"One of these days that ol' boy is gonna be one of the best head coaches this game has ever seen."

The next day, the Aggies jumped to fourth in the A.P. poll. Though Rice was the next opponent, all eyes were on the Texas game coming up in ten days, on Thanksgiving. First, though, the NCAA had some business to attend to.

The SWC had already voted to lift the probation against the Aggies, and the measure was supported by both TCU coach Abe Martin and Texas coach Ed Price. Now the eighteen committee members of the NCAA had their vote, and Bryant had few political allies. He had accused NCAA executive director Walter Byers of "selective enforcement" when the Aggies were slapped with probation in 1955. Bryant's past also worked against him. One of the committee members was a representative from Kentucky, and he was certain to lobby and vote against the Aggies. In the end, the NCAA felt that A&M had shown no ill effects from probation. Though the players were given their unconditional release, all decided to return. A&M had lost only two games in two seasons. The NCAA voted unanimously to continue the probation. The Aggies wouldn't be going to the Cotton Bowl even if they defeated Rice and Texas and the Chicago Bears in the final weeks of the season.

Instead of feeling despair, the Aggies worked themselves into a frenzy. Practices leading to the Rice game were the most spirited that Bryant could remember. All but Dennis Goehring had been able to participate in workouts. Dennis was still hobbling on two sprained ankles. He was wearing street clothes when Bryant found him standing outside the locker room Thursday afternoon, just minutes before the Aggies took the field.

He grabbed the feisty guard by the collar and ripped his shirt. "By God, you've got to practice today if you're gonna play against Rice." Goehring grabbed Bryant's shirt and virtually tore it off. The two men stood there for several minutes, virtually naked from the waist up. Then they both started laughing.

A few minutes later, Dennis was dressed in his football suit and limping toward the practice field.

The Aggies tore through Rice 21–7 as Pardee scored two touchdowns and Taylor sprinted twenty-two yards around left end for another. Osborne threw only three passes. Smash-mouth football had rendered its eighth win of the season for A&M and now the days couldn't pass fast enough before Thursday's kickoff against Texas. The Aggies were ranked number three in the A.P. poll. It was the shootout they'd been waiting for since Junction.

23

Revelation

No coach has ever won a game by what he knows; it's
what his players know that counts.

—PAUL "BEAR" BRYANT

NOVEMBER 26, 1956

Bryant scribbled on the chalkboard. "Five on our four. That's what
we're lookin' for here. We get five of our men on four of theirs and we'll
win that battle every time."

The team had gathered for Bryant's noon lecture and soon they would
be transfixed by his words and theories. Future coaches carried thick notebooks and composed page upon page of notes. Stallings already had announced his intentions to coach, and Bryant planned to hire him.

It was one of those rare occasions when the Man didn't rely upon the
power of his mystique. He was like a fatherly pipe-smoking engineering
professor as he lectured about the science of football. This professorial
side emerged during the lunch hour on Tuesday when the chalkboard was
rolled through a side door into the team's private cafeteria. The room grew
still. The players enjoyed this time with their coach because he was there

to teach, not to admonish. He was there to expound on a game that with all of its geometric angles and puzzling codes could baffle common thinkers.

In forty-eight hours, the Aggies would play the biggest game in their history on Thanksgiving Day in Austin. Bryant gazed around the room. He cleared his throat and said, "I want the Junction boys to stand up."

Eight seniors rose. They were the last of the 111 players who had boarded two buses outside of Walton Hall bound for the western edge of the dehydrated Hill Country that summer morning in 1954.

"Weasel Watson," Bryant began. "I never thought you'd fit my system. But there's not a single boy in this room, nobody in this conference, who's made more big plays than you the last three seasons.

"Lloyd Hale. If I had to fly into Russia, and I could take only one man, it would be you. I've never had a better center.

"Bobby Jack Lockett. Son, you got off to a slow start. You had some injuries. But I wouldn't trade you for any tackle in the conference right now.

"Dee Powell. You've broken your damn nose nine times this season. But you haven't missed one doggone practice or game. And you won the LSU game for us when you blocked that punt out of the end zone.

"Bobby Drake Keith. Pound for pound, you're the best football player I've ever had. The doctors say you gotta sit out Thursday because of that god-dang broken jaw. I know it must be killin' you. But our hearts will be with you.

"Dennis Goehring. Son, Smokey and I tried to run you off from the first day. Now I've got some news for ya. Jones Ramsey just informed me that *Look* magazine has named you to their All-American team. Hell, you deserve it.

"Jack Pardee. You're the toughest football player I've ever coached. Bar none. You're smilin' now. But it's true. I'm just glad you didn't decide to whip my ass in the Baylor game.

"Bebe Stallings. Boys, this is the greatest team player that ever put on his suit. Someday he's gonna be one of the greatest coaches in America. He knows the meaning of team concept. Bebes, you ain't a bad football player, either, son."

For the first time that anyone could remember, the boys saw emotion tugging at Bryant's face. He sat down, gritted his teeth, and grew silent. He pulled a cigarette from his shirt pocket and lit it. The boys studied his expression as they had so many times. They had never seen him even close to tears. They never expected this hardened man to formally say good-bye to the Junction boys. But he'd just come close.

Head down, Bryant let the spent cigarette slip slowly from his fingers, dropping into his Coke bottle. He blinked his eyes and composed himself, and then he stood and walked toward the chalkboard, where he scrawled and then circled the number 33.

"Boys. I'm gonna level with ya. Everybody's been talkin' about how we ain't beat Texas in Austin in thirty-three years. But I'm expectin' ya to go through those bastards like shit through a goose. They've won one game and that was Tulane. Hell, Oklahoma beat 'em 45-to-nothin'. TCU took 'em 46–zip. There's one more reason we're gonna win, and I'm serious about this. Everybody talks about those turds bein' rich country clubbers and us boys bein' poor folks from the country. Well, I think we're gonna win because our mamas and papas are better than their mamas and papas."

Bryant paced in front of the chalkboard, lighting another Chesterfield and formulating the words.

"I've never told you boys about the time I thought I had a sure thing at the racetrack. Well, I was coachin' at Kentucky and this bigwig alum told me 'bout a horse he had runnin' at Keeneland. He said the horse couldn't be beat and said I should bet big money. Well, I wasn't satisfied just to bet the $3,000 I had in the bank. I borrowed another $7,000. Me and Mary Harmon drove up to Keeneland, and I was pretty nervous. But I put the whole ten grand on the horse.

"Then I sat down and studied the *Racing Form* and realized the horse did look pretty good. There was nothin' in the field that could run with him. So I felt mighty good. Then they let 'em go and I couldn't find my horse in the binoculars. I soon realized he'd gotten hung in the gate and was runnin' dead last. He finished last, in fact, and I lost ten grand on a sure thing. Think about that Thursday mornin' when you're gettin' ready for the biggest game you'll ever play."

The next day, Bryant was in a whimsical mood when he sat down to tape his weekly TV show with moderator Lloyd Gregory, who had brought along a bobble-headed mascot doll in burnt orange and white. Gregory parked the Longhorn doll on the front of the desk.

"Coach," Gregory began, "tell me why y'all can't beat Texas."

"I guess it's because they hate us more than we hate them." Bryant took a swipe at the Longhorn doll, and its head bobbled wildly. Every time

Texas was mentioned, Bryant smacked the doll and laughed. The head bobbed and spun and soon the little Longhorn was lying facedown on the studio floor.

The Aggies checked into the Driskill Hotel in downtown Austin Wednesday night just as ten thousand howling Aggies in College Station celebrated the lighting of the traditional bonfire that had required three months to build. It was almost four stories high and had been topped off with an outhouse and half of a farmer's barn.

The team meal included steaks, mashed potatoes, green beans, squash, fried okra, black-eyed peas, and piles of fresh, hot rolls. Smokey peered across the table at Billy Pickard. "Boy, my hands sure been achin' lately with the arthritis." Billy didn't look up. "I been workin' so hard that I don't think these hands'll be worth a shit tomorrow." Billy's eyes focused on his steak.

Smokey sighed. He feigned an attempt to straighten his fingers. "Boy, I hope you don't get the arthritis when you get old. I can barely cut my steak."

"All right, you old fart," Billy finally said. "I'll tape all the ankles tomorrow if you'll just keep quiet."

"That's great." Smokey stood and laughed. Then he leaned across the table and stabbed the remainder of Billy's steak with his fork. He sat down and started sawing with hands as strong as a blacksmith's.

• • •

The day broke with a pale blue sky spangled with red streaks. The city felt empty as Smokey took a cab to the stadium. He spread the *Austin American-Statesman* across the taping table. Minutes later, John David Crow limped slowly through the door. Pain rarely registered on John David's face, but now it was quite evident.

John David fell into a chair as Smokey began to laugh loudly. "Listen to this quote in the paper today," he said. Smokey began to read the sports page aloud. " 'We're going to beat Texas because Coach Bryant says so,' Aggie guard Murry Trimble said. 'Coach Bryant says that our mamas and our papas are just better than their mamas and their papas.' "

Crow smiled crookedly.

"Wait till the Texas players read this," Smokey said.

Crow smiled again. "Wait till Coach Bryant reads it."

John David had broken his right foot five days earlier against Rice, and it was swollen like a balloon by Tuesday when a reporter had asked if he was going to have it x-rayed. "There's no use in it. I'm gonna play anyway."

That morning, John David could barely squeeze his foot into his shoe. "Smokey, do you think I can get a shot of that Novocain stuff? I never had one. Maybe it's time."

John David intended to play even if Smokey said no. Minutes later, Dr. Harrison worked the long needle into the blue and puffy area and the sensation was like hot water being poured into the foot. The numbness climbed all the way to John David's knee.

Loyd Taylor was also limping on a broken foot that wasn't going to keep him off the field. At five-foot-seven and 160 pounds, he had come from a hard-edged football family in Roswell, New Mexico, where two older brothers had played college ball. His father had forbade little Loyd to play football for the longest because of his size. But once Loyd got on the field, they couldn't get him off, or tackle him, for that matter. It still stuck in his craw that Texas had rejected the notion of recruiting him. "He's a good little football player," coach Ed Price had said. "But we've got some of those."

Taylor stared into the locker-room mirror that morning and growled, "Yeah, Price, but you ain't got one like *me*."

Though the Longhorns had won only one game, each of the 60,000 seats would be filled. Teasips, as they were called by Texas haters, would show up just to pick on the Aggies. Texas had won almost every athletic event outside of baseball against A&M the last decade. One of their favorite taunts was "Pooooor Agggggggies." The chant always began as the Longhorns gained a commanding lead and would echo across the stadium until the game ended. Aggies could hear it in their sleep. Every year, Longhorn fans carried a handmade sign around the stadium that read, TAMC—TEXAS ASSES AND MULE COLLEGE.

In the locker room, Bryant strode toward Bebes Stallings and extended his right hand.

"Coach, I got something I want to show ya." Bebes reached into his shoe and pulled out his mustard seed.

"Coach, I've got mine, too," Don Watson said, plunging his hand into the jeans that hung by his locker.

"Got mine right here," Pardee said.

"Still got mine," Goehring said.

All eight of the Junction Boys had brought their mustard seeds on the trip. Bryant was suddenly struck by an idea. "Give me all of them," he said. He dropped each one into his right pocket.

The Aggies were scheduled to take the field in a matter of minutes and Bryant had yet to begin his pregame speech. A game official stuck his head through the dressing room door and said, "Coach, it's time to get 'em out there. Kickoff's upon us."

"Not until they play that song."

"What song?"

" 'Eyes of Texas.' "

"Huh?"

"You tell the teasips that we'll come out after they play that goddamn song." The official closed the door and left.

For years and years, the Aggies had charged onto the field at Memorial Stadium only to have "Eyes of Texas," the famous school song, blasted in their faces. Bryant believed it intimidated the boys. This time, they would wait. Five minutes later, the official returned.

"I ain't heard the dang song yet."

The official slammed the door behind him.

The Aggies waited and waited, huddled in their locker room, and the Memorial Stadium crowd grew restless. Bryant finally heard the song. He slowly removed his hat and began the most important pregame speech of his life.

"Boys, I once told ya that you can move mountains if you have the faith of the mustard seed. I said you'd be champions before you walked off campus. I still believe that. But sometimes you act like those god-dang Longhorns are eight feet tall. Shit, they're the last-place team in the conference and their coach is probably gonna get his ass fired."

Bryant reached into his memory for a verse from the Book of Revelation: " 'Blessed is he who reads aloud the words of the prophecy, and blessed are those who hear, and who keep what is written therein; for the time is near.' "

Looking up, he could see the tops of their bowed heads. Tears welled in his eyes.

"Men," he drawled softly. "The time is near."

Metal-tipped cleats scraped the concrete floor as seventy Aggies buckled their chin straps and walked with deep resolve toward the locker-room door.

Smokey Harper stood on a chair and cleared his throat. He'd waited weeks for this moment. "I'd rather see my sister in a whorehouse than my brother at the University of Texas!" he yelped.

Some of the boys had to bite their bottom lips to keep from laughing.

The Longhorn kickoff team was already lined up at the forty when the Aggies reached the field and roared toward their sideline. This time they could actually hear their own school song being belted from the far end of the stadium.

It was too easy at first. Running on a numb foot, John David broke six tackles on a twenty-seven-yard touchdown run, and it seemed the entire Texas team was strewn across the field as he crossed the goal. The Aggies had moved seventy yards on the opening drive with thirty-three yards coming on a pass from Roddy Osborne to Bobby Marks. A&M was just getting warmed up.

The second drive, which consumed eighty yards, was even more impressive. Texas defensive players, already tired, were standing with hands on hips when Osborne slipped into the end zone from three yards out. Kern Tips told his radio audience, "It looks like somebody left the matches too close to the firecrackers. These Aggies look ready to explode." Taylor missed the extra point kick, and A&M led 13–0.

The rout appeared to be on until the Aggies were caught flat-footed by Walter Fondren, one of the most elusive running backs anywhere. The Aggies were quite familiar with Fondren's acrobatic runs. Tips: "Texas lights a firecracker of its own named Walter Fondren and he sputters into the middle of the merrymakers in the line and he explodes. This bit of Texas TNT is good for forty-three yards." Stallings was the only Aggie to lay a hand on him before he scored.

Texas A&M answered quickly. When Taylor sprinted twenty-two yards around the end for a touchdown, Tips warbled, "The little Aggie takes it all the way to the top of Longhorn Hill." It seemed to be downhill from there. The Longhorns, losers of eight games and now trailing by two touchdowns, seemed on the brink of collapse.

It was no time to turn smug. But Bryant somehow underestimated the Longhorns and their powerful hex over the Aggies. He inserted the second defensive team and quarterback Joe Clements completed three straight passes, the last one to a diving Bob Bryant for a touchdown with only two seconds remaining before halftime. Bryant could have kicked himself. The Aggies should have run away with the game in the first half but didn't. They led 20–14.

For the first time, live television cameras were capturing the action of an SWC game. Bryant thought about all of the Aggies watching and listening and swearing his team would blow it in the second half. He thought about his last conversation with Dr. John Wiedeman back in Junction:

"You know, Coach, you've got a lot of fans out here. We'll be listening to your games on the radio." Indeed they were. More than two hundred miles from Austin, families huddled around radios and a few TV sets.

The Thanksgiving dishes had been washed and put away at the Hagood house in Junction when the game came on. The large family settled into the airy living room to listen to the wood-grain RCA radio. A few miles away, the same scene was playing out at the Wiedeman home. Squirt Newby was so nervous at halftime that he decided to take a drive around Junction in his green Ford. But he kept the dial punched to the Aggie broadcast. Buckshot James restlessly paced the den floor and muttered to himself, "No wonder Bryant's got ulcers." Buckshot picked up the phone and called R. B. McKinney. "They're gonna blow it," Buckshot said. "Them Texas boys are workin' their voodoo already." McKinney, standing in his parlor, cradled the phone and gazed through a front window. He watched several pages from a newspaper tumble down the street but thought nothing of it.

The town quietly waited and prayed the dam wouldn't break once more. As he drove the streets of Junction, Squirt didn't pass a car or see a solitary soul. The empty streets reminded him of Christmas morning when families gathered around their trees to open presents. As he steered the car back into his driveway, a gust of wind unfastened a limb from a sycamore tree and it sprawled across his front sidewalk.

As a man would nervously jingle pocket change, Bryant kept the mustard seeds dancing in his pocket. The second half kickoff skittered over the dying grass, past several Aggies, and John David let it go. The ball seemed ticketed for the end zone when it bounced high at the one and Jack Pardee leaped and batted it with his right hand. As he cradled the ball and took off, Bryant yelled, "No!" But the voice was consumed by the stadium roar.

Several Longhorns were upon Pardee as his legs seemed to kick into gear. The middle of the field suddenly parted, creating a wide lane for the big fullback. Pardee had never been one to dawdle. He always bulled straight ahead. The Longhorns flew by him like fence posts past a freight train. He was at the twenty, the thirty, the forty. Now the brown field lay open before him like an empty tortilla. Clements rushed up from the rear and finally cut him down at the fifteen. Pardee slammed his fist into the ground. "How'd a god-dang quarterback catch me?" he raged. "That's stupid."

In Junction, the Hagood family listened to Tips describe Pardee's return and jumped to their feet. They didn't hear the low rumble to the south.

An hour earlier, the black clouds had started boiling up out of Mexico. The front had been gathering steam across the flatlands near Del Rio, and as it crossed the Nueces River thunderheads appeared. Winds howled as the front crawled upon the Edwards Plateau.

Rain had been as scarce as Eskimos the last six months in the Llano Valley—the worst drought on record was now approaching seven years. Weathermen had no data to suggest a dramatic climatological shift. The hurricane season had passed and there had been no variations in the jet stream. That morning, the sky had been bluer than a truck stop rest room. Only God could have called what was coming.

The southern horizon was now dusky with stalks of dry lightning. A trucker rumbling south toward Junction from Menard rolled down his window as the smell of rain flooded his nostrils. He searched a flat stretch along Main Street for an open gas station but came up empty. He pulled into Fortran Johnston's Texaco and honked his horn. There was no reply. Then he noticed the front screen door cocked half-open. He sauntered inside to find a pimple-faced teenager hovering over a loud radio.

"Town looks shut down!" the trucker yelled.

"Why, yessir. Everybody's listenin' to the Aggies. We're beatin' Texas for the first time since Grandma got laid."

"Well, son, I need some gas. And I think you'd better come outside. There's somethin' you need to take a look at."

The titanic storm was now upon downtown Junction. Raging thunderheads swirled and then boiled upward. Lightning jigged on the simmering sky, and the wind cut with a cold knife. Then they heard the first clap of thunder.

"Mister, we ain't had a good rain in so long I swear I don't even know where my slicker is."

"Well, you'd better get braced."

In Austin, Pardee's eyes still burned over the botched return as he leaned into the huddle and said, "Dammit, Roddy, give me the dern ball." He did. The big fullback waded through five tacklers, spun at the one to avoid another, and stepped powerfully into the end zone. The Aggie lead was fourteen points. It would swell to twenty minutes later when Crow and Pardee hammered the ball down the field and George Gillar scored on a one-yard run.

As the Aggies piled up the points, dust surged in low clouds along Main Street in Junction and the first tumbleweeds rolled in. A rush of wind sent the gas station boy's Aggie cap tumbling end over end down the street. The trucker decided to pump his own gas. A tarpaulin broke loose and flapped violently on the wind. Darkness cloaked the town.

Luke Hagood listened intently to the game but kept an eye on the developing storm. He had seen so many blow in and blow out without ever peeing a drop. A short piece down the road, a family gathered on their front porch and watched the wicked sky. A man licked his finger and held it aloft. The wind was straight out of the south and gaining steam. A screen door raised a popping racket.

Clements moved the Longhorns quickly down the field with precision passing and tossed a ten-yard touchdown pass to Bob Bryant, who had to wrestle the ball from Pardee. The Aggie lead was slashed to thirteen. Bryant felt the burning in his lower gut. Texas got the ball back after a punt, and Clements started slicing up the secondary again. Texas reached the Aggie nineteen with seven minutes to play. Longhorn fans roared their approval.

No one seemed to be breathing on the Aggie sideline. High in the stadium, Rob Roy Spiller, the Junction bus station boy, was dressed in his A&M Corps uniform. He had nervously stood the entire game with the other cadets. His date moved closer, and they held hands. Across the stadium, Laverne Johnston crossed her legs and her fingers. The former Miss Wool was now a junior at Texas and wore an orange dress. But a maroon-and-white corsage was pinned to her shoulder strap with the number 62 emblazoned on it. She had a date with an All-American guard after the game.

Laverne had broken Rob Roy's heart two years earlier, choosing Dennis. But Dennis and Rob Roy then became great friends and they went to the Junction horse races together and drank a lot of beer.

In the south end zone of Memorial Stadium sat a muscular and athletic-looking boy. He wore sunglasses and a cap pulled low. He had spoken to no one, and no one had recognized his famous face. He sat alone. He had driven that morning from Sugar Land to College Station. He was in the fifteenth row, but his heart was down on the field with his ex-teammates. Now Ken Hall was fighting off tears. His life had become so confusing.

Clements retreated to pass and heaved the ball into the hazy blue sky.

Lloyd Hale thought it would never come down. As he backpedaled, the ball became a black speck against the blazing sun. Hale had seen many bright afternoons in the West Texas desert. He had stood atop oil rigs and squinted into the glaring white light. He started to raise his hand to shade his eyes but knew the ball might smack him in the face. Then it appeared from nowhere and he grabbed it.

Pardee stepped into the A&M huddle and looked around. "Boys, there ain't no way they're gettin' the ball back today." The Aggies churned out four first downs and the clock ticked toward 0:00. The "Aggie War Hymn" roared down from the stands—"Hullabaloo, Canek! Canek! Hullabaloo, Cankek! Canek!"

The streets of Junction were suddenly filled with wide-eyed people running madly into the horizontal rain. Roads became rivers. Car horns sounded all over town. Squirt Newby zigzagged along the double yellow line with the windows rolled down and the Aggie broadcast blaring. Puddles of water swirled in the floorboard, and his hair was matted and his shirt soaked.

Junctionites jumped and hollered, "Gig 'em, Aggies! Whoa!" Many ranchers and farmers fell to their knees in prayer. The Hagood family headed straight for the South Llano to see what the heavens had sent. They found rancher Coke Stevenson parked in his pickup truck on the riverbank and, like many others, his windows were rolled down and the rain was blowing in.

Stevenson, the Texas governor from 1941 through '47, had lost a heartbreaking U.S. Senate election to Lyndon Johnson, who had been accused of fixing the outcome. Coke swore he'd never run again. Now as he sat next to the river, soaked to the bone, he grinned like a man who'd just swept every county in Texas.

Some folks waded into the fast-flowing South Llano and drank the water as others rolled on the ground. Radios blared from open windows. They had waited for this drought breaker for so long that some had feared it would never come. In an hour, the South Llano had risen by five feet, and it was swelling by the minute. Hundreds of people stood on the bank, holding hands.

Old-timers remembered the day the rains finally came in 1935. The South Llano quickly rose by twenty-five feet and washed out almost half of the bridge. Then the dried-up North Llano reemerged and almost took out downtown. It rained day and night, night and day. Main Street ran like a newborn tributary as water rose into the old courthouse, where thirty-five employees were trapped. They were rescued by a detachment of soldiers from Fort Sam Houston who had been on an exercise south of Junction.

Then, as now, the ranches had been badly scarred. Cowmen who still had land and money would soon be back in business. But the business of ranching would never be the same. The drought of the 1950s would be remembered as the scourge that crippled a mighty industry in Texas.

In Austin, Bear Bryant felt the spray of water in his face and was suddenly drenched from hair to alligator shoes. The Junction Boys hoisted him on their shoulders and tossed him into the Memorial Stadium showers. Then Smokey was doused.

Aggie cadets hung around the stadium for more than an hour, singing and chanting and taking pictures of the scoreboard. "Hullabaloo, Canek! Canek! Hullabaloo, Canek! Canek!" The words had been sung since the end of World War I. But no one knew exactly what they meant. Some said "Hullabaloo Cankek!" was derived from Indian language. Others thought it meant "Beat Texas!" In truth, it meant nothing. On this glorious evening, though, when the drought had broken twice, the Aggies could care less.

In the midst of bedlam, Bear Bryant raised his right hand. Silence fell upon the locker room.

"This win is for the boys who survived Junction." Voices erupted again. "They showed us that you by-God don't quit."

Two years earlier, as the single bus rolled home from Junction, he had sat alone with his thoughts. Bryant had promised himself that he would mold a champion from the slim troop of weary survivors. It had happened. But not without prayer and a blind faith in the human spirit.

The Man turned to walk away but was struck by something important. "I told you before the game to leave the Texas girls alone. I thought they were distracting. Well, hell's bells, go for it. I bet they're out there waitin' for you right now."

At another time, the Aggies would have piled into cars and pickups and headed for the Chicken Ranch. But now they had a message to carry into the streets of Austin. They had something to show the teasips. Scholz Beer Garden, a favorite watering hole for Texas students and just a few blocks from the stadium, was overrun by boys in military uniforms. The team soon arrived, and just as Bryant predicted, the pretty teasip girls weren't far behind. John David limped in with his wife, Carolyn. Weasel Watson, Bobby Jack Lockett, Lloyd Hale, Dee Powell, Bobby Drake Keith, and Jack Pardee started pounding the Lone Star beer. Dennis had one arm around Laverne and the other around Rob Roy. The Aggie Band cranked up, and soon they all swayed arm-in-arm, singing their school songs.

Back at the Driskill Hotel, a contingent of Alabama alums had showed up to sell Bryant on the idea of coming back to Tuscaloosa. But he was whisked away by Aggie moneyman Herman Heep. The next morning, the two men were deep in the country, hunting doves, when Heep pledged to Bryant a large investment in several prominent oil wells. In return, Heep wanted to hear Bryant say he was staying at A&M. They shook hands. "You stick with me," Bryant said, "and I'll stick with you."

Two days later, Bebes Stallings and Ruth Ann Jack were married in Paris, Texas.

24

The Ring

I left Texas A&M because my school called me. Mama
called, and when Mama calls, then you just have to come
running.

—PAUL "BEAR" BRYANT

DECEMBER 8, 1957

The Man's brow was deeply furrowed as he sauntered to the front of
the room and assumed his place behind the lectern. Hot white television
lights revealed dark rings below his eyes. For months, rumors had swirled
and reporters had called and now he stood before the press at the Shamrock
Hilton in Houston, ready to tell them why.

"When you were out playing as a kid, say you heard your mother
calling you. If you thought she wanted you to do some chores, or to come
in from supper, you might not answer her. But if you thought she needed
you, you ran home as fast as you could. Well, Mama called. I'm goin'
home."

Bear Bryant was going back to Alabama, where his football passion
had been born. For years he had tried to postpone the journey home and,
as late as mid-October, he had told the press and friends at Texas A&M
that he was staying put. But once-mighty Alabama, the school that had put

269

southern football on the map, had won a total of four games in three years. The state had practically dropped to its knees and begged him.

Hank Crisp, who was like Bryant's second father in Alabama, had walked into his suite at the Shamrock Hilton the previous night. It was Crisp's rumble seat that had carried Bryant from Arkansas to Alabama. It was Crisp who had fed him one-dollar bills so he could have dates with Mary Harmon. For thirty years, Crisp had been the top aide to three Alabama head coaches.

Crisp stood before his pupil and smiled. "Now come on," he said. "Get your ass back to Alabama so we can start winnin' some football games."

While Alabamians rejoiced, folks in Aggieland were left speechless. Many were angry. The 1957 A&M season had died in ashes during the final two weeks of the season when word leaked that Bryant was leaving. The Aggies had enjoyed a number-one ranking for three straight weeks before rumors started smelling like fact. They were ranked ahead of number-two Oklahoma even though the Sooners were working on a national record forty-seven-game winning streak.

The Aggies had outlived probation and apparently their own bias for self-destruction. Then came the ninth week of the season and the Rice Owls in Houston. A Saturday-morning headline blared the news that a deal with Alabama seemed imminent. For fifty minutes the uninspired Aggies played their sloppiest game of the season, losing six fumbles and trailing Rice 7–6. They got the ball one final time after Rice's King Hill punted it out of bounds at the Aggie one.

Quarterback Jimmy Wright, still the object of Bryant's frustration, had ridden the bench most of the season as Bryant had chosen the conservative route most of that year with signal callers Roddy Osborne and Charlie Milstead. But with his team now in deep trouble, Bryant relented to Jimmy and his strong arm.

Jimmy completed a string of quick passes to Bobby Marks, Gordon LeBeouf, and John Tracey. John David Crow broke a twenty-one-yard run and was inches from going all the way before stumbling and being caught from behind by Hill. The Aggies were at the Rice thirteen when Bryant called time-out and Jimmy strolled to the sideline.

"Coach, why don't we just run a draw and let Bobby Joe kick it?"

Bryant glared at Wright. "So you wanna coach now, huh?"

In truth, the strong-willed quarterback might have been right. Bobby Joe Conrad had become a dead-eye kicker in practice, but Bryant clung to the notion that field goals were for wimps. So he ordered Jimmy to throw two more passes, which fell incomplete. The Aggies' reign as America's number-one team died on fourth down at the Rice thirteen. The date of November 16 was one that would live in infamy in college football. An hour later, Oklahoma's historic winning streak ended as Notre Dame beat the Sooners 7–0.

Ironically, the hated field goal was the undoing of Bryant in his final game against Texas. On Thanksgiving afternoon at Kyle Field, Bobby Lackey booted a thirty-eight-yarder to give the Longhorns a 9–7 victory. The Aggies lost in spite of being well within Conrad's range three times. Bryant's sad legacy would be three losses in four years against Texas.

Two weeks later, Bryant was having drinks with Blackie Sherrod of the *Fort Worth Press*. They were headed to New York to celebrate the selection of the *Look* All-American team that included John David Crow and Charlie Krueger.

After another round of drinks arrived, Sherrod studied the face of the former Aggie coach. "You've changed a lot the last four years," he said.

"Nah. You just got to know me better. I never change."

The topic of conversation moved to Crow. "The best player I've ever seen," Bryant said. "He could play any position on the field."

"Any position? Guard? Tackle? Center?"

"Damn right."

Along with a slew of All-American honors, Crow had been awarded the 1957 Heisman Trophy. He had distanced second-place finisher Alex Karras, the Iowa tackle, by almost six-hundred points. Bryant had practically threatened Heisman voters not to go against his stud halfback, who had gained only 562 yards to finish fourth in his own conference. He was hardly a household name outside of Texas, but Bryant's backing didn't hurt.

"If he doesn't win the Heisman," Bryant had said, "they ought to stop giving it out."

As Crow and Krueger were appearing that weekend on the *Ed Sullivan Show* in New York, a Texas A&M search committee was interviewing candidates to replace Bryant, who had recommended Phil Cutchin from his Aggie staff.

"They need a tough sonofabitch because Texas A&M is a tough sonofabitch," Bryant told the writer. "It's a tough place to recruit. Hell, it might just be the toughest damn school in America to win at." Days later, the committee selected Iowa State coach Jim Myers, a man Bryant barely knew.

Three Aggies—Crow, Krueger, and Conrad—were invited to join the College All-Stars who played the NFL champions in July. Conrad was a great athlete but had never really defined himself at A&M, playing several positions. But he quickly ensured himself a NFL future by kicking five field goals in a 35–19 defeat of the Detroit Lions.

Conrad was surrounded by reporters after the game.

"How many field goals did you kick in college?"

"None."

"Why not?"

"Coach wouldn't let me."

DECEMBER 11, 1964

Crying could be heard from the bedroom of a hotel suite in New York where Bryant was attending a Hall of Fame dinner.

"What's wrong with Coach Bryant?" one man asked.

"He just lost an assistant coach," the other said.

"How old was he?"

"Twenty-nine."

"My God. That's terribly young. What could he have possibly died of?"

"Oh, he didn't die. He just took the head coaching job at Texas A&M."

Gene Stallings had been the light in Bryant's eye since the Junction camp. He joined Bryant's staff the day he graduated from A&M, and his first task was to "scout" the Aggies. After games, he would report all that he had observed about A&M and its tendencies, giving Bryant an idea how an enemy scout might view his own team.

When Alabama called after the 1957 season, Stallings took off with the Bryant brigade to Tuscaloosa. He had become not only an invaluable member of the staff but also Bryant's best friend. Thanks to the Alabama media, he was now called Gene Stallings. It seemed that "Bebes" had been left behind in Texas.

When news broke that Stallings was leaving Alabama and going back to A&M, Bryant received a call from Mickey Herskowitz. "I cried buckets when I heard," Bryant told the writer. "I'm just so proud that one of my little Junction boys is going back to take over. Shoot, with Bebes gone I may have to go back to work."

MARCH 23, 1967

Dennis Goehring, the new president of the Bank of A&M, paced the floor and stared at the telephone. He had prepared his spiel for more than an hour but now worried if he had the courage to deliver it. Then he grabbed the phone and started dialing.

If the bank was to succeed, Dennis figured he would need at least one heavy-hitting investor. So he called a man who had more clout than most governors and senators and already had three national championships under his belt.

"Coach, I need myself one major stockholder," Dennis said to Bryant.

"Dennis, how old are you?"

"Thirty-one."

"Aren't you a little young to be a bank president?"

They shared a big laugh.

Goehring finally asked Bryant if he would be interested in purchasing 200 shares in the new bank. There was a long pause.

"Two hundred shares?" Bryant asked incredulously. "You've got to be bullshittin' me." There was another pause. "Dennis, I got more confidence in you than that. Give me a thousand."

Dennis almost dropped the phone. Then a warm glow washed over his body as he heard Bryant's rumbling laugh. "Dennis, you once said that you were at A&M when I got there and that you'd be there when I was gone," Bryant said.

Ten years after Bear left for Alabama, Dennis was still working at the corner of University Drive and Texas Avenue at the busiest intersection in College Station. His office was all of about thirty feet from the edge of the Texas A&M campus.

JANUARY 1, 1968

It had taken Gene Stallings only three seasons to rescue Texas A&M from the slag heap of the SWC and lead the Aggies to their first championship since the Junction Boys were seniors in 1956.

He was making plans for his team to travel to the Cotton Bowl when he got a call from the opposing coach. "Hey, Bebes, we haven't found a place to practice yet when we get to Dallas," Bear Bryant said. "Got any ideas?"

"Yeah, Coach. There's a little spot about three hundred miles south. It's a little dusty and the living accommodations are pretty spartan. I think they call the place Junction."

"Kiss my butt, Bebes."

As the head coach at A&M, Stallings had followed in Bryant's footsteps to the point that he seemed to be wearing the Man's shoes. He had developed a basic hard-grinding offense and a no-nonsense defense. But he also had a flare for the dramatic and was a bit of a showman. Against Texas in 1965 he concocted a play called the Texas Special that would have football fans talking for decades.

Quarterback Harry Ledbetter tossed a quick flare pass to flanker Jim Kauffman, who allowed the ball to skip before catching it. Then Kauffman feigned disgust, stomping and shaking his head. Texas defenders didn't realize the pass was actually a lateral and that the ball was still live. Kauffman waited for the Longhorns to relax, and then he cocked his arm and heaved a pass to Dude McLean, who was ten yards behind the secondary. A ninety-one-yard touchdown pass shocked the Longhorns. Texas still won the game. But what everyone remembered about that afternoon in Austin was the "Texas Special."

As the teams prepared to play the next season, Texas coach Darrell Royal told the writers, "Stallings might beat me, but he won't trick me this time."

The Aggies ran a double-reverse on the opening kickoff, and as the A&M kick returner passed Royal on the sideline Stallings could see the Texas coach yank off his ball cap and fire it into the ground. Royal had been tricked again. The touchdown return covered ninety-five yards.

Stallings threw trickery out the window in his game plan for Bryant and the Crimson Tide in the Cotton Bowl. He installed a basic game plan with no frills. The Aggies wore down the Crimson Tide 20–16 in spite of two touchdown runs by quarterback Kenny "the Snake" Stabler.

It was the first and last time that veterans of the 1956 Aggie championship team would take sides against Bryant. John David Crow, Jack Pardee, Loyd Taylor, Bobby Marks, Dennis Goehring, and Charlie Krueger stood on the Aggie sideline. Dee Powell and Don Watson were on Stallings's staff. All of the men who had played for Bryant, and so deeply respected him, felt a little odd pulling so hard against him.

But no one was happier for Stallings than Bryant. An image from that game is still remembered by football fans across America. Bryant decided to forego the traditional postgame handshake and surprised Stallings by hoisting him onto his shoulder. Television cameras recorded the shaky ride for several seconds. It was hard to tell who was beaming more—the teacher or the pupil.

MARCH 2, 1971

Since quarterbacking the Junction Boys in 1954, Elwood Kettler had coached all over the South. He was with Bryant at Alabama in 1961 and '62 when the Crimson Tide compiled a 21-1 record.

Now, as the defensive coordinator at Mississippi State, Elwood had decided to take a short drive to Tuscaloosa to see his favorite coach. An issue had weighed heavily on Elwood's mind for almost two decades and, as he peered across the oaken desk at the living legend, he felt almost too weak to speak.

"Coach, I've come to here to say I'm sorry."

"For what?"

"For 1954. It was your only losing season."

Bryant jumped to his feet. He slapped the desktop with his right palm. "Don't ever come in here to apologize to me. You boys weren't losers and never will be. Time just ran out on you. Think of the games we almost won. I will never, ever think of any Junction boy as a loser."

APRIL 14, 1977

Ken Hall and his family had cried all the way to the state line in 1970 when they packed up and left Texas. They hated leaving their native state, but a great employment opportunity awaited Ken.

Hall's football career had ended not too long after he walked away from Bear Bryant in 1956. Hall had been offered a scholarship to play football at the University of Washington but learned three days later that his college eligibility had expired.

He played in the Canadian Football League for the Edmonton Eskimos in 1957 and then was drafted by the Baltimore Colts the next season. His career seemed poised for takeoff until New York Giants linebacker Sam Huff speared him in the back of his head, driving his head between his knees. The sixth vertebra collapsed, ending his season. Hall lost a lot of physical coordination. The next year, he was traded to the Steelers, where he spent one season. Then he was cut by the Cardinals before the 1960 season. His last stop was the Houston Oilers of the fledgling AFL, where he returned kickoffs in 1960 and was cut again.

After moving his family to the Bay Area, Hall became an upwardly mobile executive with a sweetener company in San Francisco. His sons Mike and Chuck decided to play football at Redwood High School in Larkspur. After rebuilding his life and assuring himself a great future, Ken Hall then ran headlong into his past.

The *San Francisco Examiner* was preparing a story on Ken's football-playing sons when the writer learned of the father's sad story—the one about the greatest high school player ever flaming out on the road to glory. The slant of the story wasn't so much about Mike or Chuck as it was about Ken gaining 11,232 yards in high school, rewriting the national record book, and then falling on his face. It wasn't long before someone mailed the article to Bryant, who sat behind his desk in Tuscaloosa and composed a letter:

Dear Ken:
I was so glad to read about your successful and happy life there in California. You have done well . . . Ken, I've made a lot of mistakes in my life with the young men that I have coached. But the greatest mistake I ever made was with you.
Sincerely,
Paul W. Bryant

Ken thought about the words for several days and then decided to write back.

Dear Coach Bryant:
Thank you for the letter. I, too, am quite proud of you and your wonderful accomplishments over the years. Coach, when I left Texas A&M, I was determined to prove to you that I could be a great football player. I wanted to prove that also to my family, my friends and especially to myself. A lot of things happened and it didn't work out. But life went on and I'm doing great. Now, I believe that it's time you stop beating yourself up over me. You were forgiven a long time ago.
Sincerely,
Ken Hall

MAY 18, 1979

They shaded their eyes and peered into the sky and waited for the private jet to split the puffy white clouds and set down on the narrow airstrip outside of town. The Junction Boys had arrived. They had navigated the skinny, twisting roads of the Hill Country, driving in from points all over the country. The twenty-fifth reunion was set to begin that day. All that was missing was the guest of honor.

Bear Bryant was riding the wave of his fifth national championship. On New Year's Day in the Sugar Bowl, Alabama had stuffed Penn State with a last-minute goal line stand, winning 14–7. With a lifetime record of 284-77-16, Bryant was now thirty-two victories from breaking the all-time mark of 314 set by the legendary Amos Alonzo Stagg. After the Sugar Bowl, Bryant was asked by the writers what he would like to do next.

"Get all of the Junction boys back together for a reunion," he said. "That was my favorite team." The writers almost dropped their notebooks. The 1954 season had been the sad, forgettable one. The Aggies had finished 1–9 and Bryant had walked away with his first and only losing season.

Somehow, though, the coach had remained deeply attached to that rag-tag bunch that wouldn't quit. His lectures to them about never giving up in the fourth quarter had hit home. They would become the centerpiece of his 1956 championship season at Texas A&M.

Now as they waited for the Man, the Junction Boys marveled at what they had seen on their return to the quiet little town. They were stunned at the sight of tall grass swaying drunkenly in the breeze and miles and miles of fertile farm- and ranch land. The Llano Valley was lush and green, and well-fed cattle grazed the countryside. Emerald cedars dappled the craggy green hills. A grove of pecan trees provided a cool, dark canopy behind the Adjunct where the hell camp was staged. The South Llano gurgled over a bed of white stones. Two miles away it connected with the North Llano River that had been a dry, rut-infested strip of gravel and sand when the boys last set foot in Junction. Now it was bubbly and vibrant and showing no ill effects of the seven-year drought, the worst in Junction history. The land once scarred now teemed with lakes, rivers, and creeks and cattle with shiny coats. Deer pranced across flowering pastures. Folks moved about town in new pickups, and there was an air of prosperity about the place.

The most surprising sight was the old practice field that had once been a dust bowl covered by rocks, gravel, cactus, sandspurs, and dead weeds.

Now it was acres upon acres of verdant grass where summer school students practiced golf shots.

Boys who had survived dehydration, heatstroke, broken bones, bruises, and searing heat were now men in their midforties. They wore brightly colored shirts and happy faces. Some had grown bald, and others had grown thicker about the waist. They were doctors, engineers, lawyers, bankers, coaches, entrepreneurs, educators, architects, oilmen, ranchers, farmers, fast-food deal makers, and CEOs. Many were millionaires. Some were recognized globally for their feats in high commerce.

They stood next to a desolate airstrip with a brisk wind blowing in their faces. They imbibed beer and mixed drinks. They laughed and talked like the people they really were—long-lost friends. Then a streak of sunlight reflected off the silver wing as the jet began to descend into the valley. It sailed over the high, craggy hills, and now they could read UNIVERSITY OF ALABAMA across the fuselage. A red-and-white houndstooth hat adorned the tail.

The Junction Boys drew suddenly quiet. Some hurriedly tossed beer cans into a trash barrel. Others poured mixed drinks onto the ground and hid the glasses. The laughter and loud talking ceased. They stood up straight, seemingly at attention, and watched the jet taxi toward them.

"God, I hope he's in a good mood," Don Watson said. "I sure'd hate to run gassers today." The men laughed. Then the silence returned. They stood with rigid spines as the jets were quieted and a stairway was lowered onto the tarmac.

In truth, no one was more nervous about this journey into the past than Bryant. Guilt had haunted him for almost twenty-five years and he still had sad visions of the unforgiving practice field. He often relived the day that Billy Schroeder almost died. He could close his eyes and still see the frightened boys running out of camp into the moonlit night.

The face had turned leathery, thanks to a hard life that had been filled with unforgiving pressure. Craggy lines flared from corners of his eyes to the edge of his graying hair. He was sixty-five years old. An hour after the plane touched down, he squinted into the bright sun and his eyes scanned the practice field where, according to Mickey Herskowitz, bones crunched and bodies were mangled.

"God, it just shows you what a little rain can do for a place," Bryant told Dennis Goehring. Apple green grass danced in the cool breeze. The temperature was in the seventies, and the low humidity made the day feel fresh and invigorating. He pulled a cigarette from his pocket, and his eyes studied Goehring. "Dennis, I want you to stand here beside me. Give me everybody's name when they walk up. I'm not so sure I'll recognize all of them."

A tall man with graying hair approached. "Coach, I'm sure you'll remember this guy—" Before Dennis could recite the name, though, the man wrapped both arms around Bryant.

"My God, Billy Schroeder, it's you," Bryant said. "I didn't know if you'd want to hit me or hug me."

Schroeder held the coach in his arms for several seconds. "God, it's good to see ya," he said. "I've been waiting for this a long time."

Billy told the coach about his successful law practice in his hometown of Lockhart. Then he introduced his wife, Kay.

Bryant quickly recognized Lloyd Hale, the stocky center who had volunteered to change positions in Junction after dozens of players had quit. For almost two decades Bryant had been quoted as saying that Hale was his best center ever. That opinion was reaffirmed in his autobiography, published in 1975. But Bryant's mind seemed to change after Alabama's win over Penn State, when he told the press, "Dwight Stephenson is the best center I've ever coached." Hale read the quote and stored it for later use.

Hale scratched his head and said, "Coach, there's a matter I've been meanin' to bring up to you."

"What's that?"

"I thought I was the best center you'd ever coached." Both men chuckled.

"Oh, I told the press that so Dwight'd make the All-American teams. That's all."

Player after player approached Bryant. They shook his hand and told him of their happy and successful lives. Each one delivered the same message—that Bryant had been the most influential person in his life.

Bryant was a little surprised to see John E. Wiedeman, the doctor he'd clashed with over player abuse. But Wiedeman smiled when he shook Bryant's hand. "Coach, there was a time when I told you I had more players than you did. You said that if they didn't start playin' any better I could keep 'em." Bryant slapped the old doctor on the back, and they shared a laugh.

Only a handful of Junction survivors didn't attend. Gene Stallings, who had been coaching the Dallas Cowboys secondary for the last seven years, was busy with a spring minicamp. Washington Redskins head coach Jack Pardee was also involved in off-season workouts.

Billy Pete Huddleston and Charles Hall declined invitations as minor protests to how the camp had been run. Huddleston had explained his position to Dennis Goehring over the phone. "I think everyone should be invited, including the quitters," he said. "I think this should be a time of healing." Dennis explained that plans had been made for only the survivors to attend.

Hall flatly rejected the invitation when Dennis called. He still resented Bryant's callused response to his injuries and for admonishing him for getting married.

"Dennis, I really don't care to go. My experience with Coach Bryant wasn't that positive."

"Well, Charlie, you know that Coach Bryant was like a second father to me."

"My God, Dennis. I had a good father, and I would never want to compare him to Bear Bryant."

The Junction Chamber of Commerce organized the event from start to finish. A stage was erected in the pecan bottoms next to the river. The ceremony was held just below the area where the Quonset huts were situated back in 1954. Ten of the twenty huts were stationed exactly where they had been, and a few others were scattered around the grounds, each having been freshly painted.

A month before the event, Don Watson had telephoned Mary Harmon in Tuscaloosa to ask about the coach's ring size. A commemorative ring was being designed for the ceremony. "I don't know," Mary Harmon said. "He's never worn any jewelry in his life." So Watson showed a picture of Bryant's hands to the ring maker, and he guessed size 12.

That evening, as the sun set over the craggy hills and a thousand Junctionites gathered for the ceremony, the local high school band belted out the "Aggie War Hymn." One-by-one, the Junction survivors walked to the lectern and spoke about memories of the ten-day hell camp and told how it had affected their lives.

"Coach Bryant," Dennis Goehring said, his voice slightly breaking. "If not for you, I couldn't have done the things I had to do in my life. If I hadn't been tough, I never would have made it. You are the person who made me tough."

Marvin Tate, one of the 1954 captains, asked Bryant to approach the lectern. He slid the ring onto his finger, and it fit perfectly. Bryant wiped a tear from his cheek and then proudly held the ring aloft for all to see. Many of his ex-players had suspected that a big heart was beating beyond that rawhide exterior. Now they were sure of it.

Bryant stepped to the microphone and sized up his audience just as he had done twenty-five years earlier in the Grove. Then he turned to his right, where the ex-players were seated, and studied the faces that were no longer young.

"I never had a team I was more proud of," he said. "I came here today to apologize to y'all. I shouldn't have done what I did to you twenty-five years ago. If somebody'd done that to me, I would've just walked off. Quit. I really would have.

"But now that I've seen all of you today, and heard about your happy and successful lives, I realize that maybe I did something right after all. I knew you men would be successes. But nothing like this. Hell, maybe I oughta stop feelin' guilty."

JANUARY 26, 1983

Bear Bryant had eerily predicted that he'd "croak in a week" if he ever stopped coaching. Twenty-eight days after his final game, he was gone, pronounced dead at 1:30 on a Wednesday afternoon when low clouds were spun into smoke-colored rings and the wind howled. He was sixty-nine years old.

Gene Stallings was working in his office at the Dallas Cowboys complex when he received a midafternoon call from Bryant's secretary, Linda Knowles. "I didn't want you to hear this on radio or TV," she said. "But Coach is dead." Stallings put his head in his hands and cried for several minutes.

John David Crow received a phone call at his home in Texas. "I feel numb," he said. "I feel like I just lost my father."

On learning of Bryant's death, Dennis Goehring walked into his backyard, sat on the ground, and cried.

The entire state of Alabama settled into mourning. The memorial service was held at the First United Methodist Church in Tuscaloosa and piped into two others via closed-circuit television. More than ten thousand mourners either were packed into the churches or stood solemnly outside in the misting rain.

The funeral procession covered fifty-five miles along Interstate 59 between Tuscaloosa and the Elmwood Cemetery in Birmingham. More than a hundred thousand citizens, some wearing black and others wearing crimson, lined the roadside. Several signs hung from overpasses. One sign read: WE LOVE YOU, COACH, THANKS FOR THE MEMORIES. Another simply said: WE LOVE YOU, BEAR. Truckers stood in front of their rigs, their ball caps pressed against their hearts. Buses carrying dignitaries along with past and present players followed the hearse.

Gov. George Wallace ordered all of the state flags to be flown at half-staff. Radio and television shows were preempted all morning across Alabama so the funeral could be carried live.

As he lay peacefully on a hillside outside of Birmingham, rows upon rows of mourners fanned out across the tree-lined cemetery. People were visible almost as far as the eye could see. They were black and white, young and old. Coaching peers Woody Hayes and John McKay were at the gravesite, along with Wallace in a wheelchair. Rays of sunlight broke through the low clouds as the 300-car motorcade pulled off the highway and lined the gravesite. It was the first bit of heavenly light Alabamians had seen in almost a week.

Hayes stood under a tree and recalled the day that Knute Rockne died. "I have the same feeling today," he said. "Rockne was the great coach of his era and Bryant was the great coach of his."

Bear Bryant won six national championships and 323 games, more than any other college coach. Twenty-three of his teams finished in the top twenty. No one had a greater impact on the college game for three decades. But it was the team that had gathered beneath a canopy of pecan trees next to a river back in Texas he loved the most. When the Man passed, he was wearing the only piece of jewelry that he'd ever cared about, his ring from that 1–9 Aggie team. It was a reminder that he was human and therefore capable of losing once. More important, it was a testament to a heart far more caring than most had imagined. Some men are measured in wins. In the end, Bear Bryant was remembered more for the people who loved him. The inscription on the ring he'd received four years earlier simply read: JUNCTION BOYS.

Epilogue

Just as Bear Bryant had observed at the twenty-fifth reunion, each of the Junction survivors became a success story in professional life. Some went on to fame and fortune.

Gene "Bebes" Stallings became one of the most versatile coaches of the twentieth century, returning to Texas A&M in 1965, winning a conference title two years later, and coaching there for seven years. He spent fourteen seasons under Tom Landry as the defensive secondary coach of the Dallas Cowboys. After a brief stint as the head coach of the Phoenix Cardinals, he was called home by Mama, just as Bryant had been in 1957.

When he was introduced as the head coach of the Crimson Tide in 1990, Stallings responded with typical humility. "The people love Coach Bryant and they just tolerate the rest of us," he said. But Stallings offered a connection to the past, and he became the symbolic flame keeper for Bryant. Paul Bryant Jr. approached Stallings at the press conference and said loud enough for all to hear, "This is exactly what Papa wanted."

In 1992, Stallings brought Alabama its first national championship since Bryant's death. He was named the winner of the Bear Bryant Coach of the Year award. Stallings proved to be exactly what the Alabama football program needed to regain national prominence.

He now lives on his 600-acre ranch near his hometown of Paris, Texas, with his wife, Ruth Ann, and son, Johnny. Several hundred cattle roam the ranch along with assorted wildlife.

Jack Pardee, the big, smiling fullback who played six-man football at Christoval High School, began his pro football career as a second-round choice of the Los Angeles Rams. One of the best linebackers of his time, Pardee played thirteen seasons with the Rams and was an All-Pro. Diagnosed with skin cancer in 1965, he spent that season on Stallings's coaching staff at Texas A&M.

Late in his playing career, Pardee was traded to the Washington Redskins and became part of the famed Over the Hill Gang under George Allen. He also won All-Pro honors for the Redskins and played in Super Bowl VII against unbeaten Miami.

Pardee was a head coach for two decades and won Coach of the Year honors in three leagues—the NFL, WFL, and USFL. He was honored as Coach of the Year by two NFL teams—Washington and Chicago. He spent three successful seasons at the University of Houston before coaching the Houston Oilers for six years and reaching the play-offs five times.

Still active in the American Cancer Society, Pardee lives on a 500-hundred acre ranch in central Texas with his wife, Phyllis.

Dennis Goehring, the gregarious guard whom Bryant and Smokey Harper tried to run off, has been a successful businessman in the Bryan/College Station area for the last forty years. He was the first president of the Bank of A&M. In 1980, he was named president of the College Station Economic Foundation and was recognized for transforming a small outpost into a thriving community. He is currently the president of Paynet. Of all the Junction survivors, he remains the most active in university affairs.

Like many of the Junction Boys, Don Watson spent the better part of his professional career as a coach. He was a member of Stallings's staff at Texas A&M.

In 1986, Watson was attending a stage production in Houston of *The Best Little Whorehouse in Texas* when he was struck by an idea. He fetched a Texas A&M autographed football from his car, and during curtain call he vaulted onto the stage and presented it to the actress playing Miss Mona. She seemed dumbfounded by the gesture.

"Miss Mona," Weasel said. "This is from all of the Texas A&M boys, including yours truly, who made those fun and memorable trips to the Chicken Ranch."

Miss Mona regained her composure and wrapped her arms around Watson. "Why, I'm sure all of those girls back then were real glad to see you," she said.

In 1959, two years after Bryant left Texas A&M, Smokey Harper joined his great friend in Tuscaloosa, where he became the coach's right-hand man.

"Smokey, I want you to go downtown and drink coffee with me every morning," Bryant would say. "And I want you to tell everybody what a great coach I am."

Midway through the 1961 season, Smokey sent a letter to former Texas

A&M student trainer Jerry Rhea. "We got a bunch of narrow-ass people here," he wrote. "We got no chance of winning many games." A month later, the Crimson Tide completed an unbeaten regular season, defeating Auburn 34–0 and clinching Bryant's first national championship. They topped off the season with a 10–3 win over Arkansas in the Sugar Bowl.

At Alabama, Smokey did odd jobs like filing game films and was on the athletic payroll until his death in the summer of 1971. Bryant openly wept at the funeral.

Billy Pickard, the student trainer, remains the Aggie flame keeper from the Junction camp. He graduated from Texas A&M in 1956 and was named head trainer nine years later. He became an assistant athletic director in 1987 and, during his time at the university, has coordinated the training, equipment, and facility staff. He remains one of the most visible people on the Aggie sideline during football games and is a member of the National Athletic Trainer's Association Hall of Fame.

After working his way through the coaching ranks, former Junction end Bobby Drake Keith was on the threshold of being named the head coach of the Oklahoma Sooners in 1966 when the board of regents changed its mind. The regents demanded that Keith fire all of the assistant coaches from the previous staff. When Keith refused, the regents decided to hire someone else—Jim Mackenzie from Arkansas. Keith would never coach again.

More than thirty years later, Keith said he couldn't be happier about his career change. He's the CEO of Entergy, the largest public utility company in Arkansas. A few years ago, he helped organize the biggest bond deal in the history of public utilities, worth more than $750 million.

Marvin Tate became the associate athletic director at Texas in 1967 and was promoted to athletic director in 1980. He held the job for three years before being elected mayor of Bryan. After ten years in public office, Tate retired and recently was named Mayor Emeritus for Life in Bryan, where he remains an active and popular figure.

Billy Schroeder, who almost died in Junction, graduated from law school at the University of Texas and has practiced in his hometown of Lockhart since 1961. He is very active in civic activities, including the $2.5 million restoration of the Caldwell County Courthouse, which was originally built in 1890.

In spite of winning only one game, Elwood Kettler was Bryant's favorite quarterback at Texas A&M. He then spent thirty-seven years as a coach on the college and high school level. He was the offensive coordinator at Oklahoma State for six years and the defensive coordinator at Mississippi State for three seasons. His longest tenure as a head coach was ten seasons at Texas City High, where he became the first at the school to win a bi-district championship. His right leg is still numb due to his breaking four transverse processes in his lower back in 1954. He is now retired, and his number-one goal is to catch a 100-pound catfish.

Billy "Redbird" Granberry, the smallest of the Junction survivors, still is troubled by occasional dislocations of his left shoulder. Granberry earned his law degree in 1965 and has practiced law in and around Corpus Christi for the last thirty-four years.

One of the most successful Junction survivors is Billy Pete Huddleston, who has owned and operated his own petroleum and geological firm in Houston since 1967. Huddleston and Company Inc. provides petroleum engineering consulting services for 500 oil and gas companies, gas transmission companies, banks, and other financial institutions. He has served as a visiting professor at Texas A&M since 1981.

Lloyd Hale, a petroleum engineer, is one of Huddleston's most able and loyal employees. It was Hale who volunteered to change positions in Junction after several centers quit. For more than two decades Bryant called Hale his best center ever. Hale and Huddleston have been friends since childhood, having grown up together in the small West Texas town of Iraan.

Running back Joe Schero was one of the driving forces behind Church's Fried Chicken's rise to national prominence. At the time of its inception in the late 1960s, he owned all of the Houston franchises that became the foundation for the company's success.

Don Kachtik, whom Bryant considered his second-toughest player in 1954 behind Jack Pardee, was the county agriculture agent in Orange, Texas, until 1988 and today is the largest Christmas tree grower in the world. He is somewhat of a Bryant historian and has visited the Bear Bryant Museum several times in Tuscaloosa.

Charles Hall, a running back for Bryant in 1954, once described himself as a "quiet, introverted but responsible kind of guy." He stuck it out at Junction knowing that he couldn't afford to fund the remainder of his education. Of all the survivors, he was the unhappiest player during the 1-9 season. His ill feelings for Bryant lasted well past graduation.

Hall spent twenty-nine years as a professor at the A&M Veterinary School. Shortly before retiring in 1995, he was asked by the graduating class to deliver the commencement address. He was the first veterinary professor to be chosen for that honor. Just the idea of standing before 5,000 people at Rudder Hall made him nervous. But his speech was a rousing success.

"Being an introverted person, it was beyond my imagination to get in front of that many people and even put a sentence together," he said. "It took me six months to psych myself up for it. One thing I always knew about Coach Bryant is that he had the words when he needed them, whether it was chewing you out or making a pep talk to six-thousand students at the Grove. He was the most articulate man I'd ever met."

Bennie Sinclair, the Junction survivor who didn't appreciate Bryant's foul language and was the inspiration for the "cuss bucket," became one of the country's most successful petroleum engineers and worked his entire career for Pennzoil. He was a senior vice president for the company from 1987 through his retirement in 1993.

"There is no doubt that Coach Bryant had more influence than anyone in my life outside of my parents," he said. "This ol' football business about sucking it up when times get tough is true. Very often in my life I thought of him in time of crisis."

Troy Summerlin, the student manager who became an emergency center during the '54 season, is vice president and part-owner of one of the most successful general contracting firms in Texas and has been involved in major commercial construction throughout the southern part of the state. His headquarters is Victoria.

Heisman Trophy winner John David Crow, a freshman in 1954, wasn't allowed on the bus to Junction. But he still uttered one of the most memorable lines from the trip. He was standing on the sidewalk when only one bus carrying thirty-five survivors returned to campus and pulled up to the curb next to the athletic dormitory. "Where the hell did everybody go?" he said in disbelief.

Along with the eight seniors who survived the hell camp, Crow was a large reason that the 1956 team went unbeaten and won a conference championship. After eleven successful seasons in the NFL that included four trips to the Pro Bowl, he embarked on a coaching/business career that eventually brought him back to A&M in 1983 as an associate athletic director. He was promoted to athletic director in 1988 and held the job for five years before becoming the director of athletic development. He was instrumental in the raising of $637 million from alumni and other private sources—the largest fund drive ever completed by a public university.

Ken Hall, who still holds twelve national high school football records but quit the Aggies out of frustration during the 1956 season, returned to Texas from California in 1988 and now own Ken Hall's Barbecue in the Hill Country town of Fredericksburg, about fifty miles from Junction. His hobby is painting scenes of the Texas landscape.

Jimmy Wright, the rebellious quarterback whom Bryant benched in 1956, is now retired from a long career in coaching. Bryant approached him during a meeting of SEC coaches in 1974. "I should have been more understanding with you," Bryant said. "If I'd let you throw more, we would have won a national championship."

Four Junction survivors are deceased—Gene Henderson, Henry Clark, Paul Kennon, and Billy McGowan.

Rob Roy Spiller, the bus station boy who wrote tickets to the Junction quitters, returned to his hometown shortly after graduating from Texas A&M in 1958 and has been the president of Junction National Bank the last twenty-five years. His high school girlfriend, Laverne Johnston, became Dennis Goehring's girlfriend during his days at Texas A&M. She died tragically at age thirty-eight. Dennis and Rob Roy remain great friends.

The town of Junction, which was a dust bowl during the horrific drought, has grown by only a few hundred people since Bryant brought the Aggies there in 1954. But consistent rains over the years have greatly improved the ranching, and the once-parched Llano Valley is covered with verdant grass. The citizens are some of the friendliest in the state. Visitors who come to view the site of Bryant's camps are surprised to find college students hitting golf balls and deer grazing on a grass-covered field that once was littered with rocks, gravel, cactus, and sandspurs. Junction survivor Jack Pardee said, "Junction got a bad rap when we were there in the 1950s. It's really a beautiful place."

So much has changed about Texas A&M that a 1956 graduate who moved out of the country for more than forty years would be shocked at the landscape, the coeducational student body, and the emphasis on higher education. Once known as a "cow college" with its graceless cell block buildings, Texas A&M was recently named one of the top fifty colleges in the United States by *U.S. News and World Report*. In 1954, when attendance was growing at Texas public schools at the rate of 92 percent, A&M's enrollment actually declined. A&M now has the largest full-time undergraduate enrollment (more than 45,000) in America. Only 2,200 students belong to the Corps of Cadets. For decades, A&M was known as a secondary adjunct to UT. Now it is generally considered the best public university in the state. A trip to Aggieland on a fall afternoon when Kyle Field is packed and rocking can be an exhilarating experience.

Women were admitted in 1963, and compulsory military ended for good in 1965. Still, many of the old traditions, like Fish Camp, the bonfire, and Aggie Muster remain. The story of the Junction Boys is handed down from generation to generation of Aggies and remains one of the great legendary tales in the annals of college football.

It is said that Paul "Bear" Bryant always carried a poem with him. This is one:

This is the beginning of a new day.
God has given me this day to use as I will.
I can waste it or use it for good.
What I do today is very important because I am exchanging a day
    of my life for it.
When tomorrow comes, this day will be gone forever.
Leaving something in its place I have traded for it.
I want it to be a gain, not loss—good, not evil.
Success, not failure, in order that I shall not forget the price I
    paid for it.

THE JUNCTION SURVIVORS

Ray Barrett	G	5-9	195	Sr.	San Angelo
Darrell Brown	T	6-1	190	Soph.	Liberty
James Burkhart	G	6-1	185	Soph.	Hamlin
Henry Clark	T	6-2	205	Jr.	Mesquite
Bob Easley	FB	5-11	190	Jr.	Houston
Dennis Goehring	G	5-11	185	Soph.	San Marcos
Billy Granberry	FB	5-7	155	Soph.	Beeville
Lloyd Hale	C	5-10	190	Soph.	Iraan
Charles Hall	HB	5-10	185	Sr.	Dallas
Gene Henderson	QB	6-1	175	Jr.	Sonora
Billy Huddleston	HB	5-9	165	Jr.	Iraan
George Johnson	T	6-3	200	Jr.	Ellisville, Miss.
Don Kachtik	FB	6-1	185	Sr.	Rio Hondo
Bobby D. Keith	HB	6-0	175	Soph.	Breckenridge
Paul Kennon	E	6-1	185	Sr.	Shreveport
Elwood Kettler	QB	6-0	165	Sr.	Brenham
Billy McGowan	E	6-1	180	Sr.	Silsbee
Russell Moake	C	6-3	215	Soph.	Deer Park
Bobby Lockett	T	6-3	190	Soph.	Breckenridge
Norbert Ohlendorf	T	6-3	200	Sr.	Lockhart
Jack Pardee	FB	6-2	200	Soph.	Christoval
Dee Powell	T	6-1	210	Soph	Lockhart
Donald Robbins	E	6-1	188	Jr.	Breckenridge
Joe Schero	HB	6-0	175	Sr.	San Antonio
Bill Schroeder	T	6-1	200	Jr.	Lockhart
Charles Scott	QB	5-8	160	Soph.	Alexandria, La.
Bennie Sinclair	E	6-2	195	Sr.	Mineola
Gene Stallings	E	6-1	165	Soph.	Paris
Troy Summerlin	C	5-8	145	Soph.	Shreveport
Marvin Tate	G	6-0	175	Sr.	Abilene
Sid Theriot	G	5-10	195	Sr.	Gibson, La.
Richard Vick	FB	6-1	185	Sr.	Beaumont
Don Watson	HB	5-11	155	Soph.	Franklin
Lawrence Winkler	T	6-0	225	Sr.	Temple
Herb Wolf	C	5-11	185	Jr.	Houston